The HEART RATE MONITOR BOOK

A Heart Zone™ Training Program

For Outdoor and Indoor Cyclists

Sally Edwards & Sally Reed

VELO
press

BOULDER, COLORADO USA

The Heart Rate Monitor Book For Outdoor and Indoor Cyclists
A Heart Zone Training Program
Copyright © 2000 Sally Edwards and Sally Reed

International Standard Book Number: 1-884737-80-3

Library of Congress Cataloging-in Publication Data applied for.

Printed in the USA

Distributed in the United States and Canada by Publishers Group West.

VELO
press

1830 North 55th Street
Boulder, Colorado 80301-2700 USA
303/440-0601; fax 303/444-6788; e-mail velopress@7dogs.com

To purchase additional copies of this book or other VeloPress books, call 800/234-8356 or visit the Web at www.velogear.com.

Designed by Paulette Livers-Lambert
Edited by Anne Stein

Contents

*The Danskin Women's Triathlon—Seattle awards ceremony with
Sally Reed (left) and Sally Edwards (right).*

Acknowledgments

From the heart of Sally Reed and Sally Edwards, we would like to thank the people who contributed to and helped develop this book.

On the Vietnam memorial in Sacramento, California, one plaque reads: "Some Gave All, All Gave Some." The names of those who died fighting that war, those who gave all, are inscribed on its wall.

We are happy here that the following individuals gave some; none gave all:

Lyle Nelson. Olympian and author and Marty Rudolf, for providing their retreat home in Oregon. Estelle Gray, owner of R and E Cycles, in Seattle, Washington, gourmet chef, and our consultant and venue director. Scott Reed, our star heart zone trainer. Bellevue Club for their support in the early development of this program. The people in the original Heart Cycling class, who were willing participants in the "HZT Training Lab." Sue Matyas, Fitness Director at Bellevue Club, for listening to Sally Reed for four years about this. Nancy Weninger from Marin County, California, for her cutting-and-pasting talents. Sue Dills, in Seattle, Washington, for providing the Lake Union Waterworks retreat. Jack Dills, of Mercer Island, Washington, our English professor extraordinaire. Betsy Herring, of Seattle, Washington, for her attention to editing details. Carolyn Behse, of Bellevue, Washington, for applying the science of Heart Cycling with analysis and flair. Kathy Kent, of Naperville, Illinois, for taking Heart Cycling to the midwest. Shawn Bloom, of La Crosse, Wisconsin, for reading the original manuscript and teaching it. Carla Felsted, of Austin, Texas, for being a role model and inspiration. Dorey Schmidt, of Austin, Texas, for assembling and compiling the rough draft. Anne Stein, of Evanston, Illinois, for finishing the final edit. Judy Moise, of Seattle, Washington, for her sculpting and refining. Geena Reebs and Aimee Bluhm, photography contributions, Publications Department, Bellevue Club. And, finally, Heart Cycling master trainers: Jessica Menendez, Kathy Kent, Bev Sigler, Lindsey Smith and Tracy Latham.

Heart Cycling class at Bellevue Club with Sally Edwards (center right).

Happy cyclist riding with her emotional heart.

Introduction

This is the first easy-to-follow cycling program that uses technology—a heart rate monitor—to guide you through your training. The program, Heart Cycling, uses the heart muscle as the smart motor for getting healthier and fitter on a bike. With an emphasis on indoor cycling, more than 50 indoor and outdoor workouts are provided along with key information on heart zone training and tips on using your monitor for weight management, fitness testing and fitness goals. Using a heart rate monitor is a way for the mind to see what the heart is saying.

This is a training book. It does not include information on bike set-up, maintenance, bike fit, bike handling and skills, or how to buy a bike. There are wonderful books on the market today about all of those topics. Rather, *The Heart Rate Monitor Book for Outdoor and Indoor Cyclists* is an entirely new way of training for cyclists, triathletes, cross-trainers and anyone who participates in indoor and outdoor training classes.

To help you train more effectively, we have included a CD-ROM–based software product. Adding riding software to the program allows the rider to quickly input the key pieces of data: heart rate in beats per minute, time in training (elapsed time), altitude (in total vertical change during the ride), and total ride distance (in miles or kilometers). Heart Cycling Training Software provides the reader with information such as training load by calculating Heart Zone Training points, as well as other useful data including calories burned and heart rate averages. By combining coaching, analysis and logging in an accessible package, the cyclist can track progress, get useful information easily and maximize training benefit.

Why did Sally Reed and Sally Edwards write this book? There are two answers, just as there are two authors. Sally Reed's perspective is based on her experience after taking a seminar that Sally Edwards first presented in the summer of 1996. "In the seminar, Sally Edwards encouraged us to take the material from her books on Heart Zone Training and apply it. "Heart Zone Training seemed like a perfect fit for indoor cycling. She [Sally Edwards] was emphasizing training smarter and safer. I knew there must be a way for fitness professionals to apply what world-class athletes and exercise physiologists were telling us about training. These same training principles could apply to cyclists at all levels. With permission granted to be creative, the seminar inspired me to develop the Heart Cycling program and ultimately this book."

The other version as to why this book was written is from Sally Edwards. She blames it all on Sally Reed's incredible ability to motivate others. "As the athletic director of the Bellevue Club in Bellevue, Washington, Sally Reed has more than a full-time job. She took the initiative and decided to launch a heart rate monitor test program using an existing indoor cycling program. I admire Sally Reed. She follows one of the most basic tenets of heart zone training—it's personal and individualized, just as you have your own dreams, physiology and finish lines. Just as we share the same first name, the two of us are one in our mission to help build a happier, heart-healthy society."

Prior to starting any exercise program, it's important to have a complete physical examination. Men over age 40 and women over age 50 should have a medical examination and diagnostic exercise test before starting a vigorous exercise program, as should symptomatic men and women of any age. If in doubt, consult your physician for clearance.

—*Sally Edwards and Sally Reed,* co-authors

CHAPTER 1

Let's Ride

You notice the burn in your shoulder, like a single nerve tingling. You are feeling exhilarated and it's just the smallest sensation so you push harder and faster as you gulp another mouthful of air. So it was for Sue, until her shoulder burn became unbearable pain and her daily swim workouts became mostly kick sets. The doctor ordered time off from swimming and weeks of rehab. I suggested indoor cycling with a heart rate monitor to maintain cardiovascular fitness and strengthen her legs. She agreed and so began a four-year training program that not only got Sue back in the water and setting national records, but also winning her age group in triathlons. How did she go from a great swimmer to a champion age-group triathlete? She learned how to train smarter by using a heart rate monitor and she committed to Heart Cycling, an indoor cycling class using all the concepts we write about in this book. I can't promise you the same success Sue had, but I can promise that you will be healthier, stronger and fitter for cycling or any sport you choose.

—Sally Reed

Getting healthier, getting fit, and getting your fittest: It all starts with getting on your bike and it helps to have a heart rate monitor. These watch-like devices, using the electrical signal from the heart muscle, measure the number of beats per minute your heart contracts. But if you don't have a heart rate monitor, count your pulse rate in your wrist or on the side of your neck. Using a watch or clock with a second hand, count manually for 6 seconds, then multiply by 10 (or add a zero to your count). This is your pulse rate in beats per minute (bpm). The number is the same whether you're measuring the mechanical blood flow by counting manually or letting the monitor count your heart contractions.

The basic idea is to use your own heart muscle to set the intensity for your personal training zones. Getting to know your response at each heart rate level is a first step. Ride by heart rate and use feeling, cadence and speed as support information.

It's time to get on your bike and ride. The first self-assessment helps to determine your initial riding heart zone. A heart zone is a range of heartbeats. Each zone is 10 percent of your maximum heart rate, or 10 percent of the fastest your heart can beat for any one minute. Co-author Sally Reed's maximum heart rate is 180 bpm: Her zones are:

Heart Zone Chart for Sally Reed

Zone 5	90—100 percent maximum heart rate	162—180 bpm
Zone 4	80—90 percent maximum heart rate	144—162 bpm
Zone 3	70—80 percent maximum heart rate	126—144 bpm
Zone 2	60—70 percent maximum heart rate	108—126 bpm
Zone 1	50—60 percent maximum heart rate	90—108 bpm

The anchor point is your maximum heart rate. There are four assessments to help determine 60 percent of your maximum heart rate. Those are:

A. Every two minutes go harder
B. The biggest number you have ever seen or counted
C. Using your favorite workout ride
D. Determining 60 percent of your maximum heart rate
STOP! Intermediate and advanced cyclists go to page 91, Chapter 4: Sub-max Test for Cycling

SELF ASSESSMENT A:
EVERY TWO MINUTES GO HARDER

To begin a training program, set a starting point. This point should be based on heart rate information about you. The first, and one of the simple self-assessments, is based on your subjective feeling of exercise intensity, called "perceived exertion" or RPE (rating of perceived exertion).

In the 1950s, a Swedish physiologist named Borg correlated how hard someone exercised with a verbal description or feeling of that sensation. He developed two scales, one called the RPE scale and the other the CR10, or modified scale. Both scales measure an individual's perceived exertion. We have chosen the modified scale, where a "10" is maximum exertion and a "1" is barely moving. For example, if you're at rest and I asked for your exercise intensity, you would say zero. When you start to ride slowly, just warming up, you might call that a "3" and describe it as moderate intensity. RPE is a number you give to your personal feeling of how hard you're training (Borg, 1998). As you go faster, or ride up a hill, or as you increase the exercise resistance or load, your heart rate goes up and so does the number you perceive as your exertion level. For this simple assessment, you'll spend two minutes at each number until you feel challenged or tired.

When you reach this level of exertion, slow down or remove the resistance and warm down. During the assessment, you should always be able to talk; never ride harder than that. Every two minutes record the number that best corresponds with that level of exercise intensity. Use a watch to keep track of the time. A heart rate monitor can make this test easier, but it also works if you manually count your heart rate.

Here are some descriptions of how each of the RPE numbers feel so you know what number to associate with the feeling:

1–2	Very light and easy	Very little effort, very comfortable
3–4	Moderate to somewhat strong	Easy to talk; could keep it up for a long time
5–6	Strong to heavy	Feels hard, more challenging
7–8	Hard	Tough, very challenging
9–10	Very, very hard	Uncomfortable, can't talk; ready to stop

Now you know everything you need to start. Take whatever time you need to warm up before beginning the test. We suggest using an easy gear or light to moderate resistance so your leg muscles don't fatigue before the test is complete.

Minutes	Heart Rate	Rating of Perceived Exertion
Warm-up	Fewer than 100 bpm	1–10
0–2	100–110 bpm	_____
2–4	110–120 bpm	_____
4–6	120–130 bpm	_____
6–8	130–140 bpm	_____
8–10	140–150 bpm	_____

You can stop the workout when you get to an RPE 4 in your feeling of exercise intensity. You'll have all the information needed. For most people the moderate exercise heart zone falls between an RPE of 3 and 4.

Write down your heart rate when you were at an RPE of 3: _____bpm

Write down your heart rate when you were at an RPE of 4: _____bpm

SELF ASSESSMENT B:
THE BIGGEST NUMBER YOU'VE
EVER SEEN OR COUNTED

This one is for those who are fit.

Remember a time when you were riding your hardest. Perhaps you were chasing someone, attempting to pass, or grinding up a steep mountain summit. You could hardly breathe, your legs were screaming, you had your foot on the gas pedal; in other words, you were "redlining" (close to maximum heart rate, explained in Chapter 2). If you were wearing a monitor, it would have displayed the biggest number you've ever seen. It's hard to reach this point.

If you were counting your pulse manually (palpation), it would beat the fastest you've ever felt. Count for 6 seconds and add a zero to get beats per minute, and you might be surprised that in a short 6 seconds your heart can beat 15 to 20 contractions. This number is very close to your maximum heart rate.

Biggest heart rate number you have ever seen or counted: _____ bpm.

SELF ASSESSMENT C:
USING YOUR FAVORITE WORKOUT RIDE

You probably have a training ride you love. If you're like most of us, you choose that route or workout most often because it's easy, familiar and fun. This time, we'll collect some information about your heart rate during that ride.

Strap on your heart rate monitor. Every two to three minutes observe the monitor and ask yourself what rating of perceived exertion best fits that moment. Since we are trying to correlate heart rate to a rate of perceived exertion, when your level feels like what Borg would call an RPE 4, note the heart rate number. If you were to describe that feeling you might say, "I could ride like this for a long time. It's so comfortable."

If you ride a stationary bike, follow the same procedure, but if you don't have a heart rate monitor, palpate your heart rate. Only take your hands off the handlebars to count on a stationary bike.

As you ride your favorite workout, count your pulse rate when you feel that the exercise intensity is moderate. You should be able to ride for a long period of time at that level.

Your heart rate number on your favorite ride when you are at an RPE of 3 is _____ bpm.

Your heart rate number on your favorite ride when you are at an RPE of 4 is _____ bpm.

You may have used a formula that determines your heart zones based on age. These formulas were first created in the 1930s when exercise research was in its infancy and the precision of measurement was far from accurate. Using a mathematical formula is not as accurate as was previously thought; however, it can still help determine a training zone. If you've found a workable formula, use that. All these formulas approximate a maximum heart rate used to set your training heart zones.

SELF ASSESSMENT D: DETERMINING 60 PERCENT OF YOUR MAXIMUM HEART RATE

We asked a colleague, Dan Heil, Ph.D., to examine data he and his co-workers had collected for 1500 walkers tested at the University of Massachusetts. In a computer analysis of factors that seemed related to the walkers' maximum heart rate, he discovered that three variables seemed most influential: age, body weight and gender. Using those results, he created a new and reliable formula:

211.415 minus 0.5 times your age minus 0.05 times your body weight in pounds plus 4.5 for men (zero for women).

We have simplified this to:

210 minus half your age minus 5 percent of your body weight in pounds, plus 4 for men (zero for women).

Let's use Sally Reed as an example. She just turned 52 and weighs 120 pounds. Her formula would be:

$210 - 26 - 7 = 178$ maximum heart rate

Her true and tested maximum heart rate cycling is 180 bpm.

Now calculate your maximum heart rate based on this new formula by plugging in your numbers below:

210 minus half your age minus 0.05 percent of your body weight plus 4 for men and zero for women = _____ bpm

This is your mathematically calculated maximum heart rate.

SETTING YOUR FIRST TRAINING HEART ZONE: ZONE 2, THE TEMPERATE ZONE

You now have four different ways to determine your first training zone, and it's time to apply this information to a ride. Your zones need to be based on your unique physiology, current fitness level, goals and much more.

The size or number of heart beats in your zones are keyed to your maximum heart rate. The heart rate we'll use for the first workout is 60 percent of your maximum heart rate, or RPE 4, a cool and comfortable zone where you can have fun and receive many health benefits.

Since you're not ready to start by redlining, we're going to find the average of the four measurements we just recommended and use this to anchor your personal Zone 2 of 60–70 percent of your maximum heart rate.

A. Every two minutes go harder self-assessment at an RDE of 4: _____ bpm

B. The biggest number you have ever seen or counted x 60 percent: _____ bpm

C. Using your favorite workout ride: _____ bpm

D. Using a mathematical formula to determine 60 percent of your maximum heart rate:_____ bpm

Looking at these numbers, use your best judgment to determine a heart rate number that best represents the feeling of RPE 4, or about 60 percent of your maximum exertion. Write that number here: _____ bpm.

Here's an example for Sally Reed's individual training zones:

A. Every 2 minutes go harder self test:	110 bpm
B. The biggest number you have ever seen or counted: (175 x 60 percent)	105 bpm
C. Using your favorite workout ride	105 bpm
D. Determining 60 percent of your max heart rate using a mathematical formula	107 bpm
Average of these four different measurements:	109 bpm
Her tested maximum heart rate of 180 x 60 percent =	108 bpm

STEP 1:
ESTIMATE YOUR MAXIMUM HEART RATE

To estimate your maximum heart rate simply use your 60 percent estimate and calculate its 100-percent value. The following chart makes Step 1 easy. Circle the 60 percent estimate and then write the corresponding 100 percent number that corresponds to it:

Maximum heart rate, or 100 %	150	155	160	165	170	175	180	185	190	195	200	205	210	215
60 %	90	93	96	99	102	105	108	111	114	117	120	123	126	129

CHAPTER WORKOUTS AND
TRAINING RIDES

Each chapter contains both indoor workouts and outdoor rides using your heart rate monitor. *Indoor workouts* will be based on your fitness goals. *Healthy Heart workouts* will interest those whose goals are to build an endurance base and get healthy, exercising between 50 and 75 percent of maximum heart rates for 20 to 30 minutes. *Fitness workouts* are for those who want to get fitter. The intensity is higher (50—80 percent) and the duration of the ride is longer. *Performance workouts* are for those wanting to get their fittest, with intensities

HEART CYCLING

TRAINING ZONE (% MAXIMUM HEART RATE)	FUEL BURNING	Max HR 150	Max HR 155	Max HR 160	Max HR 165	Max HR 170	Max HR 175	Max HR 180	Max HR 185	Max HR 190	Max HR 195	Max HR 200	Max HR 205	Max HR 210	Max HR 215	Max HR 220
Z5 Red Line 90%-100%	GLYCOGEN BURNING	150 ◇ 135	155 ◇ 140	160 ◇ 144	165 ◇ 149	170 ◇ 153	175 ◇ 158	180 ◇ 162	185 ◇ 167	190 ◇ 171	195 ◇ 176	200 ◇ 180	205 ◇ 185	210 ◇ 189	215 ◇ 194	220 ◇ 198
Z4 Threshold 80%-90%		135 ◇ 120	140 ◇ 124	144 ◇ 128	149 ◇ 132	153 ◇ 136	158 ◇ 140	162 ◇ 144	167 ◇ 148	171 ◇ 152	176 ◇ 156	180 ◇ 160	185 ◇ 164	189 ◇ 168	194 ◇ 172	198 ◇ 176
Z3 Aerobic 70%-80%		120 ◇ 105	124 ◇ 109	128 ◇ 112	132 ◇ 116	136 ◇ 119	140 ◇ 123	144 ◇ 126	148 ◇ 130	152 ◇ 133	156 ◇ 137	160 ◇ 140	164 ◇ 144	168 ◇ 147	172 ◇ 151	176 ◇ 154
Z2 Temperate 60%-70%	FAT BURNING	105 ◇ 90	109 ◇ 93	112 ◇ 96	116 ◇ 99	119 ◇ 102	123 ◇ 105	126 ◇ 108	130 ◇ 111	133 ◇ 114	137 ◇ 117	140 ◇ 120	144 ◇ 123	147 ◇ 126	151 ◇ 129	154 ◇ 132
Z1 Healthy Heart 50%-60%		90 ◇ 75	93 ◇ 78	96 ◇ 80	99 ◇ 83	102 ◇ 85	105 ◇ 88	108 ◇ 90	111 ◇ 93	114 ◇ 95	117 ◇ 98	120 ◇ 100	123 ◇ 103	126 ◇ 105	129 ◇ 108	132 ◇ 110

between 50 and 95 percent of their maximum heart rate and workouts lasting up to 60 minutes.

Each indoor workout format contains an introduction, the purpose of the workout and a plan or overview of the session. These sessions train your heart, muscles and energy systems to be more efficient. Whether you are a beginner, intermediate or competitive cyclist, workouts are driven by heart rate, and how you reach and maintain those heart rates is determined by your specific training goals. As an example, if your goal is to train for strength and power, you will change your training intensity using resistance and gearing. If your goal is to train for improved leg speed and suppleness, your heart rate numbers will be based on cadence or spinning. A person riding at a heart rate of 150 bpm and 60 rpm is training for strength, unlike someone riding at 150 bpm and 150 rpm, who is training for leg speed. Each rider has the same heart rate number, but two totally different physiological systems are being stressed.

When "choice" is listed in the workout, you select what you want to work on. If you want to build leg strength and have no knee problems, you may choose to use more resistance or bigger gears to reach a specific heart rate. If you want to work on your spin or leg speed, you will use less resistance and a higher cadence. A choice may also be made to sprint to a certain heart rate rather than taking the allotted time.

Indoor Workouts and Outdoor Rides

A typical heart cycling workout includes the following parts:
- Time (duration)
- Intensity (zone or percent of maximum heart rate)
- Workout type (intervals and steady state)
- Cadence (rpm)
- Body position
- (R) Resistance and/or gearing
- Pedal stroke
- Music selection (for indoor cycling only)

Time

Most indoor workouts are between 30 and 60 minutes in duration, outdoor rides may be longer. Each indoor workout is based on a warm-up, main set and warm-down section. Typically the warm-up and warm-down are each 10–15 percent of total riding time and the main set is 70–80 percent of total riding time. Warm-up and warm-down are critical elements to successful training, so do not compromise them.

Stretching is a vital part of every workout. Incorporate stretching prior to your warm-up and after your warm-down on the bike. If you avoid it, you'll pay the price down the road in the form of injuries, inefficiency and restriction in your range of motion.

Intensity

The heart rate intensities (percentage of maximum heart rate) during these workouts will range from 50—95 percent depending on your current goals and fitness level. Intensity can be measured in other ways, but for our purposes, heart rate is the measure, along with perceived exertion (how you feel).

Workout Types: Intervals and Steady State

Interval training consists of alternating different speeds and levels of effort in one session. Intervals add variety to training and result in the training effect. They are used to get the cyclist faster and fitter in a shorter period of time. Interval training has been supported by a tremendous amount of research to validate the theory that raising and lowering your heart rate or intensity during a single workout produces multiple benefits, including:

• Improved endurance or aerobic capacity, measured by the amount of oxygen you can use (VO_2 max)

• Total calories burned as you increase your intensity

• More fun, by adding variety

• Helps individuals stay on their training program

The primary reason for intervals is to train the energy systems to use specific fuels and deliver nutrients to your muscles more efficiently. You actually train your fuel systems as much as you strengthen specific muscle groups.

Steady state riding is training at a fixed heart rate number. The reason to ride at a constant speed, cadence or heart rate is to train yourself to become more efficient at this specific intensity level.

Cadence

Cadence or pedal revolutions per minute (rpm) tend to be under-emphasized but essential elements in training. Cadence is different for each person. In general, a cadence between 80 and 110 rpm on flat ter-rain and around 55–65 rpm on hills, depending on the length and grade of the climb, is ideal. Just remember that a lower cadence and higher resistance or big gears can strain knees and quickly fatigue the muscles. Maintaining 60 rpm or above when climbing hills allows you to blend power with cadence. As you get fitter and stronger, you will be able to ride bigger gears or use more resistance at the same rpm and heart rate.

Higher cadence during parts of your workout will help recruit slow-twitch muscle fibers designed for hours of use. High-speed cadence, or spinning, is also good for recovery because it promotes cir-culation and refueling of the working muscle groups.

The best way to determine cadence is with a bike monitor or com-puter. If you don't have one, you can calculate cadence by counting the downstroke of one leg for six seconds and adding a zero. A heart rate monitor with stopwatch function is handy. Some workouts contain a six-second number in the coaching notes. Use the following table as a guide for checking cadence.

Pedal Strokes Per 6 Seconds	Equivalent in rpm
4	40
5	50
6	60
7	70
8	80
9	90
10	100
11	110
12	120
13	130
14	140
15	150

Body Position

A smooth pedaling style greatly affects efficiency on the bike. Minimize extraneous movement, keeping your torso steady and letting your legs do the work. Your hips should not rock, bounce or bob from side to side. Keep your shoulders square and your back elongated and flat. Use your abdominal muscles for support while relaxing your shoulders and neck.

Body positions on the bike are individual. For some, standing is easier than sitting on a long steep hill or interval and for others the choice is remaining seated. Whatever position you choose, try to maintain good form, keeping your body as natural and relaxed as possible. Indoor stationary cycling classes offer a myriad of positions on the bike. Though fun and entertaining, not all extra space positions apply to outdoor cycling. Just accept the studio class for what it is: a group exercise setting to improve your fitness level, not necessarily a class to improve your cycling skills.

Resistance and Gearing

Don't make the mistake of thinking more resistance or bigger gears is the answer to getting fitter, faster and stronger. Heavy resistance and big gears in the beginning are a prescription for biomechanical problems such as knee injuries. Many people take up cycling because it's supposed to be good for strengthening muscles and tendons surrounding the knees, as well as a great low-impact activity. Remember, though, that too much, too soon of any type of overload strength training can be detrimental. Honestly evaluate your fitness level and cycling skills, and take it easy on the resistance or gearing in the beginning.

Initially, you should work on your pedal stroke, cadence and riding position rather than reach for heart rate numbers by excessively overloading your muscles and knees. There are several ways to increase intensity and raise your HR; resistance or gearing is just one. The workouts will show you how to raise the intensity.

If you train to improve your strength and power, you may choose to add resistance or gearing. If you want to work on improving leg speed and neuromuscular response, then high-speed cadence would be your choice. You may do a blend or alternate on intervals. You might choose to stand, sit, change hand positions or use other body positions. Raising intensity is based on your goals and choices; the coaching notes are only guidelines.

Pedal Stroke

Pedal with as smooth a stroke as possible in a circular motion, applying force through the legs to the pedals. You should pedal in circles rather than squares by dropping your heels at the bottom of the stroke and pulling back up using your hamstrings. Imagine that you have a small pencil on the inside of your ankles and the goal is to draw perfect circles on each revolution. Keeping pedal pressure constant is your objective.

Music Selection (for indoor workouts only)

What you listen to while riding depends on whatever motivates you. In most indoor cycling classes, the music is choreographed to the ride. Whether you like rock, jazz, New Age, country, hip-hop or classical music makes the workouts more fun and motivating. Listening to music while riding outdoors is reckless and dangerous.

Choose a workout based on your fitness level and goals, then do it!

INDOOR WORKOUT ABBREVIATIONS

Z1, Z2	Zone 1, Zone 2
(R)	Resistance of gearing
Max HR	Maximum heart rate
(Rec)	Recovery or decrease in intensity
(%)	Percentage of maximum heart rate
Bottom	The lowest heart rate number or percentage in each zone
Top	The highest heart rate number or percentage in each zone
rpm	Cadence or revolutions per minute
(8)	80 rpm or a count of "8" pedal revolutions in 6 seconds
HZT points	A point system to measure the workout training load by calculating the total number of minutes in each zone times the zone number.

WORKOUTS

Indoor Training

Criss Cross Zones 1 & 2

Healthy Heart 50–70 percent

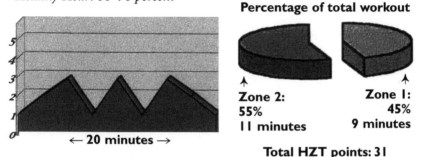

Percentage of total workout

← 20 minutes →

Zone 2:
55%
11 minutes

Zone 1:
45%
9 minutes

Total HZT points: 31

Since this is your first Heart Cycling workout, we want to make it easy and fun. If you are just getting started on a fitness program, the purpose of this 20-minute workout will help build an endurance base. Zones 1 and 2 are the healthy zones and lead to a stronger heart muscle. In addition, by riding in low zones, you will decrease your blood pressure, lower your cholesterol, stabilize your body weight and improve your self-esteem.

Purpose

The purpose of Criss Cross Z1 and Z2 is to give you a feel for the two lowest intensity zones, which are between 50 percent and 70 percent of your maximum heart rate. If this is your first time using a heart rate monitor or counting your pulse, you may be surprised at how friendly and pleasant these zones feel. These lower intensities should feel very easy, comfortable and effortless. In fact, it may seem so easy that you see little value in spending any amount of time here, but don't be fooled; they are packed with loads of heart-healthy benefits. Additionally, low heart zone training offers a much-needed sanctuary of rest and recovery from higher-intensity training. Don't expect much sweat but do expect to feel your legs and lungs working together at a moderate intensity and a rate of perceived exertion (RPE) from 1 to 5 on a scale of 10.

Workout Plan

Start with a 2-minutes of easy pedaling as you warm up. Use little or no resistance if you are on a studio bike and an easy gear, such as 39x20 or higher, for an indoor trainer.

At the end of 2 minutes, increase your heart rate (HR) to the bottom or beginning of Zone 2 (60 percent of maximum heart rate) and sustain for 3 minutes.

Your next heart rate increase will be at 5 minutes into the workout and you will increase the intensity to the top of Zone 2 (70 percent of maximum heart rate) for 2 minutes. A two-minute heart rate recovery follows to the bottom of Zone 1 (50 percent of maximum heart rate).

At 9 minutes into the workout you will criss cross (increase your heart rate) from the bottom of Zone 1 (60 percent of maximum heart rate) to the top of Zone 2 (70 percent of maximum heart rate) in 2 minutes followed by another 2-minute heart rate recovery to the bottom of Zone 1.

Criss Cross Zones 1 & 2

Elapsed time in minutes	Coaching notes	Zone	Your HR numbers	Duration
0–2	Warm up, bottom of Z1, easy pedal	1	_____	2 min.
2–5	Increase resistance (R) or cadence (rpm) to bottom of Z2 (60 percent of max HR)	2	_____	3 min.
5–7	Increase resistance (R) or cadence (rpm) to bottom of Z2 (70 percent of max HR)	2	_____	2 min.
7-9	Recover (Rec) to the bottom of Z1	1	_____	2 min.
9-11	Increase (R) or cadence (rpm) or combination to the top of Z2 (70%)	2	_____	2 min.
11-13	Recover (Rec) to the bottom of Z1	1	_____	2 min.
13-15	Criss Cross from the bottom of Z1 to the top of Z2, your choice	2	_____	2 min.
15–17	Recover (Rec) to the bottom of Z2	2	_____	2 min.
17-19	Warm down to the bottom of Z1	1	_____	3 min.
	Total HZT Points 31			

At 13 minutes into the workout you will again criss cross (increase your heart rate) from the bottom of Zone 1 to the top of Zone 2 in 2 minutes, followed by a 2-minute recovery to the bottom of Zone 2, then a warm-down for three minutes to the bottom of Zone 1, for a total of 20 minutes.

This Criss Cross interval from the bottom of Zone 1 to the top of Zone 2 may be repeated as many times as you choose. Make sure to warm down with easy pedaling for at least 10 percent of your total workout time.

Criss Cross Zones 2 & 3

Fitness 60–80 percent

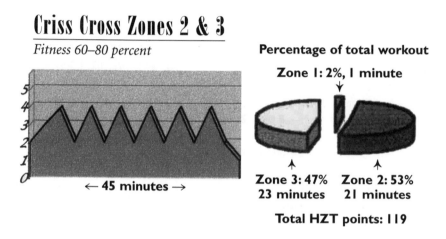

Percentage of total workout

Zone 1: 2%, 1 minute

Zone 3: 47% **Zone 2: 53%**
23 minutes **21 minutes**

← 45 minutes →

Total HZT points: 119

This is one of our favorite 45-minute workouts because you cross two zones and experience some significant physiological changes or training effects in your body. You are cycling between 60 percent and 80 percent of your maximum heart rate, which is similar to an easy-to-moderate outdoor ride. You go from being very comfortable to slightly uncomfortable and from no sweat to dripping wet. The body's choice of fuel is shifting to more carbohydrates and respiration is more rapid and deeper to meet the additional need for oxygen. Endorphins, the brain chemicals that blunt pain and are responsible for what is termed "runners high" (or what we call "spin grins") are one of the benefits of Zone 3 riding. Endorphins lead to a wonderful sense of well-being and a feeling of pleasure.

Purpose

This workout is really a tour of the two most enjoyable heart zones and should leave you feeling better than when you started. You are burning more calories and consuming lots of oxygen and your cardiopulmonary system responds by dramatically improving. By training in the fitness zones, you will get fitter and faster. The exercise high which often develops as you travel through Zone 3 results in mood improvement, reduction in anxiety and improved appetite control. The benefits last for hours after the workout and people may think you have been on vacation because of the smile on your face.

Criss Cross Zone 2 & Zone 3

Elapsed time in minutes	Coaching notes	Zone	Your HR numbers	Duration
0–5	Warm up to the bottom of Z2	2	_____	5 min.
5–8	Increase HR with resistance (R) or cadence (rpm) bottom of Z3	3	_____	3 min.
8–11	Increase HR with resistance (R) or cadence (rpm) to the top of Z3	3	_____	3 min.
11–14	Recover (Rec) to the bottom of Z2	2	_____	3 min.
14–17	Increase HR to the top of Z3. Your choice of (R) or rpm, seated	3	_____	3 min.
17–20	(Rec) to the bottom of Z2	2	_____	3 min.
20–23	Increase HR to the top of Z3. Your choice of (R) or rpm, seated	3	_____	3 min.
23–26	(Rec) to the bottom of Z2	2	_____	3 min.
26–29	Increase HR to the top of Z3. alternate (R) and rpm, seated	3	_____	3 min.
29–32	(Rec) to the bottom of Z2	2	_____	3 min.
32–35	Increase HR to the top of Z3. Alternate (R) and rpm, standing	3	_____	3 min.
35–38	3 minute (rec), bottom of Z2	2	_____	3 min.
38–41	Increase HR to the top of Z3, all out sprint high rpm, seated	3	_____	3 min.
41–45	Warm down to the bottom of Z2 then Z1	2 1	_____ _____	4 min.
	Total HZT Points 119			

Workout Plan

The workout is a total of 45 minutes including a 5-minute warm-up, a 36-minute main set with six different repetitions of approximately a 30-beat interval, followed each time by a 3-minute recovery and a warm-down. The tour includes 3 zones with intensities ranging from 50 percent to 80 percent.

Begin by warming up to the bottom of Zone 2 (60 percent), then do a 3-minute interval of increased intensity to the bottom of Zone 3 (70 percent) followed by another 3-minute heart rate increase to the top of Zone 3 (80 percent). Recover by decreasing intensity to the bottom of Zone 3 in 3 minutes, making sure your heart rate doesn't drop below 70 percent. This approximate 30-beat-plus work/recovery interval is repeated 5 more times followed by a warm-down.

30-Beat Interval
Fitness 50–70 percent

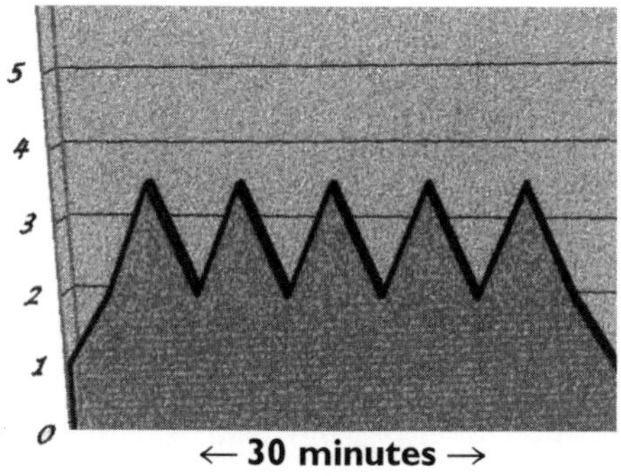

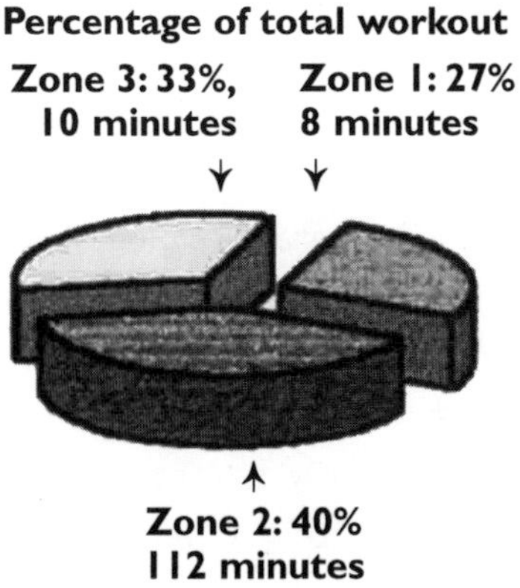

Percentage of total workout

Zone 3: 33%, 10 minutes   **Zone 1: 27%** 8 minutes

Zone 2: 40% 112 minutes

Total HZT points: 62

← 30 minutes →

If your cardiovascular goal is to get fitter and you have been working out three or more times per week, choose this 30 minute, 30-beat interval workout. If you have not done an interval workout before, they are fun and challenging. An interval is defined as alternating periods of higher intensity with periods of lower intensity. The interval in this tour is 2 minutes and the intensity is a 30-beat increase in heart rate. The recovery is a 30-beat decrease in heart rate in 2 minutes. The intensity will range from 50 percent to 75 percent of your maximum heart rate.

Purpose

Completing this 30-beat interval ride will challenge your heart muscle to respond to both time and intensity intervals. Here is your chance to put the pedal to the metal and blow out the carbon! You will reap the benefits of lowering your cholesterol and blood pressure and increase your capacity to burn fat. As you transition into Zone 3, the benefits include an increase in the size and strength of your heart and an increase in your fat-burning metabolism.

Workout Plan

This workout is a total of 30 minutes, including a 4-minute warm-up, a 22-minute main set and a 4-minute warm down. This tour includes three zones with the intensity ranging from 50 percent to 75 percent.

Begin in the Healthy Heart zone and cross the Temperate zone on your way to the mid-point of the Aerobic zone. The 30-beat, 2-minute interval begins at the bottom of Zone 2 (60 percent) and goes to the mid-point of Zone 3 (75 percent). The rest or recovery interval drops 30 beats in 2 minutes to the bottom of Zone 2.

Be aware of the following: 1. As you increase your heart rate to the mid-point of Zone 3 (75 percent), you may exceed the heart rate goal. That's fine; just remember on the next work interval you may have to "ease up" a few beats before you reach the 75 percent heart rate goal. 2. The recovery interval is what we call an "active" recovery versus an absolute recovery. In other words, you are pedaling with very little effort as your heart rate drops. Be careful not to allow your heart rate to fall below the recovery heart rate goal. The main set has five 30-beat intervals.

30-Beat Interval

Elapsed time in minutes	Coaching notes	Zone	Your HR numbers	Duration
0–4	Warm up in Z1, easy pedal	1	_____	4 min.
4–6	Increase resistance (R) or cadence (rpm) bottom of Z2	2	_____	2 min.
6–8	Increase HR 30 beats to the mid-point of Z3 (75%). Your choice of (R), (rpm) or a combination of both, stay seated	3	_____	2 min.
8–10	"Active" (rec) to the bottom of Z2, easy pedal, no (R)	2	_____	2 min.
10–12	Increase HR 30 beats to mid-point of Z3 (75 percent), your choice	3	_____	2 min.
12–14	Recover (Rec) to the bottom of Z2	2	_____	2 min.
14–16	Increase HR 30 beats to 75 percent, standing	2	_____	2 min.
16–18	(Rec) to the bottom of Z2	3	_____	2 min.
18–20	Increase HR 30 beats to 75 percent, high (rpm)	2	_____	2 min.
20–22	(Rec) to the bottom of Z2	3	_____	2 min.
22–24	Increase HR 30 beats to 75%, heavy (R)	2	_____	2 min.
24–26	(Rec), bottom of Z2	1	_____	4 min.
26–30	Warm down with easy pedal			
	Total HZT Points 62			

ONE SIZE DOES NOT FIT ALL

Salespeople in the athletic shoe business will tell you that fitting people for performance and comfort is a challenge because no two feet are the same. Similarly, there is no single perfect training program for everyone.

All exercise, like shoes, should be customized to fit the individual. Several years ago, a popular magazine named the fittest man in the world. The article outlined his training program with the insidious assumption that readers should consider following it so they could become as fit as the cover boy. That approach may sell magazines, but it is not good advice for training. You can appreciate and respect others' training regimens, but follow the one that fits you.

Let's use maximum heart rate as an example. Maggie Sullivan, Vice President of Sports Marketing for Danskin, is a 46-year-old, hard-working, very slender, tall, high-energy woman. Looking at her, it would be hard to predict her percent body fat, cholesterol level, blood pressure, metabolic rate or maximum heart rate. In a test, she wore a heart rate monitor and measured her maximum heart rate on a treadmill. Surprisingly, her maximum heart rate tested out twice at 215 beats per minute.

There are two things to note about maximum heart rate. The mathematical formula commonly used (220 minus your age) is extremely inaccurate for much of the population. For Maggie's heart rate, the error using this formula would be 220 - 42 years = 178 bpm. Compared to her tested maximum heart rate of 215, an error of 37 beats per minutes would be 20 percent—too large for practical use.

Secondly, Maggie's heart zones are unique to her. She needs to determine her training zones based on her anchor point heart number of 215 bpm, which is entirely different than,

Outdoor Training
The Tune-Up Tour

The tour consists of three outdoor rides that will allow you to become more familiar with your heart rate monitor and the information and feedback it is providing. *The Observation Trip* is an assessment of your current fitness level, *The Steady State Pace Ride* is finding your comfort zone and *The Recovery Interval Ride* is measuring your recovery levels. Remember that the power in the Heart Cycling training system is not in using a monitor but rather in your ability to use the information it provides.

for example, Sally Reed's maximum heart rate of 180 bpm. As they say in the shoe business, if the shoe doesn't fit, don't wear it.

The same is true for group exercise programs. We put groups of individuals together, make them follow the same workout programs and expect them all to do well. It is common in aerobics classes or Masters Swim workouts. The coach or instructor leads the group through the same intensity, duration and frequency of exercise. Some do well and others don't. If there are a few stars in the class who lose a lot of weight or win a race, the coach is considered brilliant. We don't consider the participants who fail to accomplish their goals and say that the coach is a failure. We should. The coach has failed the group if he or she hasn't individualized the workout to meet everyone's unique needs.

This is common in indoor cycling classes, where the fittest riders hop on the bikes nearest the instructor and the last row can barely hold onto the workout. This tends to happen out of intimidation or fear. Many of these indoor cycling workouts are called "high, hard," because participants hold a high heart rate for long periods. Just as in a pack of road riders, the unfit fall off the back and quickly out of the program. We lose them because they're burned out.

In contrast, heart zone training, which might be called individualized zone training with heart, is totally based on your individual physiology—your heart zones. Honoring your individual goals, individual physiology, unique sports history, interests and special needs, heart zone training is totally about you. Your heart sets the tempo and the pace. Yours is the smart heart.

Your heart rate monitor is the link between your mind and body, allowing your mind to see what your heart is saying.

The Observation Trip

All of us have a favorite ride. Most of these rides have names. It might be the lunch time ride or the river ride or the Tuesday night ride. Your first ride with a heart rate monitor is to simply ride and observe your heart rate. Ride just like you always do and ride comfortably. Don't change a thing. There is tendency to disagree with your heart rate monitor on your first ride and say it is not working. In most of the cases the monitor is right and the person is wrong. As humans, we tend to want something different. A higher number here, as in bike speed, and a lower number there, as in heart rate, and more of this, like altitude changes, and less of that, like the time that it takes to finish the ride. Most of us react this way.

On your observation trip just ride and look and be detached from the numbers. They don't really have a lot of meaning until they are all put into relationship with each other. Don't have an opinion; it's called riding with detachment. Be in the present and just look, feel, wonder and think. Don't fight with what you are observing or argue with yourself about it. For now, just accept the information.

When you finish this first trip, note the following bits of information by entering them in your training log book or similar place.

Today's date
Elasped time—(Chrono on watch, heart rate monitor or bike monitor)
Distance
Average speed—(bike monitor)
Maximum speed—(bike monitor)
Peak heart rate—(highest number you saw)
Average heart rate—(if your heart rate monitor has this function)

That's it. That's all you have to do. Just note this information and get ready for the second ride.

Steady State Pace Ride

This one is easy and fun. You simply will ride according to your feel and will hold a constant speed that is comfortable. If we were to say ride in your "comfort zone," which might be a heart zone that you can maintain while still talking continuously, that is the intensity level to ride. Try not to vary your pace or speed. The goal is to hold the speed constant throughout the trip. Ride at a steady state for a fixed distance. Five miles is recommended if you are a beginner, 10 miles if you are an intermediate rider and if you are more experienced, such as a century rider, then do a 25-mile ride. What is key is not the distance, but that you keep your pace the same throughout.

At the end of the ride, there is only one key number to record: your average heart rate. Note that number in your log book.

The Recovery Interval Ride

How quickly you recover is a measurement of how fit you are. The faster your heart rate can recover, the fitter your cardiovascular system. This is an assessment you'll periodically do to see if the promise of getting fitter is a reality, and if your training system is working for you, not against you (that is called "over-training").

This ride is a series of intervals. An interval is simply a series of hard to easy bouts within a workout set or session. For trip No. 3 (there are a lot of variations once you understand the importance of both interval training and the power of recovery), you will do 3 intervals of hard effort and 3 intervals of recovery. Warm up for a period of 15 to 20 minutes or until you feel ready to ride hard. Ride hard for 5 minutes at a fixed speed. For beginners use 12 mph; for intermediate riders use 18 mph; and for advanced riders use 20+mph. Then drop the speed by 5 mph for 5 minutes. This is the recovery time. Repeat this hard effort recovery interval 2 more times. Finish by riding easy and warming down. Record the following information:

Average heart rate:

Chrono time (elapsed time):

Average speed (mph or kph):

The first three rides are about setting some bench marks or starting points. Using your heart rate monitor allows you to measure your improvement and individualize your training. That's what we call "smart training."

REFERENCES

Borg, Gunmar. *Borg's Perceived Exertion and Pain Scales.* Champaign, IL: Human Kinetics, 1998.

Wilmore, Jack and David Costill. *Physiology of Sport and Exercise.* Champaign, IL: Human Kinetics, Revised, 1999.

Edwards, Sally. *The Heart Rate Monitor Book.* Helsinki, Finland: Polar Electro Oy, 1993.

Sally Edwards (left) and Cathy Anderson-Meyers riding in the Sierra Nevada Mountains.

Co-author Sally Edwards (right) winning silver medal at the Nike Masters World Games.

CHAPTER 2

Your First Week

Paul Yale is a brilliant software developer, teacher and author. Success in business came easily for him, but successful fitness had been a challenge for years.

When I met Paul through my Heart Zone training seminar, he was a couch potato who belonged to a prestigious athletic club but never worked out. He gained weight each year and didn't like it. He traveled internationally, so it was hard to stay in shape when the speed of his life was accelerating.

He attended his first seminar alone but later brought many relatives and his whole business team. After three years, he's completed his first triathlon, run a marathon in less than five hours and started to ride to get in better shape. He's gained muscle, lost fat and lost total body weight. I'm thrilled by the improvement I've seen in his health and his life.

We asked Paul why, like so many others, he continues to come to the seminar and bring more people. He answered that business and cycle training share qualities that make it possible for him to integrate both. He applies the way we train and race as competitive athletes to how he conducts his small business.

Paul's first discovery was in the "g" word: goals. This chapter will teach you how athletes set achievable, attainable goals by training. We rarely exercise. When we do, we move for the joy or benefit of the movement itself. That's important. When we train, we move to accomplish a goal. That's critical. For athletes to succeed, we use goals for motivation.

Business and most other aspects of life are similar in that if you set goals, the chance to accomplish more increases enormously. But more important than mere goal-setting is the feeling of personal accomplishment, self-esteem and satisfaction when you cross the finish line. The feeling that you did it is one of the best rewards that comes from the process. You set a goal, you write and execute a plan and you joyfully reach the finish line. That process can empower each of us. Becoming an athlete by practicing the Heart Cycling system gives you access to that feeling and ability. You can apply the same process to every other aspect of your life. In *The Art of Happiness* (Riverhead Books, 1998), the Dalai Lama describes this process:

"(In) an approach to bringing about positive changes within oneself, learning is only the first step. There are other factors as well: conviction, determination, action, and effort."

In the 10 Steps to Heart Cycling (page 29), you'll go through each of the steps that almost all successful athletes follow, whether they finish first with a gold or with a finisher's medal. The process, not the position, is what's important.

I know this is true because I volunteer to finish last in all the Danskin women's triathlon races. I've finished last in more than 30 races in the last five years. I swim with the last swimmer, bike with the last cyclist and run with the last runner so that no one else has to come in last. I have the privilege of being the sweep athlete.

Finishing dead last isn't as much fun as finishing somewhere else in the field, of course. But what counts is that you set goals and accomplish them. Reebok® once had an advertising campaign with a slogan that I loved: "Life is not a spectator sport." I'd like to rewrite it positively as "life is a participant's sport." You are the athlete. An athlete in my playbook is anyone who trains.

Paul has applied the principles he's learned through Heart Zone Training to his successful business. The training system delivered on the promise: the company and Paul both got better, experiencing more energy and happiness.

You can experience this kind of improvement not only in your athletic performance, but also in your life. Follow this systematic process and you will realize the outcome by saving time and getting more benefit. In your workout and in your life, you will increase productivity.

—Sally Edwards

The 10 Steps to Heart Cycling

Step 1:	Estimating your maximum heart rate	Chapter 1
Step 2:	Setting your heart zones	Chapter 2
Step 3:	Choosing your goals	Chapter 2
Step 4:	Determining your weekly riding time	Chapter 3
Step 5:	Determining your training spokes	Chapter 3
Step 6:	Determining your current level of fitness	Chapter 4
Step 7:	Writing a training plan	Chapter 6
Step 8:	Analyzing your training plan	Chapter 6
Step 9:	Logging your workouts and rides	Chapter 8
Step 10:	Reassessing your fitness level	Chapter 10

STEP 2: CHOOSING YOUR GOALS

Start by choosing your athletic goals. As a framework for making those choices, you need to ask if your goals are specific, measurable, attainable, realistic and timely. You also need to decide on short-term and long-term goals.

Next, write down your goals. Determine what it will take to accomplish them. What are your resources? What support systems do you need to have in place? What tools and skills will you going to need to be successful? Go get them. Then realistically assess the amount of time you'll need.

Once you've done this, commit your goal requirements to paper or disk in the form of a written plan. We'll call this a training plan. Use it to detail your workouts and how you'll complete them. Record your training in a log or log book so you can track how well you're doing. In the world of commerce, this kind of planning and recording is called a business plan.

Complete a self-assessment. This is a measurement (see Chapter 4) that gives you a starting point for later comparison. For example, what's your current fitness level? That will be one of your starting points.

It's sometimes wise to get a medical check-up before you begin. Keep a copy of the records; don't just leave them in your physician's files, since they belong to you. Take charge of your health and accept responsibility for its improvement. Athletes and coaches call this your personal "performance evaluation." Reinforcing the business-sports

Goal-Setting Model for Athletes

Steps	Goal chain	10 Steps to Heart Cycling
1	Making your choices	Determining your maximum heart rate
2	Setting your choices	Setting your heart zones
3	Choosing your goals	Choosing your goals
4	Determining your current position	Determining your riding times in zones
5	Determining your resources and needs	Determining your training spokes
6	Getting resources	Determining your current level of fitness
7	Writing a plan	Writing a training plan
8	Analyzing the plan	Analyzing your training plan
9	Logging your execution	Logging your workouts and rides
10	Managing and measuring the plan	Reassessing your fitness

connection, an employer calls it the same thing, a personal performance evaluation.

Finally, measure progress at intervals in your training. This procedure helps you see improvement and better manage your training
program. You'll be getting healthier, fitter, faster and stronger. Realizing and enjoying the changes in yourself will also motivate you.

How Athletes Use Goals In Their Lives

To put the athletic goal-setting process into a model, we need to
bring the big picture into view. The following chart will help you
understand the process of setting goals.

Your goal-setting process leads you up to the big moment when
you realize you're prepared to face the challenge. Throughout your
training, you will have built a structure that puts you on the line—the
starting line. You will reach the starting line ready and confident
because you have trained like an athlete, and you are an athlete in every
mental, physical and emotional way.

Almost every year, somewhere in the world, Sally Edwards races
in an Ironman triathlon. She has completed 16 Ironman races over the
past 20 years. People frequently ask her why she continues to enter that
difficult race after so many years.

Her answer: "I love challenges and accomplishments. I prefer the
hard races—the multi-day adventure races like the Eco-Challenges and
the bicycle race across the United States called RAAM, because it is as
much who I am as what I want to learn and gain from the experience.
Each year, I set my own big and little goals.

"To reinforce this lifestyle, I carry with me the memory of how I feel
as I head toward the finish banner. The crowds are cheering and a smile
of joy radiates from my face. I look up at the finish clock and read the
number I'd set in my goal process, the finish time I committed to when I
set my goals. And at that moment, I know who I am and the satisfaction
in my heart and soul of accomplishing the goals that I set and believed in,
which is why I continue to participate in sports and business."

For Sally and so many others, such as former couch potato Paul
Yale, that's success. This can become success for you, too.

UNDERSTANDING MAXIMUM HEART RATE

In Chapter 1, your first workout was to determine the bottom of Zone 2 (60 percent) of your maximum heart rate. When you tried all four measurements, you came up with an average heart rate number for yourself. You rode three different workouts in varying lengths (time) and intensities (zones) to get the feel of riding by heart rate. You are now well on your way to combining your head and heart to create smart training.

To ride with heart, you need to know your maximum heart rate. Here are some important characteristics of maximum heart rate:
• Genetically determined; you are born with it
• Altitude-sensitive
• A fixed number, unless you become unfit
• Affected by some medications
• If high, does not predict better athletic performance
• If low, does not predict worse athletic performance
• Has great variability among people of the same age
• Serves as the anchor we use to set an individual's training zones
• Sport specific

COMPARING THE FIVE
HEART RATE ZONES

All zones have structure, weight and size. Structurally, the top and bottom of a zone are like a ceiling and floor. The ceiling of Zone 3, for example, is structurally the same number as the floor of Zone 4. All zones have size. They all are 10 percent of your maximum heart rate, with a midpoint halfway between ceiling and floor. The nature of all zones is to have a name relating to the benefit derived from riding within its structure.

Each zone is unique. What happens physiologically changes between them, such as the fuels consumed, your feeling while in the zone, the amount of time you can spend in it and the training effect that results.

Zones are not cumulative. You can't get the benefit of Zone 1 by training in a higher zone such as Zone 4. You only get the benefit of the specific zone you are experiencing. Zones have weight or value that corresponds to the number of the zone. The higher the number of the zone, the heavier the weight or multiplier value. All zones are part of a wellness continuum from health to fitness to performance. All zones are relative, which means they are specific to your maximum heart rate and nobody else's.

Here is an overview of each of the five zones:

Zone 1—The Healthy Heart Zone

Zone	Zone name	Percent of max HR	Fuels burned	Calories burned per minute	Description
1	Healthy Heart Zone	50–60%	10% carbohydrates 85% fat 5% protein	3 to 5 calories	Easy. Don't sweat. Fun. Relaxing. Recuperative. Sustainable for long periods of time. Breathing is effortless.

This is the kickoff zone for those new to training. The reason you start a cycling program with mostly Zone 1 time is that it builds a healthier heart. Your heart muscle gets stronger and more efficient. Not a lot of total calories are burned, but those that are come primarily from dietary and body fat stores.

If you are in shape, the Healthy Heart Zone is a great place for a gentle recovery ride. Some of the health benefits from training here include lower blood cholesterol, lower blood pressure, improved self-esteem and ideally, a stabilized body weight. You will no longer gain that one pound per year that is so common in even the most conscientious person. Because Zone 1 is such a low-intensity zone, you'll have plenty of time to enjoy the sights and smell the flowers while you ride.

Zone 2—The Temperate Zone

Zone	Zone name	Percent of max HR	Fuels	Calories burned	Description burned per minute
2	Temperate Zone	60–70%	15% carbohydrates 80% fat 5% protein	6 to 8 calories	Cool zone. Breathing is comfortable. Known as the moderate zone. Gain muscle mass. Realize more health benefits.

This zone has such a strong character that it is known by a variety of names, including the moderate zone, the comfort zone, the cruise zone, and sometimes (though inaccurately) the fat-burning zone. Benefits you'll get from training in the Temperate Zone are increased skeletal muscle mass and decreased body fat. In this moderate zone, you train your body to efficiently metabolize fat, which includes fat mobilization, transportation and utilization. You can read more about this in Chapter 5.

Oxygen is plentiful in this zone, so you will realize improved aerobic function. As you spend more and more time in the Temperate Zone, you will increase your capacity to burn fat by increasing the number of mitochondria, or energy factories, in each muscle cell. In other words, training in Zone 2 allows you to open your fat cells and let the fat out of them, while turning on the demand for fat by muscle cells. Simultaneously, because of the body's adaptation to the exercise, your muscles are increasing the number of fat-energy-burning factories.

Zone 2, the Temperate Zone, like its name, is a cool and comfortable zone to ride.

Zone 3—The Aerobic Zone

Zone	Zone name	Percent of max HR	Fuels burned	Calories burned per minute	Description
3	Aerobic Zone	70–80%	55% carbohydrates 40% fat 5% protein	9–11 calories	Cardiovascular zone— improvement in the number and size of blood vessels, in respiratory functions, in cardiac function, endorphins released, shift in fuel utilization toward carbohydrates. You sweat.

Zone 3 gives you the biggest fitness benefit in the least time. In the Aerobic Zone, you maximize your efforts because you are burning many calories in the form of carbohydrate and fat. Simultaneously, your body is consuming lots of oxygen and your cardiopulmonary system dramatically improves. Endorphins, the brain chemicals that blunt pain and are responsible for what's termed the "runner's high" are released. These opiate-like stress reducers can increase up to five-fold from the resting state training here.

It is the key fitness zone because you get fitter and faster when you train within it. During this training time, you dump many of the emotional and physical stored-up toxins. You build resistance to fatigue and increase your endurance. Zone 3 riding builds cardiovascular efficiency while sparing the carbohydrates and burning the fats. The exercise high or state of euphoria arising from training here results in mood improvement, reduction in anxiety and improved appetite control. Its beauty is that all these benefits last for hours after the workout.

Zone 4—The Threshold Zone

Zone	Zone name	Percent of max HR	Fuels burned per minute	Calories burned	Description
4	Threshold Zone	80–90%	70% carbohydrates 25% fat 5% protein	12–14 calories	Improved oxygen consumption, increased tolerance to lactic acid production (the burn). Breathing is more difficult. High calorie consumption and many carbohydrates utilized as fuel.

When you cross over into the Threshold Zone, you enter a new territory of high heart rate numbers. Zone 4 leads to improved sports and fitness performance. If you want to get really fit, you need to spend some riding time in this zone. If you want to stay fit, you never need to cross this threshold.

Somewhere in this zone for most individuals you pass from aerobic to anaerobic exercise. At this point, most are exercising so hard that the muscles become hungry for oxygen. You can continue to exercise without enough oxygen. As a result, you may feel a burning sensation in the working muscle groups because without enough oxygen there is a build-up of lactic acid.

The Threshold Zone is high-intensity training. It is much too stressful for the beginner, but for anaerobic workout junkies who spend all their riding time hanging out here, producing endorphins and eating up lactic acid as if it were chocolate, it's a delight. This isn't an easy training zone to stay in because it is hot; it has high heart rate numbers and high intensity. Even for the really fit, it's a challenge to stay in this zone for more than 60 minutes. Your muscular energy factories, called mitochondria, are working at full capacity, burning every calorie that comes their way without distinguishing fat from protein or carbohydrate. You might just think of the Threshold Zone as one with a high thermostatic climate.

Zone 5—The Redline Zone

Zone	Zone name	Percent of max HR	Fuels burned	Calories burned per minute	Description
5	Redline Zone	90–100%	90% carbohydrates 5% fat 5% protein	15–20 calories	Extremely high intensity zone. Important for maximizing speed and strength but potentially damaging to the physiology. High total calories burned. Labored breathing patterns.

The Redline Zone is only for competitive athletes. You may have experienced Zone 5 by accident if you ever had to sprint to catch the bus, when your heart is beating so hard and your breathing is so labored that you feel you will burst. Redlining is a training zone beyond the anaerobic threshold junkie's favorite. This is the territory where athletes suffer pain as they try to deliver the maximum metabolic demands of the muscles. It's not a sustainable training zone because your heart muscle can't and won't contract at or near its maximum intensity for long. For every second spent in this zone, you are taxing your oxygen capacity, your fuels, heart and skeletal muscles to their limits. And, of course, payback comes later during recovery with sore muscles, fatigue, possible injury, potential aerobic capacity damage and much more.

This zone is where you face your maximum heart rate. Stay too long and you will reach complete exhaustion. The Redline Zone is tantalizing because if you don't visit it often enough, you can't reach your highest performance levels. But if you overstay your visit, your body won't readily invite you back.

Each of the five physical heart zones has its own face, name and character, as unique as you and I. You'll find a reason to spend time with each and accomplish different specific goals by doing so. That is what is so attractive about them and about the training system. If the endorphins don't get you in Zones 3 to 5, the fat-burning will seduce you in Zones 2 to 3.

STEP 3: SETTING YOUR ZONES

Maximum Heart Rate Chart

Heart zone percent	Number of beats per minute
100 percent maximum heart rate	_186_ bpm _186_
90 percent maximum heart rate	_167_ bpm _167_
80 percent maximum heart rate	_148_ bpm
70 percent maximum heart rate	_130_ bpm
60 percent maximum heart rate	_111_ bpm
50 percent maximum heart rate	_93_ bpm

Zone Name	Heart Zone	Beats per minute	Zone Number
Redline Zone	90–100% max HR	_167_ to _186_	5
Threshold Zone	80–90 % max HR	_148_ to _167_	4
Aerobic Zone	70–80 % max HR	_130_ to _148_	3
Temperate Zone	60–70 % max HR	_111_ to _130_	2
Healthy Heart Zone	50–60 % max HR	_93_ to _111_	1

When Paul Yale was asked why he liked to ride, he replied he wanted to lose weight and get healthier by riding in the Health Zones. A year later, after repeating the seminar, he said he wanted to get fitter and was riding in the Fitness Zones. He then trained and finished his first marathon. After his third seminar, he wanted to race, training in the Performance Zones. He's now realized all his goals and was rewarded for the work he spent on setting and pursuing them, in business and in cycling.

WORKOUTS

Indoor Training

5 x 2

Fitness 50–80 percent

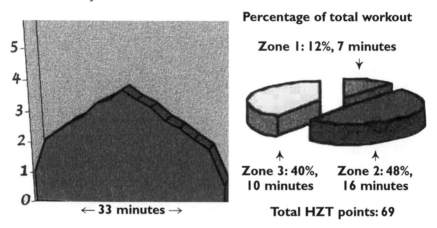

Percentage of total workout

Zone 1: 12%, 7 minutes

Zone 3: 40%, 10 minutes

Zone 2: 48%, 16 minutes

← 33 minutes →

Total HZT points: 69

This is a fun but challenging 33-minute workout, just like climbing up a ladder every 2 minutes and increasing your heart rate 5 beats. The training intensity can be adapted to your goals by moving the top rung of the ladder either higher or lower. To lengthen the workout, change the time to 5 beats every 3, 4 or 5 minutes. The goal is to go up and down the ladder at least one time.

Purpose

Ladders teach your cycling-specific metabolic systems to adapt to changing workloads every 2 minutes, forcing your cardiovascular system to get stronger by adapting to the progressive overload. Reaching the top rung is only half the battle; coming down in a controlled manner is sometimes harder.

Workout Plan

Subtract 40 beats from your maximum heart rate to determine the top rung of your ladder and subtract 70 beats from your maximum heart rate to determine your starting point, or bottom rung of the ladder. Warm up for 5 minutes in Zone 1, then begin by starting at 70 beats below your maximum heart rate.

Sustain that heart rate number for 2 minutes, then add 5 bpm in intensity every 2 minutes until you reach the top rung of the ladder, which is 40 beats below your maximum heart rate.

Decrease your heart rate every 2 minutes as you come back down the ladder. It is your choice on how to increase heart rate. You may use cadence, resistance or any combination you can think of. You may sprint to the next heart rate or you may gradually increase heart rate as long as you reach each 5 bpm increment every 2 minutes. Be careful coming back down as you decrease your heart rate 5 bpm every 2 minutes. When you get close to the desired heart rate you will have to work harder so as not to drop below the 5 beats. The more you do this workout the better you get at it.

Note: 5 x 5 is a longer duration workout (60 min.) at a higher intensity for those wanting to get fitter. Try maximum heart rate minus 20 bpm as the top rung and maximum heart rate minus 50 bpm as the starting point. Make sure you have plenty of water, as this is a long and challenging workout. It is designed for the person who is fit and wants to improve fitness and performance.

5 x 2

Elapsed time in minutes	Coaching notes	Zone	Your HR numbers	Duration
0–6	Warm up in Z1	1	111	6 min.
6–8	Increase HR to max minus 70 bpm	2	116	2 min.
8–10	Add 5 bpm	2	121	2 min.
10–12	Add 5 bpm	2	126	2 min.
12–14	Add 5 bpm	2	131	2 min.
14–16	Add 5 bpm	3	136	2 min.
16–18	Add 5 bpm	3	141	2 min.
18–20	Add 5 bpm	3	146	2 min.
20–22	Drop 5 bpm	3	141	2 min.
22–24	Drop 5 bpm	3	136	2 min.
24–26	Drop 5 bpm	2	131	2 min.
26–28	Drop 5 bpm	2	126	2 min.
28–30	Drop 5 bpm	2	121	2 min.
30–33	Warm down, Z1	1	111	2 min.
	Total HZT Points 69			

Tail Wind

Fitness 60–90 percent

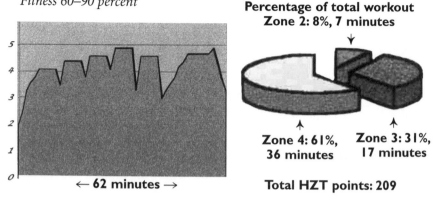

Percentage of total workout
Zone 2: 8%, 7 minutes

← 62 minutes →

Zone 4: 61%, 36 minutes

Zone 3: 31%, 17 minutes

Total HZT points: 209

Tail Wind is one of those words you love to hear as a cyclist. It means the wind is at your back as you coast along effortlessly, enjoying the moment and knowing that at any minute the wind could change. This 62-minute workout is full of moments drifting like a leaf in the wind followed by hard efforts when the wind is again in your face and the riding is hard.

Purpose

This is a true interval workout with brief bouts of moderate to high intensity followed by brief periods of recovery. You are training your cycling specific metabolic systems with over 60 percent of the workout in Zone 4. This session is loaded with various challenges. Vary the work bouts by changing cadence, position on the bike, adding resistance or changing gears. For example, you may want to "spin" your way up the first two-thirds of the work interval, then "power" (add resistance or gearing) your way the last one-third as if you were passing everyone as you crest the hill, knowing relief is on the way (a tailwind).

Workout Plan

This ride is 62 minutes with a 5–7 minute warm up, 45–50 minute main set followed by at least a 5-minute warm down. You may alter the total time; just remember that the warm-up and warm-down are each about 10 percent of the total time.

The main set begins by adding 5 heartbeats every minute until you reach the bottom of Zone 4. Sustain the bottom of Zone 4 for 4 minutes; then a 2-minute tailwind drops you back down 10 heartbeats.

The next 4-minute work interval takes you to your maximum heart rate minus 30 heartbeats, which is about the mid-point of Zone 4, followed by a tail wind that drops you back down 10 beats.

There are a series of four more work/rest intervals, each taking you a little higher in intensity. You may choose to change the intensity of the workout to meet your goals by dropping down a zone for each work/recovery interval.

Note: This is a great workout for visualizing a series of hills with steep descents on each side. Use your imagination and creativity to attack each hill differently. I imagine everyone passing me as I start up the hill, saving my legs until the last third where I stand, then power my way past them as I crest the hill.

Tail Wind

Elapsed time in minutes	Coaching notes	Zone	Your HR numbers	Duration
0–5	Warm up to the bottom of Z2	2	_____	5 min.
5–7	Add 10 bpm with cadence (rpm)	2	_____	2 min.
7–11	Add 5 bpm each min. with cadence (rpm)	3	_____	4 min.
11–15	Sustain HR at the bottom of Z4	4	_____	4 min.
15–17	Two min. recovery (rec) to mid-point of Z3 (75%)	3	_____	2 min.
17–22	Sustain max HR minus 30 bpm, your choice	4	_____	5 min.
22–24	(Rec) to mid-point of Z3 (75%)	3	_____	2 min.
24–29	Increase HR to mid-point Z4 (85%), sprint	4	_____	5 min.
29–31	Decrease HR to bottom of Z4, 90 rpm (9)	4	_____	2 min.
31–36	Increase HR to the top of Z4, sprint first 3 min. then heavy (R) last 2 min., 60 rpm (6), standing	4	_____	5 min.
36–38	Decrease HR to max HR minus 50 bpm and sustain	3	_____	2 min.
38–43	Add 25 bpm, your choice	4	_____	5 min.
43–45	(Rec) to bottom of Z3	3	_____	2 min.
45–50	From the bottom of Z3, add 5 bpm each min.	3	_____	5 min.
50–56	Add 10 bpm and sustain, your choice	4	_____	6 min.
56–57	Increase HR to the top of Z4, your choice	4	_____	1 min.
57–58	Decrease HR to the bottom of Z4	4	_____	1 min.
58–59	Decrease HR to the bottom of Z3	3	_____	1 min.
59–62	Decrease HR to the bottom of Z2	2	_____	3 min.
	Total HZT Points 209			

Top Spin

Fitness 50–90 percent

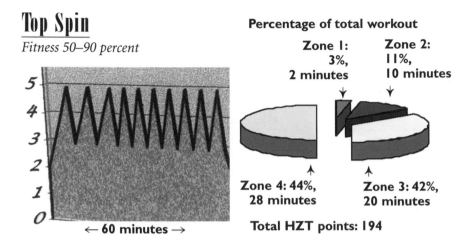

Percentage of total workout

| Zone 1: 3%, 2 minutes | Zone 2: 11%, 10 minutes |
| Zone 4: 44%, 28 minutes | Zone 3: 42%, 20 minutes |

Total HZT points: 194

← 60 minutes →

This is one of our favorite workouts and a play on words if you are a tennis player. You will spin yourself to the "top" of four zones in 60 minutes. This workout can also be changed to meet your goals by dropping down a zone on each 4-minute interval, which makes it a great workout for those wanting to get fitter. The last 10 minutes will challenge your sprint and recovery capabilities and give you a taste of how fit you really are.

Purpose

Top Spin is designed to improve your ability to respond to approximately 20-beat and 40-beat intervals. It will also help you measure your fitness level by timing recovery rates. You may choose to do the 20-beat intervals by increasing cadence or adding resistance. If you choose resistance, keep a steady tempo or cadence. Do an "active" recovery by soft pedaling or easy pedaling back down. The 40-beat intervals are your choice in terms of using cadence, resistance, body position or combinations that increase heart rate; do whatever it takes to get up to the top fast and back down. This is a good workout to do monthly to see if your recovery times are improving.

Workout Plan

This is a series of approximately 20- and 40-heartbeat repeats. The work to recovery ratio is 2:1, meaning for every 2 minutes of effort there is a 1-minute recovery. The last 10 minutes of the main set is very challenging seeing how many times you can do the 40-beat recovery interval. The most times up and down we have seen in heart cycling

43

classes is 8 times—just to give you something to shoot for.

Note: This is fun to do with a group of people, especially the first 10 minutes when everyone is sprinting and recovering at different times. Bring your towel and water bottle for this workout.

Top Spin

Elapsed time in minutes	Coaching notes	Zone	Your HR numbers	Duration
0–5	Warm up to the bottom of Z2	2	_____	5 min.
5–10	Increase HR to the top of Z2 with cadence (rpm)	2	_____	5 min.
10–14	Increase HR to the top of Z3 with (R)	3	_____	4 min.
14–18	Increase HR to the top of Z4, your choice of sprint, (R) or combination, seated	4	_____	4 min.
18–20	Recover (rec) to the top of Z2	2	_____	2 min.
20–24	Increase HR to the top of Z3 with (R), standing	3	_____	4 min.
24–28	Increase HR to the top of Z4, your choice of sprint, (R) or combination, first two min. seated, second two min. standing	4	_____	4 min.
28–30	(Rec) to the top of Z2	2	_____	2 min.
30–32	Seated sprint to the top of Z3	3	_____	2 min.
32–34	Standing sprint to the top of Z4	4	_____	2 min.
34–36	(Rec) to the top of Z2	2	_____	2 min.
36–38	All-out sprint to the top of Z4	4	_____	2 min.
38–40	(Rec) to the top of Z2	2	_____	2 min.
40–42	All-out sprint to the top of Z4	4	_____	2 min.
42–44	(Rec) to the top of Z2	2	_____	2 min.
44–54	Number of times to top of Z4 and (rec) to the bottom of Z3 in 10 min., your choice	4	_____	10 min.
54–60	Warm down to the bottom of Z2	2	_____	6 min.
	Total HZT Points 194			

OUTDOOR TRAINING

The safest way to take a true maximum heart rate test is in exercise or human performance labs. This test is available in most major cities in the world and the price for it varies. If you don't have access or don't want to go to an exercise lab, you can determine your own true and tested maximum heart rate at your own risk. Do these three rides only if you are fit, have no history or symptoms of cardiac, respiratory or vascular conditions and are under the age of 50 for women and 40 for men.

The Biggest Number

This is an easy and quick assessment that takes you near your maximum heart rate. Turn on your bike monitor or bike computer and warm up completely. Start your stopwatch and every 15 seconds, increase your heart rate 5 bpm until your heart rate no longer goes up. When you reach a point of near exhaustion, slow down and recover. If your heart rate monitor does not store peak heart rate, mentally record the highest number you see. Always have a friend with you for both safety and motivation. Ride on roads with little vehicular traffic or interruptions.

The All-Out Trip

This is another maximum heart rate test that takes you to a point near your maximum heart rate. Find a 1000-meter or half-mile measured distance that is flat and without obstructions. Warm up adequately. Sprint the distance as hard as you can at full speed with a friend riding nearby to encourage you. Motivation is an essential factor in trying to get close to your true maximum. Do this two times. The second time should be more difficult than the first and probably will be the lower of the two numbers. Use the higher of the two numbers as your maximum heart rate for cycling.

Hill Sprints

Select a hill that will take you approximately one minute to "sprint" to the top of. Do three all-out sprints to the top with very little rest in between. Use the highest number you see on your heart rate monitor as your maximum heart rate.

Note: When performing maximum heart rate tests, make sure you are fully rested in order to get your most accurate measurement.

Wellness Is A Continuum

Wellness is a state of well-being. Given that simplistic statement, it's hard to say who is well or how well they might be, since we lack a consistent definition of wellness. Wellness is difficult to measure; it may be easier to measure happiness than gauge the level of an individual's wellness. To compound the problem, health behaviors such as diet, stress management and physical activity are equally difficult to assess. Trying to compare the wellness states of two different individuals also presents problems. One way of understanding wellness is not to view it as a fixed point or level, but to think of it as a continuum that allows for changes in state or condition.

The Heart Zone Training system consists of three different parts that combine to form a whole—a wellness continuum. The three parts are typically the three goals of training: to become healthier, to get fitter and to perform better. Each part corresponds to heart zones that provide different wellness outcomes.

If, when asked why you ride, you answer that you want to manage your weight, then you probably need to ride in the lower heart zones, 1 through 3, because the exercise intensity in those zones enhances fat loss. If you say you want to improve your muscles and endurance, you'll train in Zones 2 through 4. To train for high performance like an athlete, you'll train almost entirely in Zones 3-5, with an emphasis on the upper two zones and Zone 2 for recovery.

Training in different zones is designed to accomplish different personal goals at different times. Occasionally riding in order to stay fit, but not get fitter, is called maintenance, and is accomplished by training in the Health Zones.

Within the wellness continuum of the five heart zones, there are no good or bad zones. If your cycle training program has the three Ms—managed, monitored and measured —all the heart zones are beneficial.

The following table emphasizes:
- Distinctly different benefits derived from each zone.
- That zones display no hierarchy of superiority. The Health Zones are merely different from, not better than, the Performance Zones.
- That benefits are not associative. You can't spend all your time in the Performance Zones and expect to get the good benefits of the Wellness Zones.
- That the Fitness Zones provide the biggest benefit with the fewest risks.

Characteristics of the Three Wellness Zones

Wellness Zone	Zone number	Improvement benefits and name	Negative aspects
Health Zones	Zone 1: Healthy Heart Zone 2: Temperate Zone 3: Aerobic	Lower blood pressure, weight loss, stress management. Overall health improvement: smoking cessation, lowers risks such as heart attacks, decreases substance abuse. Improved blood chemistry (cholesterol, triglycerides). Improved muscle mass.	Maintain, but don't gain fitness. Performance does not improve. Burn rate of total calories is low.
Fitness Zones	Zone 2: Temperate Zone 3: Aerobic Zone 4: Threshold	Increase in the following: delivery of blood, oxygen, and other nutrients to the muscles. Increase in the number and size of mitochondria, the number and size of blood vessels. Increase in the size and strength of the heart. Increase in lung function, oxygen consumption.	High percent of fat burned as fuel but low total calories
Performance Zones	Zone 3: Aerobic Zone 4: Threshold Zone 5: Redline	Improved volume of oxygen consumed, better tolerance to lactate, increased anaerobic threshold, increase muscle speed to contract, improved muscle strength. Optimum athletic performance.	Overtraining potential: increased red blood cell destruction, increased risk of injuries, diminished ATP energy renewal, potential damage to aerobic capacity and enzymes, potential damage to the immune system.

The winner is the one who has the most fun!

CHAPTER 3

Your First 30 Days

I'll never forget my first studio bike exercise class in the mid-1990s. Instructor Maureen Rusty had just finished Johnny G's (originator and trademark owner of Spinning®) Madd Dog Athletics training. Twenty black-metallic Schwinn spin bikes sparkled in the mirrors of the athletic club's former aerobics room, where every enthusiastic shout was amplified.

The real power of that experience came not from the instructor's enthusiasm, the fancy new bikes or knowing a club had made an early commitment to invest in this valuable form of exercise. The information from my heart rate monitor during the workout was what totally consumed me.

A monitor, spin bike, great instructor and rocking music are 95 percent of the formula needed to create an exceptional workout; the other 5 percent is the personal attitude it takes to be willing to suffer a little to enjoy the physical sensations of a high, hard and hot session. Without a monitor, I would not have known that for almost 60 minutes, I was redlining at above 90 percent of my maximum heart rate.

The pool of sweat under the bike should have shown I was nearing exhaustion. I was competing mentally with the cyclist next to me, who was also redlining and couldn't speak. As a matter of fact, everyone in the room seemed to feel the same way: Ride until you drop.

With the monitor, I not only perceived how hard I was working; the constant display of my current heart rate confirmed it. My maximum heart rate on a bike is 185 bpm. Throughout the workout, my hamstrings and quadriceps were spewing lactic acid as I experienced total muscle depletion. Rather than ease back if it seemed too hard as the instructor had suggested, I decided just to ride and watch my monitor.

Sure, I fried. So did all the other riders. I could barely walk after dismounting, but it was such an exercise "high," I promised myself that day to write, lecture and teach others how to enjoy indoor group exercise cycling without frying. Training smart allows you to realize all the benefits without the penalties.

—*Sally Edwards*

It seems easier for highly competitive athletes to fry when they train. We know our competition is training hard, so we train harder. But to train that hard and that high for so long leads to an increased potential for muscle and immunity system impairment and possible damage. Training is all based on how your individual body responds to what exercise scientists call training workload, or training load.

TRAINING LOAD

An effective workout has four parts: frequency, intensity, time and type of workout. When you add up the four parts, you get the acronym FITT and the result is how much total exercise you are experiencing, or your training load. Your first 30-day workout consists of integrating these four components into an individualized plan.

TRAINING ACTIVITY

Training is highly sport-specific. To be a great cyclist, you need to ride your bike and train your specific bike muscle systems and their complementary energy systems. Similarly, to improve as a triathlete, you must train your specific triathlon muscle systems, teaching them how to efficiently metabolize fuel. Sport-specific training is important. However, complementing that training with rest days for the sport-specific muscles and activity days for your auxiliary systems can take you to even higher levels of fitness. Such a training program is called sport-specific cross-training.

WORKOUT TYPES

Your training may encompass two basic workout types: a continuous, steady state workout session and an interval workout session. Both continuous and interval workouts can be divided into subcategories based on the length and heart zone of that workout. First, a definition for each:

Continuous or Steady State Workouts. Mainly confined within a narrowly described heart zone, or at, about, or around a heart rate number for the workout. A good example would be cycling a 10-mile time trial at the midpoint of Zone 3; or 75 percent of maximum heart rate. Such an aerobic ride would be designated a steady state Zone 3 workout.

Interval Workouts. A training technique alternating between short, intense efforts of exercise and periods of rest. They are designated short intervals, middle-distance intervals, and long intervals, and are measured by either time or distance. As the interval time lengthens, the sustainable heart rate typically decreases.

The type of workout, whether continuous or interval, is one part of the 30-day program. You need to blend the two together at different heart zones to realize the different benefits of each heart zone.

CYCLE TRAINING PLAN

Since no one knows your physiology and psychology as well as you, it's essential that you learn to write your own 30-day program. You know your schedule and can best assess your strengths and weaknesses, goals and ambitions, diet needs and support system. If a coach or personal trainer with cycling expertise is available, get feedback on your plan. Incorporate all or some of these elements:

Balance . . . . .Your training fits your life; it doesn't consume it. For example, it must realistically reflect the amount of time you have available.
Appropriate . . . . . .for your current level of fitness.
Relevant . . . . .Consistent with your goals and values.
Reward-based . . . .Compensates you for your investment.
Realizes obstacles . .and designed so you can overcome them.
Individualized . . . . .to fit your unique and special qualities, including the emotional and physical. Comes from the heart as much as the head.
Joyful . . . . .Offers pleasure and some celebration.
Milestones . . . . . . .Offer feedback and test events because you can best manage what you can monitor and measure.
Step-by-step process .to save you time and enhance your life.

Given those parameters, it's time to design your personalized 30-day cycle training program. You will love the process of planning, making decisions and committing to a schedule. You'll even enjoy the rewrite phase after you finish the 30 days and realize you need to fine-tune your plan. For now, your first venture into building a viable long-term training plan is to use a calendar.

For many busy people, a 30-day calendar works well because it gives you a look at your other commitments such as family, travel and meetings. Remember that a training program needs to fit into your life, not the reverse.

Using a calendar or the template on the next page, drop in your already planned favorite training rides. For example, some people ride Tuesdays and Thursdays when organized rides are offered. Since you're just getting started, your ride frequency should be three to five times per week, for 30-120 minutes, in Heart Zones 1 to 3. Consider cross training about two times per week. Decide how you will train on your non-riding days—stretching classes, weights, complementary training such as swimming, skiing/snowshoeing, running or skating—and add those to the weekly activities on appropriate days along with a day of complete recovery or rest.

Sample 30-Day Training Program for an Intermediate Cyclist

Week:	Monday	Tuesday	Wednesday	Thursday	Friday	Saturday	Sunday
1	Ride, Zone 3, continuous, with Mike at 10 a.m. for 30 minutes Take a 1-hour stretching class at 6 p.m.	Take a 1-hour stretching class at 6 p.m.	Ride, Z2—4, indoor cycle class at the club 6—7 a.m.	Rest day.	Out of town meetings all day—no training time available, going out with the family in evening	Ride, Zone 2—3, continuous pacing for one hour, at 7 a.m. with Judy	Ride Zone 3—4 hills. Leave the house at 8 a.m. with Tom for 2-hour ride at his pace
2	Rest day	Ride, mountain bike for 60 minutes, Z3 on trails near the house	Ride. Heart Cycling class at the club, Z 3—4, 45 minutes, all intervals	Cross Train: swim 20—30 laps after a Z2 warmup for 15 minutes	Ride, Z2—3 after work with Liz, continuous, midpoint Z3 100 minutes	Ride indoor trainer, "5x2."	Rest day.
3	Ride, Zone 3, continuous, with Mike at 10 a.m. for an hour	Take a 1-hour stretching class at 6 p.m.	Ride, Z2—4, indoor cycle class at the club 6—7 a.m.	Rest day.	Rest day.	Do "Tail Wind" workout for 60 minutes.	Ride Z3—4 hills. Leave the house at 8 a.m. with Tom for 3 hours at his pace
4	Rest day.	Ride mountain bike for 1 hour, Z3 on trails near the house	Ride. Heart cycling class at the club, Z3—4, 45 minutes, all intervals	Cross-train: swim 20 laps with Zoomers after a Z2 warm-up for 15 minutes	Ride, Z2—3 after work with Liz, continuous, midpoint Z3 for 90 minutes	Ride indoor trainer, intervals 5 minutes Z3, 5 minutes Z4 for 45 minutes	"Criss cross," Z2—3 workout for 60 minutes.

Note: This is designed for an intermediate cyclist who has ridden for more than one year, is currently fit, healthy, and has no injuries or other complications.

Your goal and challenge at this point is to create your program so it works. Don't fret over details or spend too much time creating the program at this point. Just commit to it for 30 days. Keep the heart rate intensities variable so you can gain the maximum benefit. You should also put in your riding partner's names, if any. Finally, try to commit to a time of day. If you know you're going to indoor cycle on Wednesday with a group, write down the time and show up, which is half of being successful; the rest is to have a goal and a plan.

As you plan your first 30 days, keep in mind: frequency, workout type (interval or continuous), intensity, time of day, mode (indoor or outdoor) and training partner, including his or her fitness level. Use the following schedule as a guideline to setting up your 30-day program.

Some training partners or students will ask their partners or coaches to write their workouts. Asking them to review, analyze and question you on your work is okay. This book's role, however, is to teach you skills and drills of cycling, train your physiology and show you the principles of the 30-Day Training Program so that you can write your own workout plan. Your satisfaction in your written decisions and their tangible results—in literally becoming the author of your training—justifies the early struggle you may experience to adequately fill those 30-day calendar spaces.

STEP #4: DETERMINING YOUR WEEKLY RIDING TIME—30 DAY TRAINING PLAN

Total:

	1	2	3	4	5	6	7	
WEEK 1								
WEEK 2	8	9	10	11	12	13	14	
WEEK 3	15	16	17	18	19	20	21	
WEEK 4	22	23	24	25	26	27	28	
WEEK 5	29	30						
						Total Weekly Training Time:		

TIP: ADVANCED TRAINING CONCEPT—
EXERTION FACTOR

Different types of activities have different weights or values based on the nature of the activity. For example, does running for 20 minutes at 150 beats per minute equal a 20-minute bike ride at 150 beats per minute? Are the two workouts equal in their training value, workload, calories burned, and effects on the muscles and cardiovascular system?

No. Running is harder on the body's skeletal system because of the impact forces of the activity. Running also consumes more oxygen and thus burns more calories per minute than cycling. You know from running that it's a jarring sport and stresses your legs and feet tremendously. You also don't have the rest phases of downhills or backing off the cadence as you do with cycling.

As a result of these jarring or impact forces, the recovery time from running is longer than from cycling. This "impact" factor, along with the stress of using different muscle groups in different activities, results in the determination of an "exertion factor." This factor differs by sport activity as well as the intensity level of the workout. Using an exertion factor allows you to compare workouts in different sports to each other.

Impact impairment from running, for example, increases as the speed increases. The faster you run the greater the impact. The faster you cycle, the more joint stress. So if you are running or cycling at high heart rates, the impact-stress or exertion factor of the activity is higher. The slower you move and the lower your heart rates, the lower the exertion or impact factor. Some training software considers exertion factor when evaluating the workout.

TIP: ADVANCED TRAINING CONCEPT—
TRAINING VOLUME AND TRAINING LOAD

Training volume is how long you exercise or how far you ride, usually measured in minutes/hours or by distance in yards/meters. Think of volume as the size of something: a mass and duration or distance traveled. Your weekly training volume is the workout frequency times the distance or total amount of training time for the week.

If you ride four days a week for 60 minutes each and it's approximately 18 miles each ride, your weekly training volume is:

Weekly training volume (by duration) = 4 days x 60 minutes = 240 training minutes for the week
Weekly training volume (by distance) = 4 days x 18 miles = 72 miles per week

Training load adds one additional key factor to the analysis: heart rate or intensity. Training load is more important to monitor because it includes how hard you exercised during that 72-mile week or 240 minutes. While it can be calculated different ways (some people total thousands of heartbeats), in the Heart Zone Training System we simply multiply by the time spent in each of the zones to determine the training load, expressed in Heart Zone Training Points.

Using the example above, let's say all the workouts were performed in Zone 3. The individual workload for the week is:

Weekly training volume (by duration) = 4 days x 60 minutes x 3 (Zone 3) = 720 HZT Points

Computer software such as Heartware is designed around the Heart Zone Training system and automatically calculates weekly, monthly and yearly workload or HZT Points for you in a more precise way. But for now, you have a way to analyze your training dosage in an easy to understand way.

TRAINING BALANCE

By now, you may have realized training involves more than glancing at a flashing heart icon and pushing your heart rate to maximum. It is common to make the mistake of using a heart rate monitor like a speedometer to see how hard and fast we can go. In reality, a monitor is more like a tachometer, showing us what's really happening under the hood and how our body is responding to stress. The more feedback we have, the better our chances of making good decisions in training and riding. You can use a heart rate monitor to balance your training.

Do you know people who think they haven't gotten a good workout unless they've pushed themselves so hard they can barely finish? They spend their training time in a big black anaerobic hole, never glimpsing the daylight of rest and recovery. While high intensity training has a purpose, at some point the body will rebel against abuse. You simply can't cycle in Zones 4 and 5 all the time without adequate rest and recovery.

If you don't allow your body recovery time to rebuild itself, you'll develop the classic symptoms of overtraining: persistent fatigue; leaden legs that balk at walking or climbing stairs; irritability; insomnia; an increase in resting heart rate; head congestion; and decreasing performance. You may be on the fast track to becoming less fit and possibly seriously damaging your body.

Spend time in each zone based on your fitness goals and training program and you will reap the benefits each zone has to offer. Your training program will change as your goals change; your goals change because your life changes. Sometimes we ride into unexpected bends in the road that help make choices for us.

Training balance is important to your success. Brian was one of those people who pushed themselves to the limit. He showed up in Sally Reed's Heart Cycling class, heart rate monitor in hand and ready to ride. What he failed to tell Sally was what motivated him to be there several weeks later. Brian had recently undergone an angiogram followed by an angioplasty, followed by triple bypass surgery. His heart muscle was strong from previous years of training as a triathlete so the doctor's orders were to continue to exercise and change his diet. Over the past two years, Brian has rarely missed a class. His motivation to be stronger and fitter comes from seeing friends who didn't survive their first heart attack. It's not just his heart that Brian wants to make stronger, but his whole body. He's not waiting to get serious about being fit and healthy. For Brian, it's not a question of eventually getting fit. He wisely says: "Today is my later and I can't let it go by!"

F.I.T.(T)

How do we fit our goals into a training schedule that will work for us? How do we quantify our training sessions to ensure we're growing progressively fitter and not under or overtraining? One way to answer these questions is by using the formula FIT. This acronym stands for frequency, intensity and time, the three key factors in designing and measuring your training. FIT is a way of evaluating how often, how hard and how many minutes someone trains.

In the past, there were four ways to measure exercise intensity: blood lactate, VO_2 (gas exchange), perceived exertion (RPE) and pulse. The first two methods are fairly accurate but require special equipment and are usually expensive and applied primarily in a clinical setting. Perceived exertion is commonly used for many activities, but is very subjective and unreliable. Pulse rate taken manually can vary 10 to 15 beats either way. The most accurate, easiest way to measure intensity is with a heart rate monitor.

Now that intensity is readily measurable, workouts can be quantified. To measure the total quantity of exercise dosage we use the formula, F x I x T = Workload.

Quantifiable workload:

F = Frequency or "how often" or number of workouts per week (one per day is a frequency of seven workouts).

I = Intensity or "how hard" or the number of the zone in which you are training.

T = Time or "how many minutes" in each zone. In Heart Zone Training it is called "TIZ" or time in zone (in minutes).

(T) = Type or mode of training such as swimming or cycling.

This formula measures the total exercise dosage applied to the individual and quantifies the workload in Heart Zone Training Points, currently one of the only ways to measure applied workload.

Example:

5 days/week x Zone 3 (70 percent of maximum heart rate) x 30 minutes = 450 Heart Zone Training Cycling Points

(5 x 3 x 30 = 450)

The American College of Sports Medicine recommends exercising most days of the week at an intensity range of 60 percent to 90 percent of your maximum heart rate for a minimum of 30 minutes to get fit. These guidelines cover a wide range of activities. The ACSM also recognizes that lower intensity levels are beneficial in reducing degenerative diseases. Healthy adults must work at higher frequencies and intensity levels for additional benefits.

It's important to remember that you'll be working out in multiple zones and for varying times, and that each person will have a different exercise capacity. Competitive athletes may have more than 3000 Heart Zone Training points per week, compared to someone who just wants to get healthier and fit with 100 to 1000 points per week. Each workout in this book gives you a percentage of time in each zone followed by the total points for the workout. You will decide your magic number of Heart Zone Training points each week based on your goals.

THE FIVE TRAINING SPOKES

Training is a cyclic process. For most, there's a start of the training season, different phases within a training season and an end. This cycle of training is called the "training wheel" because it resembles the wheel of your bike, with spokes dividing the training into distinct parts. And like a bike wheel, it's these spokes that separate and distinguish each part of training.

In the center of the training wheel is the hub—the focus, a connection piece through which each spoke threads. Symbolically, the hub might represent your training goals. There are five spokes to the training wheel:

- base training
- endurance training
- strength training
- interval speed training
- power training

THE TRAINING WHEEL MODEL

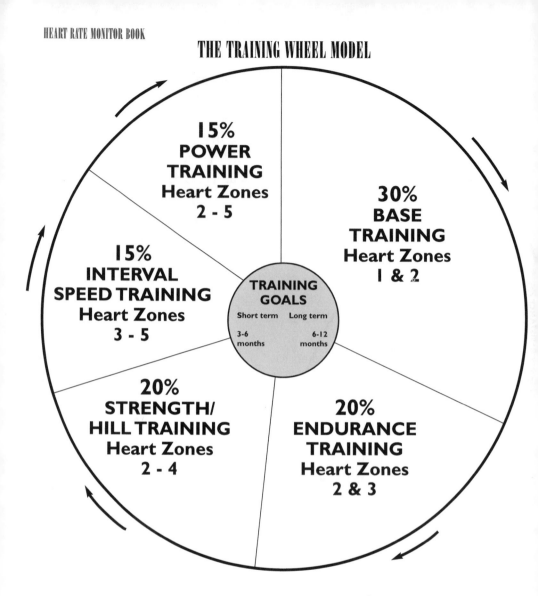

15%
POWER
TRAINING
Heart Zones
2 - 5

30%
BASE
TRAINING
Heart Zones
1 & 2

15%
INTERVAL
SPEED TRAINING
Heart Zones
3 - 5

TRAINING
GOALS

Short term   Long term

3-6   6-12
months   months

20%
STRENGTH/
HILL TRAINING
Heart Zones
2 - 4

20%
ENDURANCE
TRAINING
Heart Zones
2 & 3

The rim of the training wheel represents time, that all too precious commodity that is both free and an equalizer. We all have exactly the same amount of time in every day; managing it best means using a training system for guidance.

Unlike on a bike wheel, as the chart shows, the spokes are not spaced equally apart. You spend different lengths of time between spokes, depending on your individual needs and goals. If you are new to cycle training, spend more time in the first two spokes: base and

TRAINING WHEEL GOAL EXAMPLE

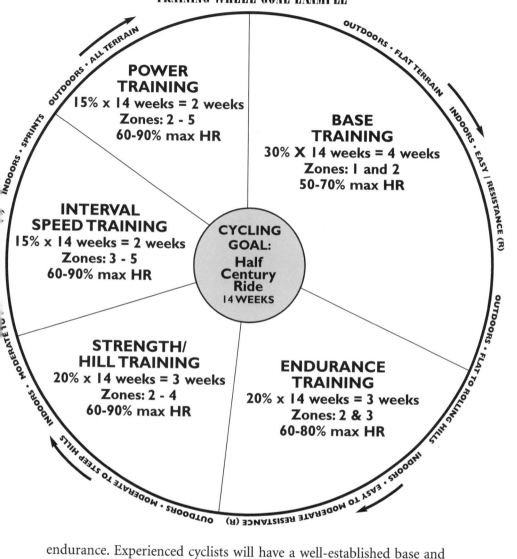

POWER TRAINING
15% x 14 weeks = 2 weeks
Zones: 2 - 5
60-90% max HR

BASE TRAINING
30% X 14 weeks = 4 weeks
Zones: 1 and 2
50-70% max HR

INTERVAL SPEED TRAINING
15% x 14 weeks = 2 weeks
Zones: 3 - 5
60-90% max HR

CYCLING GOAL:
Half Century Ride
14 WEEKS

STRENGTH/ HILL TRAINING
20% x 14 weeks = 3 weeks
Zones: 2 - 4
60-90% max HR

ENDURANCE TRAINING
20% x 14 weeks = 3 weeks
Zones: 2 & 3
60-80% max HR

OUTDOORS • ALL TERRAIN

OUTDOORS • FLAT TERRAIN

INDOORS • SPRINTS

INDOORS • EASY / RESISTANCE (R)

INDOORS • MODERATE TO

OUTDOORS • FLAT TO ROLLING HILLS

OUTDOORS • MODERATE TO STEEP HILLS

INDOORS • EASY TO MODERATE HILLS

OUTDOORS • EASY TO MODERATE RESISTANCE (R)

endurance. Experienced cyclists will have a well-established base and can cycle through them in a short time to the other three spokes: strength or hills, intervals or speed, work and power (a combination of all the spokes).

It's easy for you to build your own training wheel if you consider what specific short-term or long-term goal you have set. To determine how many weeks to spend in each spoke, count back from the goal and establish the number of weeks you'll be riding in each spoke as follows:

Weeks in the Training Wheel

Spoke name:	Percentage of total training (14 weeks)	Example: 14-week training season	Weeks and months for my training wheel	Primary training Heart Zone
Base	30%	4 weeks	_____	Zone 1–2
Endurance	20%	3 weeks	_____	Zone 3
Strength	20%	3 weeks	_____	Zone 2–4
Interval/Speed	15%	2 weeks	_____	Zone 3–5
Power	15%	2 weeks	_____	Zone 2–5
TOTAL	100%	14 weeks	_____	

This is an individual cycle training program, so make it fit your schedule. If you have a particularly long training season, it's a good idea to build a front and a back wheel on which to mount your racing bike. Training is a blend of art and science, and research shows that you should progressively vary exercise load by training in different spokes during different phases of your fitness improvement.

The key point to improve your fitness is to change your training. By moving from one spoke on the training wheel to the next you'll get fitter. As you become fitter, you will get faster and your training heart rates at the same bike speeds will lower.

STEP 5: DETERMINE YOUR SPOKE

Select which one of the five training spokes best fits your current riding ability.

In this process of five different spokes surrounding your training hub—your goals—you'll be adding different types of rides emphasizing different heart zones and different training regimes. Read this description of the five different spokes. With reference to the indoor and outdoor training rides, you should incorporate the following into your week:

Base Rides

Early season training rides, short to medium in length or time. All in the low heart zones (Zones 1 to 3). Fun, easy, and aerobic. You'll be in your base period from two to eight weeks; each week, you'll be building your cardiovascular aerobic system.

Outdoor Rides

Flat to gentle hills. Ride at a higher rpm and easier gears.

Recommended Indoor Workouts
Spokes

Base spoke 50–70% of max HR	Endurance spoke 60–80% of max HR	Strength spoke 60–80% of max HR	Speed spoke 60–90% of max HR	Power spoke 60–90% of max HR
Change of Heart	Heartbeat	The Zipper	Red Shift	Happy Feet
Criss Cross Z1&Z2	Ladder to Success	Tail Wind	Winners' Circle	Pumped
Recovery Intervals	30 Beat	Afterburner	Top Spin	30-20-10
Peak-a-boo	A Positive Spin	Seattle Ridge	Happy Feet	Red Shift
Talk Is Cheap	Fast Lane	Spentervals	Pumped	Braveheart
5 x 2	Criss Cross Z2&Z3		30-20-10	Winners' Circle
Lancelot				Top Spin

Recommended Outdoor Rides
Spokes

Base spoke 50–70% of max HR	Endurance spoke 60–80% of max HR	Strength spoke 60–80% of max HR	Speed spoke 60–90% of max HR	Power spoke 60–90% of max HR
The Observation Trip	Criss Cross Z3	The Heat Is On	Biggest Number	Saturday Night Fever
Steady State Pace Ride	Recovery Interval Ride	Hill Sprints	All Out Time Trial	Rock 'n' Roll
Noodling	Crusin'	The Spoke n' Word	Anaerobic Threshold Ride	Sign Here Press Hard
Doublemint	Paceline Ride	All Out Trip	Need For Speed	S Squared
Steady Eddy	S.O.S.			
	Pyramid Scheme			

Endurance Rides

You've developed your base aerobic capacity and are ready for longer, slightly harder rides that push the heart rate intensity. Building a bigger and more powerful base is instrumental to the rest of your training season as the aerobic foundation supporting the other training spokes. Your goal in this two to six week training spoke is to develop muscular endurance.

Outdoor Rides

Flat to gentle hills. Ride at a higher rpm using easy to moderate gearing. Increase your time in the saddle.

Strength Hill Rides

In this training spoke, you'll work on developing muscle strength—or your muscles' ability to generate force against resistance— to give your sport-specific riding muscles more power. The best way to do this is to ride with resistance up hills, into the wind, or by standing out of the saddle. Ride this training spoke for two to six weeks.

Intervals

One of the best ways to get faster on your bike is to ride repeatedly faster for short periods of time. That's interval training. This is one of the most important times to use your monitor, because you'll be riding into the highest of heart zones, redlining into Zone 5. Doses of high intensity training improve your recovery and your ability to sustain high heart rates—your ability to train at or above your anaerobic threshold.

Power Rides

During this training, you'll combine all three spokes into your weekly program—endurance, strength and speed. You'll train for acceleration, top speed and top endurance. This combination of high intensities, speed, hill intervals and endurance can lead to overtraining, so pay attention to your morning heart rates.

Outdoor Rides

Ride hills, do the time trials and the "S.O.S." workout in Chapter 8. Use the big chainring to develop strength and power while being careful with your knees.

INTERVAL TRAINING

Interval training is a fast way to becoming fitter and faster. It builds strength and speed and packs a lot of punch into a short period. Defined simply, interval training is periods of work followed by periods of rest or recovery. Intervals can be aerobic or anaerobic. Aerobic intervals typically take place in Zones 1, 2 and 3, anaerobic intervals in Zones 4 and 5. Keep in mind this depends on your fitness level and anaerobic threshold. The fitter you are, the longer you can stay aerobic and the higher the percentage of maximum heart rate cycling you can handle before crossing over into anaerobic training.

Outdoor cycling is not a steady state or one effort type of sport. You are constantly adapting to changing terrain and environment, so the more you can train your body to adapt, the better you'll be. Interval training will make you accelerate faster for "breakaways" and "jumps"—even escaping unexpected dogs. You'll be stronger climbing hills and faster on the flats as you increase your power and speed.

Intervals are rated by time and intensity or heart rate. They may involve concentrating on a specific position or skill, such as standing for the duration or spinning at high rpm. The following chart shows some interval techniques and skills often used in indoor cycling classes to make the workout more varied and fun. These can be incorporated in the chapter workouts when appropriate.

You can take your training workouts to yet another level. For advanced riders, each spoke can be divided into more parts that lead to more advanced training programs. Whether or not you choose this option, the basic training principles will lead to your becoming a better-trained rider.

Interval Training Skills and Techniques

Technique/Definition	Cycling Benefits
Isolated Leg Training (ILT) Pedal with only one leg; rest the other on a box, stool or just dangle it at the side. Use only one leg at a time	Improved strength, speed and pedaling techique
Spin Ups Increase cadence progressively by 5 to 10 rpm at regular intervals	Improved neuromuscular adaptation, leg speed
Power Starts From a slow spin or stopped position, seated or standing, expend 10 seconds all-out effort with heavy resistance or hard gear. 20-second recovery, alternate lead foot	Improved power, acceleration, balance
Surges Moderate to heavy resistance with 30 second cadence increases, then back to original cadence	Improved muscle recruitment, strength and power
Hill Climbing Put front wheel on a 4-inch block of wood to simulate climbing	Improved specific strengthening of hill climbing muscle groups and body position
Pedaling Circles Concentrate on a round pedal stroke, minimizing the "dead spot" at the top of the stroke by pulling up and across the top	Improved suppleness, pedaling efficiency and muscular endurance
Ups and Downs Number of times up to a certain heart rate and recover back down to a given heart rate in a period of time	Improved muscular power, speed and endurance. Test for recovery heart rate
Tempo Steady cadence with increases in resistance, gearing	Improved muscular strength and endurance
Lactate Threshold Maintain the highest sustainable heart rate for a period of time	Improved oxygen and fuel utilization and lactate clearance systems. Getting fitter, faster and stronger
Jumps 1. Alternate riding standing and seated to a count; 2. Seated or standing, short, fast accelerations	1. Improved strength, balance, muscle recruitment 2. Improved power, acceleration and balance
Hovers Hover just above the seat with the body weight over the seat post	Improved strength, balance, muscle recruitment
Slides From a hover position, slide weight forward over handlebars, drop toes, then slide weight back over saddle dropping weight over the heels. Usually done to a count	Improved strength, balance, muscle recruitment
Tricep Pushups Rpm = 80 or less, elbows and palms facing out. Push up and down on handlebars. Usually done to a count	Improved upper body strength, balance
Ladders Incrementally increase heart rate during certain periods of time	Improved physiological adaptation to an increasing workload at different periods of time
Pyramids Incrementally increase and decrease heart rate during certain periods of time	Improved adaptation to increasing work load at different periods of time, during controlled recovery periods
Repeats Repeat effort and recovery intervals a number of times	Improved muscular strength and endurance

INDOOR TRAINING

Does indoor training have to be boring? Cycling indoors can be fun and motivating when your workouts have a purpose and a plan. Indoor cycling is one of the most time-efficient and inexpensive ways to train during the winter months or off-season; some cyclists train throughout the year using indoor training to work on specific aspects of their conditioning.

Sitting on a bike and sweating for 60 minutes for no apparent reason is not "training." In contrast, riding with a specific purpose and goal in mind is.

How do you stick with an indoor training program? Start by calling your exercise *training*. Set some goals, individualize your workouts using a heart rate monitor, and write a training program.

Indoor training is important unless you live in a land where the sun shines 24 hours a day and snow, ice and rain are not in the local weatherman's vocabulary. The question is not whether to train indoors but how, where and on what. The "how" is what heart zone training and using a heart rate monitor are all about: training most efficiently and effectively indoors or out. The "where" is your choice of a health club setting or investment in home equipment where you can follow your own schedule. The "what" is the type of training equipment you'll use.

In a health club, you have the advantage of training on various kinds of equipment and with others in a group exercise format such as studio or indoor cycling. If you haven't tried indoor cycling or a Spinning® class, it's recommended. Bring your heart rate monitor so you can measure the intensity level and adapt the class to meet your goals. Classes can be lots of fun, and some people find they work harder when someone is coaching them through a workout. Many people like to share the fun and sweat with a friend or group.

Training at home may require more discipline, but one of the main advantages is using your own bicycle on an indoor trainer. The following is a guide to some of the more popular trainers listing approximate cost, phone numbers and Web sites.

Guide to Indoor Trainers

Trainer	Price	Phone/Web site
Blackburn TrackStand Defender	$230	800/456-2355
		www.blackburndesign.com
Performance Travel Trac 2000	$220	800/727-2453
		www.performancebike.com
CycleOps Fluid+	$299	212/924-6724
		www.cycle-ops.com
Cateye CS1000 Cyclosimulator	$350	800/522-8393
		www.cateye.com
Elite Volare Fluid Drive	$260	360/692-6540
		www.elite-it.com
Minoura MagTurbo ERGO-10	$130	800/601-9592
		www.minoura.co.jp
Tacx Cycleforce Excel	$659	847/465-8200
		www.tacx.nl
Kreitler Wind Trainer	$350–$375	800/333-5782
		www.kreitler.com
RacerMate CompuTrainer	$1000-2000	800/522-3610
		www.computrainer.com
QuickStand C-Force	$279	800/727-9377
		www.biketrainer.com

Rollers, a type of indoor trainer, is not recommended for beginning cyclists. It is an excellent training tool for advanced cyclists because it requires advanced skills.

Types of Trainers

Trainers come in two types: a conventional trainer where you mount your bike after taking off the front wheel, or a trackstand trainer where your rear wheel is cradled and your front wheel is left on. Which you use is a matter of personal choice. Ask your local bike shop to recommend one and if possible, try one before buying.

On an indoor trainer, resistance devices can be either fan, magnetic or fluid. Resistance fans are typically cheaper and noisier. Magnetic-type resistance devices usually offer more resistance for very strong riders, but aren't necessarily better. Rollers are designed more for balance and spin technique than strength work.

Sally Reed trains and teaches on a studio bike, or what some call a spin bike. The disadvantage to a studio bike is usually fit and feel.

While designed to fit a wide range of body type and size, it's difficult to get a good fit if you are short (under 5 feet 2 inches) or very tall (over 6 feet 5 inches). The flywheel on the bike weighs between 30 and 47 pounds, and the resistance is usually a belt or pads that apply pressure to the flywheel. These bikes are fun but are strictly "fixed gear," meaning the pedals go around with the flywheel and thus offer no coasting—only spin. To date, studio bikes lack fancy gadgets or gears; a resistance knob or lever adjusts the resistance to them.

If you're considering a spin bike, you can contact one or more of the most popular spin bike companies. Take a class or try one out before making a commitment to train on one. Plan to spend between $600 and $900 to purchase a new bike. Check with local athletic clubs for old bikes for sale; you can sometimes find these for between $200 and $400. Again, ride them first to make sure they haven't been ridden into the ground.

Indoor Cycling: Studio Bicycles

Spin bike	Price	Phone/Web site/Address
Reebok	$600–$800	Reebok CCS Fitness www.ccsfitness.com; 800/344-0444 16401 E. 33rd Dr., Ste. 40, Aurora, CO 80011
Schwinn	$600–$1000	Schwinn Fitness Products www.schwinn.com; 303/939-0100 1690 38th St., Boulder, CO 80301
Keiser	$600–$800	Keiser Corporation www.keiser.com; 800/888-7009 Fresno, CA 93706
Star Trac V-Bike	$600–$800	Star Trac by Unisen Inc. www.startrac.com; 800/228-6635 14410 Myford Rd., Irvine, CA 92606
Greg LeMond Revmaster	$700–$900	Stairmaster www.stairmaster.com; 800/635-2936 12421 Willows Rd. NE, Ste. 100 Kirkland, WA 98034-8736

WORKOUTS

Indoor Training

Peak-A-Boo

Fitness 50-80 percent

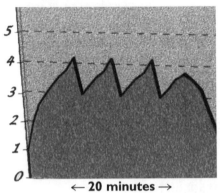

← 20 minutes →

Percentage of total workout

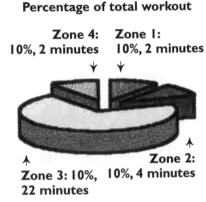

Zone 4:
10%, 2 minutes

Zone 1:
10%, 2 minutes

Zone 3: 10%, 22 minutes

Zone 2: 10%, 4 minutes

Total HZT points: 84

This 30-minute workout gives you a taste of four zones with the majority of time in Zone 3. Three times you take a "peak" at Zone 4 staying just a short time, then you go back down to the bottom of Zone 3.

Purpose

In cycling you must constantly adapt to changing workloads such as hills and wind. This workout will help you do just that by gradually changing the intensity every minute. As you pedal through Zone 3 you'll transition from the Healthy Heart Zone to the Fitness Zone. The ride becomes more challenging as you near the top of Zone 3 and "peak" into Zone 4. Working out in these zones enhances your cardiovascular capacity. That means an increase in the number and the size of blood vessels, an increase in vital capacity, an increase in size and strength of your heart and an increase in endorphins (spin grins!) Zone 3 is also a great zone for teaching your body to metabolize fatty acids. A high percentage of you outdoor workouts will be in Zone 3.

Workout Plan

You will spend the first 5 minutes warming your way up to the bottom of Zone 3, then you will do a five-beat increase every minute as you reach the top rung of this ladder with a peak into Zone 4. A short, 1-minute stay is all you get, then a 2-minute recovery to the bottom of Zone 3. You can test your recovery time by counting the number of beats you drop in the first minute of your 2-minute recovery. Make a mental note and try this on each recovery interval. Record your recovery heart rate, and the next time you do this workout the time to reach this number should be less if you are getting fitter.

This ladder is repeated three more times, but on the last ladder stop before reaching Zone 4, near the top of Zone 3. Then, recover with a warm-down. You can add more warm-up and warm-down time plus another ladder interval if you want to increase your workout time and your total Heart Zone Training Points.

Peak-A-Boo

Elapsed Time in Minutes	Coaching notes	Zone	Your HR numbers	Duration
0–2	Warm up to the top of Z1	1	_____	2 min.
2–4	Warm up to mid-point of Z2 (65%)	2	_____	2 min.
4–5	Increase HR to bottom of Z3 (70%), increase	3	_____	1 min.
	cadence (rpm)	3	_____	
5–9	Increase HR 5 bpm every min., choice	4	_____	4 min.
9–11	Recover (Rec) bottom of Z3, easy pedal, no (R), timed (rec), (number of beats dropped in 1 min.)	3	_____	2 min.
11–15	Increase HR 5 bpm every min.,	3	_____	4 min.
	(R), seated	4	_____	
15–17	(Rec) bottom of Z3, easy pedal, no (R), timed (rec)(number of beats dropped in 1 min.)	3	_____	2 min.
17–21	Increase HR 5 bpm every min., cadence (rpm)	3	_____	4 min.
21–23	(Rec) bottom of Z3, easy pedal, no (R), timed (rec)(number of beats dropped in 1 min.)	3	_____	2 min.
23–26	Increase HR 5 bpm each min. for 3 min., choice	3	_____	3 min.
26–28	Drop 5 bpm each min. for 2 min.	3	_____	2 min.
28–30	Warm down to bottom of Z2	2	_____	2 min.
	Total HZT Points 84			

Heartbeat

Fitness 60–80 percent

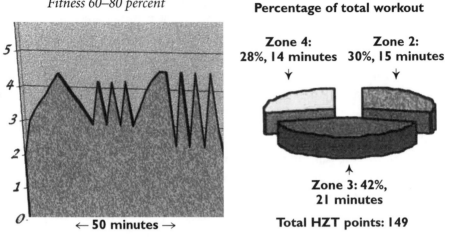

Percentage of total workout

Zone 4:
28%, 14 minutes

Zone 2:
30%, 15 minutes

Zone 3: 42%,
21 minutes

Total HZT points: 149

← 50 minutes →

This 50-minute workout had no name until Sally Edwards had a new, fast custom bike made for her to race in the 1998 Ironman. She was out to win her age division with her new secret weapon, "Heartbeat." This workout gives you four internal sets. It starts with a 5 x 2 ladder then a 20-beat criss-cross of Zone 3, followed by a set of power intervals. The fourth interval set is a 40-beat criss cross of Zones 3 and 4.

Purpose

The 5 x 2 ladder will train your physiology to adapt to a changing workload every 2 minutes, much like a long hill that gets steeper and steeper. It also includes a controlled recovery back down the ladder to help you keep your mental focus. A two-minute 20-beat interval follows to train your aerobic system in Zone 3. The next interval pushes the heart rate higher as the heart and muscles are trained to respond quickly in 10-second sprints followed by 20-second recoveries. The last interval is a final push through two zones against the clock, training for power and fighting off fatigue.

Workout Plan

Pedaling easily, warm up to the bottom of Zone 3 in the first 10 minutes.

A 5-beat, 2-minute ladder starts at the bottom rung of Zone 3 (70 percent) and climbs to the middle of Zone 4 (85 percent) then back down to the bottom of Zone 3.

A short 1-minute rest follows, then 3 more times increase heart rate 20 beats with a 1-minute recovery in-between.

Finish with a 3-minute recovery at the bottom of Zone 3, then begin a series of 5 standing power sprints (10 seconds all-out with a 20-second recovery) followed by 3 minutes of recovery.

Heartbeat

Elapsed Time in Minutes	Coaching notes	Zone	Your HR numbers	Duration
0–5	Warm up to the bottom of Z2	2	_____	5 min.
5–10	Increase HR to bottom of Z3, cadence (rpm)	3	_____	5 min.
10–20	Add 5 bpm every two min., choice of (R) or (rpm), seated	3	_____	10 min.
		4	_____	
20–25	Drop 5 bpm every min. for 5 min. to the bottom of Z3	4	_____	5 min.
		3	_____	
25–33	From the bottom of Z3 to the bottom of Z4 in 1 min, your choice, followed by a 1 min. (rec) to the bottom of Z3, repeat 3 times with a final 3-min. Recovery (rec) at the bottom of Z3. Count (rec) beats	3	_____	8 min.
		4	_____	
		3	_____	
		4	_____	
		3	_____	
		4	_____	
		3	_____	
33–36	Power starts with heavy (R), standing for 10 seconds, 20 second seated (rec) x (5). Last 2 power starts above 85% (mid-point of 2⁴)	3	_____	3 min.
		4	_____	
		4	_____	
		4	_____	
		4	_____	
36–39	Easy pedal (rec), bottom of Z2	2	_____	3 min.
39–45	40-beat increase from the mid-point of Z2 (65%) to the mid-point of Z4 (85%). Count number of times in 6 min.	2	_____	6 min.
		4	_____	
45–50	Warm-down to bottom of Z2	2	_____	5 min.
	Total HZT Points 149			

The final assault is as many 40-beat intervals as you can complete in 6 minutes. The interval starts at the mid-point of Zone 2 (65 percent) and goes to the mid-point of Zone 4 (85 percent). Recover back down to the mid-point of Zone 2 and start the next 40-beat interval. We call these repeated 40-beat intervals "ups and downs." If you want to do more, extend the workout by trying 10 minutes and see how many times you can do it.

Note: This is a great workout to show the fun and power of using a heart rate monitor. Recovery time should be increasing as your heart and legs get stronger. Make sure you are recovering at the same resistance or gearing. If you find your recovery time is not increasing and you don't feel you are improving, you may want to change your training schedule. This could be an indication you are overtraining or that there are other stresses in your life. Consider a day off or a recovery workout that allows your body to rest and rebuild.

Spentervals

Fitness 60–90+ percent

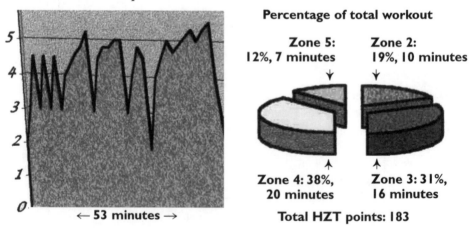

Percentage of total workout

| Zone 5: 12%, 7 minutes | Zone 2: 19%, 10 minutes |
| Zone 4: 38%, 20 minutes | Zone 3: 31%, 16 minutes |

Total HZT points: 183

This 53-minute workout is guaranteed to make you feel totally "spent" when completed. It has a great combination of hard intervals, tempo work, sprints, super spins, and a 5km time trial to finish. Bring plenty of water to this workout and expect to see some high numbers on your heart rate monitor.

Purpose

Fifty percent of your total time will be spent in Zone 4 and Zone 5. The intensity is hard and high so apply the 48-hour rule: You must take a 48-hour break from training in these high zones again on your bike. Your sport-specific cycling muscles and heart need a chance to rest and recover. This recovery process takes approximately 48 hours so take a break or do a short active recovery workout in Zones 2 and 3. Spentervals will stress your energy system, cardiovascular system, and your muscles. It has a little bit of everything with a tough finish.

Workout Plan

Start with a 10-minute warm-up to the bottom of Zone 3 (70 percent) followed by (3) 1-minute hard effort 30-beat intervals. Check your cadence and make sure you are cycling at about 100 rpm or a (10), which means 10 pedal revolutions in six seconds.

Five minutes of tempo work follows with a steady cadence of 80-rpm (8) adding 5 bpm every minute.

The next set pushes you into Zone 5. It is hard and uncomfortable so hang in there. Your perceived exertion should be between 7 and 9 on a scale of 10. These are 10-second intervals of heavy resistance with 10 seconds of recovery for a total of 5 minutes. You may choose to alternate standing and sitting or combinations of both. Give a hard effort knowing you have a 3-minute recovery to the bottom of Zone 3.

Your heart and legs have worked hard so the next interval will help flush out the lactic acid and give your legs a reprieve. Six minutes of 30-second super spins at 120 rpm or more, or a (12), followed by 30-second recoveries.

The last challenge is a 5-minute time trial. If you are competitive, you will see very high heart rate numbers. The time trial begins with a fast, hard effort off the starting line for 1 minute to the beginning of the first 1-minute hill. The first 30 seconds of the hill is seated with high rpm or (12). The last 30 seconds is standing with (heavy resistance) powering yourself up and over the top. A slight downhill follows dropping only 3 bpm every 30 seconds, sustaining 80 rpm (8). Next comes a super spin of more than 120 rpm or (12+) for 30 seconds. Keep your heart rate in Zone 5 with a 1-minute all-out sprint to the finish line. Once you have crossed the finish line look at your monitor and don't be surprised if it continues to go up for a few seconds.

After you cross the finish line and are celebrating your finish, keep pedaling for a couple of minutes and gradually pedal back down to the bottom of Zone 2.

Spentervals

Elapsed Time in Minutes	Coaching notes	Zone	Your HR numbers	Duration
0–5	Warm up to the bottom of Z2	2	_____	5 min.
5–10	Increase HR to the bottom of Z3	3	_____	5 min.
10–16	From the bottom of Z3 add 30 bpm, hard	4	_____	6 min.
	effort, 100 rpm (10) for 1 min., (rec) 30 bpm	3	_____	
	in 1 min., easy pedal. Repeat interval two	4	_____	
	more times [30 bpm up and 30 bpm (rec)]	3	_____	
		4	_____	
		3	_____	
16–21	Tempo work beginning at the bottom of Z4.	4	_____	5 min.
	Hold 80 rpm (8), add 5 bpm every min. for 5	4	_____	
	min. Stay seated	5	_____	
21–24	(Rec) to the bottom of Z3 (Drink water!)	3	_____	3 min.
24–29	10 seconds hard effort standing (R), 10 sec-	4	_____	5 min.
	onds easy pedaling, seated. Repeat 15 times	4	_____	
	total. Last two times go 5 beats into Z5!	5	_____	
29–32	(Rec) to the bottom of Z3. (Drink more water)	3	_____	3 min.
32–38	30 sec. all-out sprint, 30 sec. easy pedal (rec).	4	_____	6 min.
	Repeat 12 times total, alternate standing and	4	_____	
	seated	4	_____	
38–42	(Rec) to the bottom of Z2. (water!) Mental	2	_____	4 min.
	prep for 5km, relax			
42–47	5-min., 5k time trial. Use your imagination or	4	_____	5 min.
	follow script. Ride at AT or higher	4	_____	
		5	_____	
47–53	Warm down to the bottom of Z2	2	_____	6 min.
	Total HZT Points 183			

OUTDOOR TRAINING

The Distance Improvement Ride

Do you want to go further and at a lower heart rate in less time? That is what this ride is all about. After an adequate warm-up you will start at 70 percent of your maximum heart rate if you are a beginner, 75 percent of your maximum heart rate for an intermediate rider, and 80 percent if the goal is performance and getting your fittest. Record your distance traveled in 15 minutes at your chosen heart rate percentage using your bike computer. As you get stronger and fitter the distance you travel should become greater. When you retest to check your improvement make sure your are cycling under similar conditions such as wind, heat, humidity and the same course. Record your results in your log and compare them once a month or however often you want to measure your improvement.

Cruisin'

Pick a relatively flat course. This ride consists of three to five intervals between three to 12 minutes in duration at an intensity between 60 and 85 percent of your maximum heart rate. The goal is to improve your ability to ride in a relatively big or hard gear at a relatively high cadence for an extended period of time building muscular endurance.

The work intervals will build in intensity from the bottom of Zone 2 to the mid-point of Zone 4, or from 60 to 85 percent of your maximum heart rate, followed with a recovery to the bottom of Zone 2 (60 percent). Once you have recovered to the bottom of Zone 2 immediately begin the next interval. Repeat this interval three to five times. Warm down gradually to finish.

Steady Eddy

On a relatively flat course, ride continually at 70 percent of your maximum heart rate without recovery and at a cadence between 75 to 95 rpm. Avoid roads that have heavy traffic and stop signs. Start with

MULTIPLE ZONES GIVE MULTIPLE BENEFITS

Who said you can't have your cake and eat it too? The Heart Zone Training System provides just that—all the benefits of health, fitness and performance if you apply it in your daily life.

As you know from Chapter 2, each of the heart zones is part of the wellness continuum from health (Zone 1–Zone 3) to fitness (Zone 2–Zone 4) to performance (Zone 3–Zone 5). If you want health benefits, you train in the Health Zones. If you want fitness benefits, you train in the Fitness Zones. Performance resides in the Performance Zones, the high-hard zones of Zone 3–Zone 5. If you want all of these benefits, you have to train in all the zones.

Wouldn't it be wonderful if training benefits were associative, allowing you to train in Zone 3 while reaping the benefits of Zone 1 and 2? This isn't possible, because each zone features its unique specific metabolic and stress characteristics. If you wondered whether training only in Zone 5 would enable you to lower your blood pressure and triglycerides, the answer is

30 minutes and build to 60 minutes or more. This ride may be done several times a week as a part of your endurance training spoke or drop down to 60 percent of your maximum heart rate and use this as a recovery ride. The purpose of this ride is to build your muscular endurance.

no. The fact is you would increase your blood pressure, by riding all of your time in Zone 5 because your are adding huge amounts of exercise stress to your other daily stresses.

However, you certainly can train each day in a different zone and derive all the wellness benefits that way. You should enjoy variety in your training so you can realize the different benefits. One day, cycle in Zone 1 and use this as a recovery day—a fun, non-intense, calorie-burning workout. The next day, ride in and out of Zone 5 (intervals) and use this as your supercompensation day, where you train your physiology to its highest ability so that it can recover to a higher fitness level. The following day, train in Zone 2 for the benefits of improved self-esteem, effortlessly burning a lot of fat with little to no pain. Then train in Zone 3, the aerobic zone, multiplying your mitochondria. Take off the next day for a full rest and recovery. Resume with training in Zone 4 in different sports, and cross-train so you'll get fitter in your cycling.

Variety is the spice that allows us to maximize benefit and time. You can have and eat that cake; but first, write a 30-day training plan to make it happen.

REFERENCES

American College of Sports Medicine. *ACSM's Guidelines for Exercise Testing and Prescription.* 5th Edition. Baltimore: Williams & Wilkins, 1995.

Francis, P., M. J. Guono and A. Stavig. *Physiological Response to a Typical Spinning Session.* ACSM's Health and Fitness Journal 3 (1): 28–34, 1999.

Rippe, J., MD. *Counting Pulse Rate Compared to Heart Rate Monitor.* University of Massachusetts, 1991. (unpublished)

Putting it all together.....racing with a heart rate monitor.

CHAPTER 4

Assessing Your Fitness with Your Monitor

Heart monitors make formidable management tools, yet too frequently, we just strap them on and casually use them to judge our performance. We look at the number and hastily decide it's too low or too high, but our judgment isn't based on facts about our personal fitness.

Paul Camerer is an example of how numbers can be wrong. On our way to celebrate his 80th birthday last week, he proudly exhibited his new monitor, displaying his average heart rate for his indoor cycling workout that day: 152 bpm for 60 minutes.

Paul had happily debunked the old "220 minus your age" formula. Paul had been using a monitor that automatically calculated his maximum heart rate based on that formula: 220 minus 80 = 140 bpm, which predicted that his maximum heart rate should sink lower as he gets older. Yet for an hour, Paul had maintained an average heart rate 12 bpm higher than the old formula said he could maintain for even a minute.

When I first tested Paul's maximum heart rate at age 72, it measured 188 bpm. Today, his maximum heart rate is still 188 bpm. Maximum heart rate, at least in some people, doesn't decline with age; instead, our fitness level drops with age as we lapse into a more sedentary lifestyle. Paul has continued to train and though his volume of oxygen has probably changed and his muscle strength may have declined, his maximum heart rate remains the same.

—Sally Edwards

The American College of Sports Medicine regularly issues position papers recommending how people should exercise. Citing 262 scientific references in its report *The Recommended Quantity and Quality of Exercise for Developing and Maintaining Cardiorespiratory and Muscular Fitness and Flexibility in Healthy Adults,* the ACSM specified how much exercise is enough and what type of exercise is best for developing and maintaining fitness.

Although the report is long, it's worth reading. One of its key points is the need for standardization of testing and measurement procedures. Each researcher uses different ways of testing; as the article states in one very long sentence:

Despite an abundance of information available concerning the training of the human organism, there is a lack of standardization of testing protocols and procedures, of methodology in relation to training procedures and experimental design, and of a preciseness in the documentation and reporting of the quantity and quality of training prescribed, making interpretation difficult (ACSM, 1998).

In other words, there is no one universally agreed-on way to measure fitness, including using heart rate measurements for showing changes in fitness. Fitness is measurable in many different ways, and this is true for ways to use monitors espoused by different researchers.

STEP 6: DETERMINING YOUR FITNESS LEVEL

Despite the confusion, a few simple tests and measurements can be reliably used to determine some baseline and thresholds of fitness. Remember that the definition of fitness is the individual's ability to perform moderate-to-vigorous levels of physical activity without excessive fatigue. A heart rate monitor is an ideal tool to help you measure your current level of fitness.

Since one component of FIT(T) is frequency, the heart monitor might well be one of the best tools we have for measuring fitness outside the laboratory, for a capital investment of less than $100.

Resting Heart Rate

Resting heart rate is taken in the morning, usually before rising from bed. After awakening, simply count your heart rate before you get up, stretch or perform other activities. The rate should vary within a range of 5 bpm in day-to-day readings. Measure your resting heart rate for 5 consecutive days and average those measurements for your baseline resting heart rate value. If you note that your heart rate exceeds this number sometimes, you may be experiencing some change in your physiology. Likely causes for the increase or decrease in heart rate may be response to stress, overtraining, a poor night's rest, a startle response to awakening too quickly, or nutritional deficiency.

Ambient Heart Rate

A key heart rate indicator for stress measurement, your ambient heart rate is measured with your body in a sedentary position but biologically awake. You're in ambient heart rate mode when you are reading or watching television or in a quiet conversation with friends. The lower your ambient heart rate, the better for your health and fitness (see chart below). Ambient heart rate can decrease quickly with improvements in your physical fitness. Ambient heart rate improves dramatically when you remove the stressors in your life, which can be anything from food allergies to lack of sleep or time.

You can measure ambient heart rate several ways. The easiest is to wear your monitor all day and periodically observe it when you are sitting and inactive. Note the number. Take a half dozen or more measurements and average them. Compare the daily changes using your monitor as a type of window into your heart. Like a window, it affords you a view of what's happening to your internal physiology.

To more accurately assess your ambient heart rate, measure the total number of beats over an extended period. In *Precision Training: Training Programmes for 27 Sports Using Heart Rate Monitors* (Reed Books, 1998), author Jon Ackland describes wearing his monitor for a 24-hour workday that included 8 hours of sleep and a 30-minute run. He reported his average heart rate for the 24 hours was "61 bpm (30 percent maximum) with a maximum heart rate during my 'up-tempo' run of 175-180 bpm. My heart beat 87,840 times in the day." To complete your recording of ambient heart rate, you'll need a heart rate monitor that can either sample heart rate or count each individual heart beat for several hours. Several models provide this feature, many in downloadable models.

Perform this measurement on yourself several times throughout the month. If your ambient heart rate is dropping because you are getting more of the stress out of your life, you'll notice that the total number of heartbeats in a 24-hour period will decrease. This happens because your stroke volume is higher and you are more efficient, so your heart doesn't need to beat as often to supply the nutrients required.

Delta Heart Rate

The Greek word for change is *delta*. This heart rate measurement shows the change in heart rate as a result of a change in body position. Also known as the orthostatic test, delta heart rate is simple and doesn't take much time in return for the information it generates. Lie down and remain still for about two minutes, noting the lowest heart rate number in this position. As you slowly stand, note that the spike in the heart rate, which gradually drops to a standing heart rate number. Subtract the prone heart rate number from the standing and you have your delta heart rate. The higher the number, the more stressed the body. Here's a general range of scores for you to compare with your delta heart rate for assessing your training:

Delta Heart Rate	Recommendation
Over 30 bpm	Take the day off from training. This is not a good number.
20-30 bpm	This is a cautionary range. It's high and you should note this. Train at least one zone lower than you had planned and make it a recovery day.
10-20 bpm	Normal; everything is fine.
0-10 bpm	Excellent. Be happy that you are in a healthy state with regard to your heart's ability to respond to a change in body position.

Use the delta heart rate assessment to help you recognize the amount of training and other stress you might be experiencing. Here's the heart rate profile from the delta heart rate assessment.

Delta Heart Rate = A - B
Delta Heart Rate = 70 - 60
Delta Heart Rate = 10 bpm

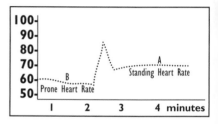

R-to-R Variability

This is a highly sophisticated measurement that is only available on very high-end heart rate monitors and Holter monitors. It measures the variability in the time between heartbeats known as the beat-to-beat variation. The greater the variability, the better the cardiac muscle responsiveness to small changes. When a person is highly stressed, there is very little beat-to-beat variability because the heart muscle simply doesn't respond to minor changes.

Heart rate changes can be used as a diagnostic measurement. This is different from using heart rate for testing fitness. Rather, changes in the heart rate values can indicate certain health changes.

Using a Heart Rate Monitor for Diagnosis

Resting heart rate	Lower the better. Indicates that you are in low stress and physically fit.
Ambient heart rate	An indicator for the current amount of stress in your life.
Delta heart rate	Same as above
R-to-R variability	The greater the variability the healthier the total physiological system.

Heart rate monitor information is valuable for measuring improvement on your bike. The following several rides show you how to measure fitness gains using your monitor.

Speed Test/Time Trial Test

This simple test uses three variables for determining improved fitness: speed, heart rate and time. Hold any two variables constant and measure the changes in the third. For example, you can use a fixed distance test. A good distance for cycling is a 1km loop, completing from 5 to 10 loops. Warm up and hold a constant heart rate such as 80 to 85 percent of your maximum heart rate for a fixed distance, such as 5km or 5 loops. Note the average speed. The higher the speed you can ride with distance and heart rate constant, the fitter you are.

Similarly, hold your speed constant along with your heart rate and notice the change in distance traveled. Finally, maintain a constant speed and distance over a measured time and note the changes in heart rate. This is one of the best ways to test true cardiovascular improvement without the need for lactate or gas analyzers, which measure the concentration of lactic acid in your blood or the volume of oxygen you consume.

Average Heart Rate Test

Average heart rate is an important feature for your monitor to display because average exercise intensity seems to be one of the best measurements to determine training benefits. Knowing your average heart rate, regardless of whether it's an interval session or a steady-state continuous workout, helps you to quantify your training load.

You can also use average heart rate to determine if you are getting fitter. That improvement test is simple: hold a constant time, speed, and course and compare the average heart rate. If it's lower, you may be getting fitter; if it's higher, you may be less fit or worse, overtraining.

Average heart rate data is especially useful for the indoor cyclist. Hold your heart rate at a constant number—say 140 bpm—for a fixed period of time from 5 to 30 minutes. As your training progresses, note whether your distance traveled for this identical workout increases—a clear indication that the training effect is working for you.

More advanced heart rate monitors feature average heart rate per lap or split. This can be useful if you are doing interval training or want to know your average heart rate per mile or kilometer during an event.

Neil Craig, one of Australia's best sports physiologists and author of *Scientific Heart Rate Training* (Pursuit Performance, 1998), writes in his newsletter *Performance Matters* (June 1999):

Why is average heart rate an important reading? Well, look at the following exercise and training principle: the average relative intensity of training dictates the extent of adaptation regardless of whether the training is done continuously or intermittently. This principle was formulated back in the mid 1970's and revisited by Canadian researchers in 1992 who looked at the value of either training continuously at anaerobic threshold or continuously but with alternating intensities above and below the anaerobic threshold. Their results confirmed that neither method was superior and that it is the average relative intensity of exercise that is the key to getting a good aerobic training effect.

In other words, for aerobic training at least, it doesn't matter whether your training is continuous or intermittent or interval in nature; provided the average heart rate is similar, you will get similar aerobic exercise benefits.

You can collect other good average heart rate examples by riding on a hilly course, resting on the downhills and working hard on the uphills. A key number to know would be the average of those hard and then easy periods, so you know whether you accomplished your training goal for that session.

If you are multizone training, average heart rate is valuable to know. For example, let's say you like to warm up at 65 percent of your maximum heart rate for 5 minutes, then your workout design calls for 10 minutes in Zone 3, 5 minutes in Zone 4 and 2.5 minutes in Zone 5 plus a cool-down of 10 minutes at 55 percent of your maximum heart rate. You can use your lap split feature to give you your average for every zone and time period as well as for the entire workout.

Hill Climb Test for Maximum Heart Rate

We all receive genetically specified distinguishing biomarkers within our DNA code. One of those is our individual maximum heart rate. As you now know, there are a number of different protocols to determine maximum heart rate. Connie Carpenter and Davis Phinney recommend using a hill climb for their protocol:

Select a hill and do several hill sprints with little rest on a day when you are feeling good (don't try this when you are fatigued). Make each effort harder than the last, and use a heart-rate monitor or take your heart rate after each sprint. After several sprints, your pulse will peak at or near your maximal heart-rate value (Carpenter and Phinney, 1992).

For indoor cycling, a test that resembles an abbreviated graded exercise test seems to be the most accurate.

Indoor Graded Maximum Heart Rate Test

Warm up adequately. Comfortably cycle at 120-130 bpm until you are ready to begin the test. Hold cadence steady and slowly increase resistance every 15 seconds. Carefully control the resistance so that heart rate increases five beats every 15 seconds. A typical test will last between 2 and 4 minutes. Toward the end of the test, your effort will require support from others to encourage you to continue to reach true maximum effort. You'll be able to hold your maximum for between 5 and 30 seconds before you reach exhaustion. Cool down completely before you dismount.

Assessing your fitness with your heart rate monitor is one of the most valuable reasons to use one. Paul Camerer learned that as he got older he could ride harder than the mathematical formulas that predicted, inaccurately, his maximum heart rate. Get the most out of your monitor by using it for measuring your current fitness and your fitness improvement

WORKOUTS

Indoor Training

Recovery Intervals
Fitness 50-70 percent

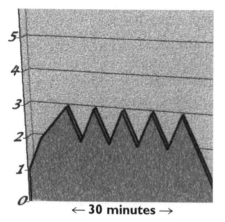

← 30 minutes →

Percentage of total workout

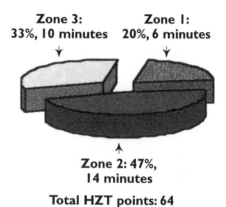

Zone 3: 33%, 10 minutes

Zone 1: 20%, 6 minutes

Zone 2: 47%, 14 minutes

Total HZT points: 64

This 30-minute workout can be used as a recovery workout on a day when you still want to ride but need to keep the intensity in the lower zones and let your heart and legs recover. It is also a great workout to measure your "active" recovery heart rate. If 30 minutes isn't long enough add more two-minute intervals.

Purpose

During the main set you will be riding between 60 and 70 percent of max HR, which means this is an ideal workout for getting your heart healthy. It can also be extended and done as a recovery workout, staying below 70 percent and allowing your muscles and legs to remain active while giving your heart a rest from high intensity training. Keep the resistance low and "noodle" (easy spin) your way up and down the intervals. Time your recoveries. Count how many seconds it takes for you to drop from 70 percent to 60 percent. As you get fitter it takes fewer seconds to recover so retest in a month or two. Another way you can do the recovery test is to see how many beats you drop in two minutes. You may go below 60 percent and that is fine; you'll just have further to go back up to 70 percent. Make sure your recovery cadence is the same on each recovery and that you are working with little or no resistance or easy gearing.

Workout Plan

Warm up for 7 minutes in Zones 1 and 2. Steadily increase intensity to the bottom of Zone 3 (70 percent) and sustain for 2 minutes. Take all the resistance off and easy pedal as you time your recovery from the bottom of Zone 3 to the bottom of Zone 2. Make a note of the number of recovery seconds. Once you reach the bottom of Zone 2, sustain that heart rate until the next work interval begins (2 minutes). Repeat a total of five times, then warm down the last 5 minutes in Zone 2 and Zone 1.

Another option is to time your recovery from the bottom of zone 3 to the bottom of Zone 2, and when you hit the bottom start your next work interval. See how many times you can complete the work/recovery interval in 20 minutes or however many minutes you choose.

Recovery Intervals

Elapsed Time in Minutes	Coaching notes	Zone	Your HR numbers	Duration
0–3	Warm up, easy pedal	1	_____	3 min.
3–5	Warm up, easy pedal to the bottom of Z2	2	_____	2 min.
5–7	Increase HR to mid-point of Z2 (65%)	2	_____	2 min.
7–27	Increase HR steadily to bottom of Z3 (70%) for 2 min., "active" recovery (rec) for two min. to the bottom of Z2 and sustain. Remember number of sec. to recover. Repeat a total of 5 times	2	_____	20 min.
27–30	Warm down to Z1	1	_____	3 min.
	Total HZT Points 64			

*Recovery may be timed and a new interval started once the bottom of Z2 is reached. Count the number of completed work/recovery intervals in 20 min.

THE SUB-MAX TEST FOR CYCLING

This method uses your "feeling" of intensity level—the "rating of perceived exertion" combined with your fitness level and your actual heart rate using a heart rate monitor. This test is designed for an indoor stationary bicycle. An increase in cadence or resistance may be used to increase exercise intensity.

Administering the test

Warm up for a minimum of five minutes at about 100 bpm. The test begins at level 1 by increasing the heart rate to 110 bpm and maintaining that for two minutes. At the end of the two minutes record the RPE number and begin level 2 by increasing the heart rate to 120 bpm. At the end of the two minutes record the RPE number and begin level 3 by increasing the heart rate to 130 bpm. (The test may stop after this level if the RPE number is 7 or higher.) At the end of two minutes record the RPE number. Begin level 4 by increasing the heart rate to

Testing Chart

A Words	B RPE BPM	C Add BPM	D Feeling	E Percent of max HR
Very little effort	1	90	Rest	
	1.5	85		
Very comfortable	2	80	Easy	Less than 35%
	2.5	75		
Easy to talk and no problem to continue	3	70	Moderate	35–50%
	3.5	65		
Could keep this up for a long time	4	60	Somewhat Strong	50–60%
	4.5	55		
Still somewhat comfortable	5	50	Strong	60–70%
	5.5	45		
More challenging, not as comfortable	6	40	Heavy	70–80%
	6.5	35		
Tough, feels very heavy, must push self	7	30	Very Strong	80–85%
	7.5	25		
Challenging, breathing deeper and rapid	8	20	Hard	85–90%
	8.5	15		
Uncomfortable, breathing deep and rapid	9	10	Very, very hard	90–95%
	9.5	5		
Ready to stop	10	0	Extremely Strenuous	95–100%

Sub-Max Test for Cycling

Levels	RPE (match with column B from testing chart)	Heart Rate	Add BPM (from Column C from testing chart)	Add Heart Rate (from 2nd Column to bpm from 4th column)
#1 (2 minutes)	_____	100 bpm	+	=
#2 (2 minutes)	_____	110 bpm	+	=
#3 (2 minutes)	_____	120 bpm	+	=
#4 (2 minutes)	_____	130 bpm	+	=
#5 (2 minutes)	_____	140 bpm	+	=
#6 (2 minutes)	_____	150 bpm	+	=
#7 (2 minutes)	_____	160 bpm	+	=
#8 (2 minutes)	_____	170 bpm	+	=
#9 (2 minutes)	_____	180 bpm	+	=
#10 (2 minutes)	_____	190 bpm	+	=
Average of HR levels to determine MaxHR				

140 bpm and maintain 140 bpm for two minutes. At the end of the two minutes record the RPE number. (The test may stop after this level if the RPE number is 7.) Begin level 5 by increasing the heart rate to 150 bpm and maintain 150 bpm for two minutes. At the end of the two minutes record the RPE number. Continue up the levels until you receive an RPE number of 7.

Warm down for a minimum of five minutes until your heart rate is below 100 bpm.

BPM, which means "beats per minute," are then added to the various levels using the accompanying chart. Maximum heart rate estimates are then averaged to determine maximum heart rate.

2 X 20 Anaerobic Threshold Test

Fitness 50-90 percent

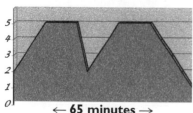

← 65 minutes →

Total HZT points: 242

Percentage of total workout

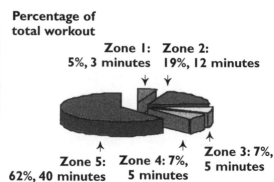

Zone 1: 5%, 3 minutes
Zone 2: 19%, 12 minutes
Zone 3: 7%, 5 minutes
Zone 4: 7%, 5 minutes
Zone 5: 62%, 40 minutes

Anaerobic Threshold Chart

RPE	Feeling	Sedentary	Fit	Superfit	Words	Zone	% of max HR
1	Rest				Very little effort		<35%
2	Easy				Very comfortable		<35%
3	Moderate				Easy to talk and comfortable		35–50%
4	Somewhat strong				Could keep this up for a long time	1	50–60%
5	Strong	X			Respiration deeper	2	60–70%
6	Heavy	X	X		More challenging, not as comfortable	3	70–80%
7	Very strong		X		Tough but breathing is still rhythmic	4	80–85%
8	Hard		X		Challenging, breathing is deeper and more rapid	4	85–90%
9	Very, very hard			X	Uncomfortable, rapid and deep breathing	5	90–95%
10	Extremely strenuous				Rapid breathing, cannot talk, ready to stop	5	95–100%

Note: "X" indicates the anaerobic threshold RPE and percentage of maximum heart rate for a sedentary, fit or superfit individual.

This is an anaerobic heart rate test designed by David Martin, Ph.D. at Georgia State University. The goal of this workout is to sustain the highest heart rate number you can for 20 minutes followed by a 5-minute recovery and then sustain the same number again for 20 minutes. After completing both 20 minute intervals, answer the question: Was that the hardest I could work for the duration of time (40 minutes)? If the answer is yes, then that heart rate number is an excellent estimate of your anaerobic threshold heart rate.

Purpose

Anaerobic threshold testing is one of the ways of measuring fitness. The higher the percentage of maximum heart rate you can sustain for the duration of the test, the fitter you are. This translates into being able to cycle faster for a longer duration. If you have never done this test before you may want to be conservative the first time until you get the feel for what is happening and what is expected. Retest in a month or six weeks to see if you are getting fitter. It is important that you are fully rested before doing this test and that you give yourself a minimum of 48 hours of rest from riding above heart Zone 3.

Workout Plan

Warm up for 5 minutes to the bottom of Zone 2, then gradually increase heart rate for the next 5 minutes until you reach the heart rate number that you think you can sustain for 20 minutes. Sustain that number for 20 minutes. You may choose to use cadence, resistance/gearing or any combination you wish to sustain the heart rate. After 20 minutes, recover to the bottom of Zone 2 for 5 minutes. Make sure you drink plenty of water and allow your legs and body to relax.

After 5 minutes of recovery begin to increase your heart rate again over the next 3 minutes until you have reached the same heart rate number that you sustained for the first 20 minutes. Sustain that heart rate for a second 20 minutes, then warm down over the next 7 minutes to Zone 1.

2 x 20

Elapsed Time in Minutes	Coaching notes	Zone	Your HR numbers	Duration
0–5	Warm up to bottom of Z2	2	_____	5 min.
5–7	Increase heart rate, bottom of Z3	3	_____	2 min.
7–10	Gradually increase heart rate to highest sustainable heart rate number		_____	2 min.
10–30	Sustain heart rate goal, choice of rpm or resisance (R)		_____	20 min.
30–35	Recover (Rec) to the bottom of Z2, easy pedal	2	_____	5 min.
35–36	Increase heart rate, bottom of Z3	3	_____	1 min
36–38	Gradually increase heart rate to highest sustainable heart rate number		_____	2 min.
38–58	Sustain heart rate goal, choice of rpm or resistance (R)		_____	20 min.
58–65	Warm down gradually to Z1		_____	7 min.

OUTDOOR TRAINING

The All-Out Time Trial

Find a 5- or 10-mile course that you can ride with no stop signs and limited traffic. Pick a day when there is no wind and the roads are dry. Make sure that you have the same weather conditions when you retest.

This time trial means "all out," as fast as you can go for the entire course. Make sure you have a good warm up. I like using a downloadable heart rate monitor for this one so I can save the printout and compare it with the next time I do this time trial. If you don't have a downloadable monitor the next best thing is to use one that will calculate average heart rate. Elapsed time or chronograph functions are also handy.

Record your results, elapsed time and average HR and make a note in your logbook of the weather, time of day/year and how you felt. As you get fitter you will notice the time to complete the course decreases and your heart rate declines. That's good because you can generate more power at a lower heart rate. If your average heart rate goes slightly higher, it means that your anaerobic threshold is higher. Good. You are fitter.

The thought of this sends shivers up my spine and pain deep into my quads! Lactic acid swims like a school of sharks in my bloodstream and I wonder why am I doing this?

When I forget the pain for just a moment the answer comes to me; so I can measure if I'm getting fitter and faster! If that is the goal then there is no better way than putting the pedal to the metal and see the results. It is extremely motivating and the pain is soon forgotten when you see that your training is working.

Paceline Ride

An important part of outdoor training is the ability and skill of being able to ride a paceline. Paceline riding is not for the beginning cyclist, but as you become more experienced and daring you will find it's a great way to ride faster with less effort and at lower heart rates. It's like being in a wind shadow and you quickly realize the savings in effort. It does not come without its risks, though, and you will need to weigh the benefits against the occasional mishaps. An excellent chapter on group riding and paceline etiquette by Geoff Drake comes from the *Complete Book of Road Cycling Skills.* Here are a few tips from the chapter:

- As the leader, visualize a string tied between your saddle and the following rider's handlebars. Sudden accelerations will break the string (leaving your pal behind) and quick stops (causing them to

RECOVERY HEART RATE—INTRARECOVERY AND INTERRECOVERY

There are two types of recovery heart rate. Intra-recovery heart rate occurs between sets of interval sessions. Inter-recovery heart rate changes between workout days and daily recovery episodes.

Training is a series of physiological stresses followed by recovery, which results in improvement of your riding energy systems. For training to lead to improved fitness, an appropriate cycle of physical stress and recovery needs to be applied to obtain the training effect.

Recovery is the ability of your physiological system to return to a normal or pre-exercise state, or homeostasis. Depending on the type of physical stress applied and the dosage of it, recovery can be immediate or take as long as several days or weeks to occur.

Here are a few simple rules to follow when using recovery times and recovery heart rate to improve or diagnose your training:

Rule 1. The harder the workout, the longer the recovery time needed

This is the principle of high, hot, hard training rides. If you spend long periods of time in Zones 4 and 5, you must allow a longer recovery. High heart zones are physiologically stressful, but it's appropriate to train there as long as you complement them with recovery overlap your wheel and launch on the tarmac) will make it slacken. Your job is to keep it taut. This doesn't necessarily mean maintaining the same speed. Instead, concentrate on exerting the same pedal pressure. This means slowing slightly for hills is okay.

- If you must break hard, such as for a dog, announce "stopping!" or "slowing!" Another way to control speed is to simply sit up and let the wind slow you. In any case, keep pedaling.
- Holding a line. Ride as if you are on rails. On occasion, this means going over a bump that you would otherwise swerve to avoid. Large obstacles, such as parked cars, and road debris merit verbal and hand warnings.
- Climbing. Shift to the next higher gear before standing to compensate for the slower cadence and maintain pressure on the pedal so your back doesn't move "backward" relative to the rider behind. The same thing applies when you sit down. Downshift and concentrate on maintain pedal pressure to any abrupt change in speed.

---

rides in the lower heart zones. A good way to measure if you have achieved sufficient inter-recovery is to measure your waking or resting heart rate. If it approaches five beats per minute of normal you have probably recovered adequately.

Rule 2. Inability to recover indicates insufficient recovery time

If your heart rate doesn't recover between workouts, you may be overtrained, or you may not have recovered from the previous ride. You could be experiencing some effects from medication or environmental conditions, or have compromised your immune system. Another possibility is that you may be feeling physiological effects from other life stresses.

Rule 3. Shortened intra-recovery time means greater fitness

Measure with your monitor and your watch the time required between intervals for your heart rate to recover to a designated percentage of maximum heart rate. If this period decreases from week to week, you are probably getting fitter—your body can recover more quickly from a period of physical stress.

Both inter-recovery (between workouts) and intra-recovery (within workouts) can be used to fine-tune your training because they help measure your improvement.

- Following. Never overlap wheels. Stay at least 6 inches behind a smooth, reliable rider and much further back if you don't know the person. Look through the lead rider, scanning for trouble rather than being mesmerized while staring at the wheel in front of you.
- Handling traffic. Announce an overtaking vehicle, particularly if one of your pals is out in the road to far. A quick "car back" will let those ahead know it's wise to tuck in so traffic can pass.
- Pulling through. In any situation where you are sharing the work by alternating the front position, don't surge. Maintain the same speed as your pull through.

If you want to give paceline riding a try, we suggest you find an experienced and predictable rider that is willing to teach you the "ropes" or in this case the string approach to group riding. The more you practice paceline riding the more comfortable you will become. Never get so comfortable you forget how quickly things can happen. Stay attentive and follow the golden rule: "You are responsible for the person behind you!"

When riding a paceline it helps to have your monitor mounted on the handlebars or somewhere where you won't have to turn or move to see it. If you are drafting correctly your heart rate will drop significantly.

As a final reminder, always let the rider ahead of you know that you are "on their wheel" or in a drafting position. If they don't know you are there they can't lead or respond accordingly.

The Pyramid Scheme

You will think "scheme" as this ride gradually gets more and more challenging. The work intervals increase in time and intensity while the recovery time is equal to the preceding work interval. Pick a flat to rolling course and begin the pyramid climb after completely warming up (15 to 30 minutes).

The work intervals are 1-, 2-, 3-, 4-, 4-, 3-, 2-, 1- minutes building to more than 90 percent of maximum heart rate. Warm down gradually to the bottom of Zone 2 (15 to 30 minutes).

The ride looks like this:

1 minute at 60 percent of maximum heart rate with 1 minute of recovery
2 minutes at 65 percent of maximum heart rate with 2 minutes of recovery
3 minutes at 70 percent of maximum heart rate with 3 minutes of recovery
4 minutes at 75 percent of maximum heart rate with 4 minutes of recovery
4 minutes at 80 percent of maximum heart rate with 4 minutes of recovery
3 minutes at 85 percent of maximum heart rate with 3 minutes of recovery
2 minutes at 90 percent of maximum heart rate with 2 minutes of recovery
1 minute at more than 90 percent of maximum heart rate with recovery warm down

Note: You may choose to go to a certain heart rate percentage then drop down in intensity rather than continuing to go higher. At this point the pyramid becomes more of a ladder as you increase then decrease intensity. Time remains the same.

REFERENCES

American College of Sports Medicine Position Stand. *Medicine and Science in Sports and Exercise.* 30: 975–991, June 1998.

Ackland, Jon. *Precision Training: Training Programmes for 27 Sports Using Heart Rate Monitors.* Auckland, New Zealand: Reed Books, 1998.

Carpenter, Connie and Phinney, Davis. *Training for Cycling: The Ultimate Guide to Improved Performance.* New York: Perigee Books, 1992.

Susan Smalls, Don Cox, and Sue Dills riding a Heart Cycling class on two different types of indoor cycles.

CHAPTER 5

Fat-burning Zones and Fuels

Marie was like so many of us, trying to lose that elusive 10 pounds, after gaining 20 in five years due to trauma and health challenges. She went through menopause, had a bilateral mastectomy, and experienced a severe ankle fracture. After 20 sedentary years, cancer compelled her to begin working out with other cancer survivors. She lost 10 pounds but had reached a plateau.

A quietly intense and competitive person, Marie was using a heart rate monitor and confessed to spending a lot of her training time in the higher zones. As you will see, she was more successful when she changed that approach.

—Sally Edwards

Burning nutrient and calorie-packed fuels is important to the successful cyclist. This isn't simple. It requires effort to combine a healthy diet with a physical and psychological training program to become a better cyclist. Eating optimally combined with training soundly can result in an entire lifestyle shift towards a healthier and longer life.

Eating optimally always leads to the question of the role of dietary and body fat as well as fat-burning. One of the questions Sally Edwards is most frequently asked is what heart zone(s) burn the most fat. She prefers to broaden the question to how fuels are utilized in each of the different heart zones.

Countless magazine articles and reports give us conflicting explanations and information about the fat-burning zones. In fact, there's only one best answer to this complex question about fat. Because it's a major issue for those interested in weight management, the process of burning fuels, including fat, is important to understand clearly.

Different types of fuels are burned in different percentages depending on the zone. The three principal types of calories used for cycling are protein, carbohydrates (also known as sugar, muscle glycogen and blood glucose) and fat (also known as free fatty acids and triglycerides). When you ride in different heart zones, you burn a different ratio of carbohydrates (carb) and fat. In practical terms, the percentage of protein used for energy remains relatively constant (about 5 percent) in each heart zone. The higher the heart zone, the higher the percentage of carbohydrates and the lower the percentage of fat that is burned. As a matter of fact, you burn the highest percentage of fat compared to total calories when you're asleep! In Zone 5, for most individuals, no additional fat is burned; all additional calories consumed are from carbohydrates. No *additional* fat means that most people are burning as many fat calories in Zone 4 as in Zone 5. You burn more *total* calories in Zone 5.

Another important point is the difference between total calories burned and the percentage of calories burned. The higher the exercise intensity, the more total calories burned in one minute. For example, as a rough estimate, in one minute of exercise, a 150-pound rider would burn the following number of calories from combined protein, fat and carbohydrates:

Calories Burned by a 150-Pound Rider

Heart zone 1   >5 Calories burned (per minute)
Heart zone 2   >8 Calories burned (per minute)
Heart zone 3   >11 Calories burned (per minute)
Heart zone 4   >14 Calories burned (per minute)
Heart zone 5   >20 Calories burned (per minute)

That same person burns a different ratio of calories in each of those heart zones. The higher the exercise intensity, the more glycogen or muscle sugar (carbohydrates) are burned, and the lower percentage of fat calories burned.

FREQUENTLY ASKED QUESTIONS: FUELING THE ZONES

The following are Sally's 10 answers to frequently asked questions about the fat-burning heart zones. As you read the answers, remember that each person is unique and we display highly individual differences in our response to foods as fuels. As a result, we burn fat, carbohydrates and protein in an individual way and each according to a number of different factors.

1. In what heart zone do I burn the most fat?

The fitter you are, the more fat you burn in each of the heart zones. The less fit you are, the lower the heart zone. For example, if you are unfit, the zone that burns the most fat is in the lower range, from Zone 2 to 3. If you are tremendously fit, you'll burn the most fat in Zone 4 or Zone 5. For long-term weight management goals, the total number of calories you burn matters more than percentage of fat.

Oxygen must be present for fat to burn. When you exercise aerobically, with plenty of oxygen and without shortness of breath, you burn a high percentage of fat. As soon as you cross over to the anaerobic exercise intensity, the point where there is not enough oxygen to sustain the exercise, you don't burn any *additional* fat as the source of calories fueling your muscles. The following chart shows the percentage of calories utilized in each zone and an example of a 30-minute bike ride in each heart zone:

Calorie Consumption for a 30-Minute Ride

Zone	Percent of max HR	Wellness zones	Fuels burned	Calories burned for 30 minutes	RPE	Description of the feeling
5	90—100%	Performance	90% carb 10% fat 1% protein	450—600	9—10	Very, very hard to extremely strenuous
4	80—90%	Fitness/Performance	85% carb 15% fat 1% protein	<420	7—8	Very strong to hard
3	70—80%	Fitness	50% carb 45% fat 5% protein	<330	5—6	Strong to heavy
2	60—70%	Health	25% carb 70% fat 5% protein	<240	3—4	Moderate to somewhat strong
1	50—60%	Health	10% carb 85% fat 5% protein	<180	1—2	Very light, easy

2. Which fuels are burning in each heart zone?

As mentioned earlier, a different ratio of fuels is burned in each of the five heart zones. The higher the heart zone or the level of exercise intensity, the higher the percentage of carbohydrates oxidized. The lower the zone, the higher the percentage of fat calories used. If you are training for weight management goals, are you interested in burning a high percentage of fat calories or a high number of total calories? Research is still unclear today as to the best answer to that question, but what there is suggests that burning a high number of total calories better promotes a successful weight management program.

To help clarify the question about the best form of fuel utilization in the heart zones, the following chart shows the five different heart zones and the percentage of calories burned in each one:

Heart Zone Training Fuels

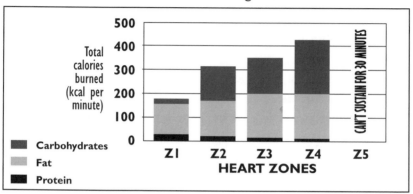

The simple conclusion is that it's best for weight loss or maintenance to exercise longer periods of time in heart zones that you can sustain.

3. Do We All Burn Calories the Same Way?

No. There are enormous individual differences. If you've ever read or thought that a calorie is always just a calorie, think again. It's not simply the way we metabolize or burn energy. Energy balance is highly individual-specific. Recent research shows that burning fuels is more complex than previously thought (Blair, et. al, 1985).

If you want to achieve an "energy shift" that results in successful weight management, you can change many factors influencing your individual energy balance:

1. The *ratio of fuels* in your current diet. If you eat a high-fat diet, you'll burn a higher percentage of fat calories when you train.

2. Your current *fitness level*. The fitter you are, the more fat you'll burn at the same exercise intensity.

3. What you have *just eaten*. If you just ate food and are training or racing with that fuel simultaneously being digested, it will affect the ratio of fuels burned.

4. Your current *body composition.* Your percentage of body fat to lean body weight affects fat-burning capacity. Those with a higher percentage of body fat burn more fat as a percentage than those who have lower body fat.

5. The amount of *alcohol* in your diet. Alcohol is a diuretic. It provides 7 kcal/g of nutrient-free calories. Acute alcohol ingestion results in adverse performance, impairing both psychological and physiological ability.

6. The length of *time* you exercise. How long you ride affects your requirements for fuel. Before, during and after a workout, fueling depends on frequency, intensity, type and duration of exercise.

7. *Gender* plays a role in weight management. For the female, different hormonal levels result in different ways fat is utilized and deposited. Further, water retention varies at different times in the female menstrual cycle. The female athlete's energy requirements are lower than men's. According to Butterfield and Gates, "provision of a high carbohydrate diet as recommended for the male endurance athlete may not be realistic for the female athlete, given her requirements for other micro- and macro-nutrients."

8. Food palate or *taste preference.* The joy of eating food needs to be respected, as well as the need for a varied and balanced diet, which provides adequate nutrient intake.

9. Total *daily number of calories* consumed. An adequate energy intake is required to prevent fatigue and low individual energy levels. Excessive fuel intake results in an energy balance shift and eventual body fat accumulation.

10. *Genetic makeup* is significant. Though complicated, genetics greatly affects your body composition.

11. *Environment.* Factors such as rural versus city residing, pollution and a sedentary job without support for human-powered transportation can affect your energy balance and overall health.

12. *Past sports experience.* If you've been fit before, it's sometimes easier to get fit again not only because of the familiarity, but also due to the emotional impact of fitness improvements.

13. *Stress.* A high-stress lifestyle can lead to an energy shift toward holding back on fat release (hoarding), because the body responds to stress by automatic preservation of body fat.

You have a degree of control over many of these factors. Understanding and adjusting them can have an impact on how you refuel and manage weight. That is the basic tenant of energy shifting for body weight changes.

4. How does fat burn in each of the heart zones?

Fat comes in two basic forms: the kind we burn in the form of fat calories for basic metabolic and movement requirements, and the kind that's stored in different parts of our bodies, such as in adipose tissue, our blood and the fat that protects our organs. For most, liberating the stored fat in the adipose tissues is a major goal. To do this, your metabolic pathways must allow for fat cells to release triglycerides, transport the fat to the working muscles and then burn it off preferentially. We want to burn fat before we burn any of the other sources of fuel.

To do this successfully, low heart zone exercise has been found to be the most effective. Though it burns fewer total calories per minute, it results in the improvement of metabolic fat-burning pathways, which depend on the presence of aerobic enzymes. Low heart zone training high in oxygen availability effectively allows fat out of the fat cell (called fat release) and then allows it to be successfully transported to the muscle (fat transportation). When these same molecules of fat reach the working muscles, low intensity exercise easily permits the cell membrane to open and allow the fat gram, packed with nine calories of energy, to be burned by the body's energy factories (the mitochondria).

Burning body fat is a complex process that takes time to occur. Short, brief Zone 5 bursts of energy can't match longer, slower, less-energetic heart zones 1 to 3 workout sessions for burning fat. If you want to burn fat preferentially and in sizeable amounts from your stored body fat, then train in low heart zones for longer periods of time and, simultaneously, have more fun.

5. Is cycling the best activity for fat burning?

If you are a cyclist, probably yes. If you are a swimmer, the best fat-burning activity is probably swimming. This isn't because one activity burns fat better. Each burns different amounts of fat based on several factors. However, what's known—and fairly easy to guess—is that those who stick with an exercise program tend to burn more fat long term than those who quit. This is called "exercise compliance," or the ability of the exerciser to stay on a training program. Compliance strongly relates to the enjoyability of the experience. If you love to ride your bike, your compliance to bicycle riding will be high. If you train in the fitness heart zones, you'll burn lots of fat, lots of calories, stay on the training program and achieve results. If you're a cyclist who turns to running and doesn't find joy in it, your unwillingness to stay on the running program may derail your success.

Ultimately, it comes down to whether you are training at all, not which zones you occupy. The most recent review of the scientific literature shows that those who are overweight usually get too little exercise; they *don't* overeat.

You'll probably experience a direct and absolute relationship between exercise and weight loss. Training on your bike can result in steady, slow but long-term, effective weight loss and weight maintenance. That's the best way to reach your weight-management goal.

6. What about bike weight versus body weight?

One of the nice things about riding a bicycle is that your body weight is supported by your bike frame and tires rather than your skeletal frame. Cycling may be easier on your joints, but sooner or later that extra weight must go up a hill! That's where you might say the rubber meets the road. Extra weight (either as body fat and muscle or bicycle weight) can slow down the cyclist on hills. Since climbing a hill is work against gravity, a lighter climber is simply pushing fewer pounds and thereby gaining an advantage over a heavier cyclist.

According to Arnie Baker, M.D., "a 5-percent loss in either body weight or bicycle weight or a combination of both could result in as much as three minutes in an hour's climb" (Baker, 1996). That may not sound like much, but it could mean the difference between winning the race or coming in last. It could mean the difference of being able to keep up with the gang, or dropping off to grind your way to the top alone.

Three things will get you to the top of the hill faster. You can buy your way to the top with expensive equipment (which doesn't work very well if you're not fit) or you can train your way to the top by losing extra fat pounds and gaining muscle strength. A third option might combine technology with training. Train with a heart rate monitor and train in your aerobic heart zones. In this way you can train in less time, burn more fat, and enjoy your cycling more.

7. What are the best foods to eat before, during and after cycling?

It's up to you to decide what fuels are best suited to your body and its metabolism, whether off or on the bike. Let's briefly examine a couple of your nutritional choices. Carbohydrates are one of the most important energy sources to enhance athletic performance. They are absolutely essential for cycling and prolonged endurance activities. Exercise scientists have long known that a diet rich in carbohydrates and a body trained to utilize blood glucose improves performance and endurance. The more glycogen you can pack into your muscle cells and the more stored, readily accessible fuel you possess, the less you fatigue during long rides.

Your daily energy needs for cycling will depend both on the duration and the intensity of your training. The harder and longer you cycle, the more calories you'll need to consume to maintain the same pace for longer periods. Beware though: Cycle training is not an invitation to eat anything and everything. Training smart means eating the right mix of food from the three major fuel sources to ensure proper energy. Current research supports a nutrient-rich diet of between 60–65 percent carbohydrate, 25–30 percent fat and 10–15 percent protein, with a calorie intake adequately geared to intensity and duration on a daily basis.

As already noted, only carbohydrates and fats are used extensively during cycling. Your working muscles prefer burning carbohydrates because their energy contents are easily and quickly released and used by the body.

In general, your pre-ride meal should be high in carbohydrates and low in fats and proteins. It should contain adequate amounts of fluid to ensure that you are well hydrated. Pancakes, waffles, cereals, pasta, bagels, toast, fruit, fruit juices and liquid carbohydrate and food supplements are all good food choices. For those with no time to feast, an energy bar can suffice but isn't a replacement for real foods. It is important to eat before cycling, so forget about skipping breakfast— it's too important.

For rides lasting more than one hour, consume about 100 to 150 calories of carbohydrate every half hour throughout the ride. Most 8- to 12-ounce servings of sport drinks provide about 300 to 400 calories of carbohydrate and fat, so drinking 8–12 ounces every 30 minutes should help fight off the bonk.

Fluid supplementation such as energy drinks during long rides provides electrolytes, water and carbohydrate. Water is the most critical because dehydration greater than 2 percent of body weight greatly reduces performance. Energy drinks also provide sodium, an electrolyte, which enhances water absorption from the intestine into the bloodstream. Most energy drinks are between 5- and 10-percent carbohydrate, which is the percentage to optimize fluid absorption and provide carbohydrate to power your muscles. If you can grab a cool energy drink, do it. Cool fluids empty faster from your stomach than warm fluids.

If you are riding over several hours, you might consider some solid food such as energy/sport bars. Drink several ounces of fluid with the energy bar. Choose high-carbohydrate energy bars low in fat and protein. Select bars that are more than 80-percent carbohydrate and less than 10-percent fat. Another energy source is high-energy concentrated carbohydrate gel, which offers quick energy for sustained performance. Each package is premeasured carbohydrate and relatively easy to consume on the bike. It can also be used immediately after exercise to help with recovery. They are not designed to replace food, energy drinks or bars, however. A better choice might be to eat real food—bananas, fruit cookies, bagels, peanut butter sandwiches and nuts.

Carbohydrate-rich foods like fresh fruits, breads, cereals and energy bars, along with energy drinks, are important tools. The secret is to try different forms and find out which works best for you.

What and when you eat after a long ride can be as important as what you eat before and during it. You may require up to 24 hours to resynthesize muscle glycogen, provided ample carbohydrate is consumed. Try to eat carbohydrates as soon as possible after a ride. If you aren't hungry, drink an energy drink or high carbohydrate beverage to replace needed fluids. By ingesting them at the end of a ride, you stimulate glycogen replacement, thereby shortening recovery time, leaving more available energy for the next day.

8. How much water should I drink?

Don't leave home without water. Your car can't run without it and your body won't either.

How much to drink invites another "it depends": on intensity, duration and environmental factors of the ride such as heat, humidity and wind. It also depends on how your body dissipates heat produced by fuel metabolism. It depends on how many workouts per week you do and their intensity.

Hydration is the key to prolonged activity and performance. If you fail to drink enough during a long ride, you'll suffer dehydration and an inability to sweat, which means a rise in body temperature and premature fatigue. Excessive dehydration can also increase the risk of heat exhaustion and even heat stroke.

Your cycling speed declines often because dehydration reduces the water portion of the blood (plasma), decreasing blood volume. Less blood is sent to the muscles for fuel and oxygen and to the skin to help with cooling, and heart rate and body temperature climb. Your heart rate monitor indicates dehydration when your heart rate drifts upward with no increase in effort. This phenomenon is called cardiac drift.

The key to reduce dehydration is to drink often, before you are thirsty. Drink at least 10–20 ounces every 30 minutes, or about a standard water bottle's worth every 30–45 minutes. You should carry two water bottles on your bike for long rides and plan a stop to refill. A water pack on your back can carry considerably more water; try it out first on short rides. For rides longer than an hour, you'll need extra carbohydrates and electrolytes to help maintain your blood glucose levels and your electrolyte balance.

9. How do I lose weight cycling by using my heart rate monitor?

If it were possible to distill the basics of what research and experience have shown to be the world's best weight plan, it would read something like this: Lower the amount of fat you eat and increase the amount of fat you burn exercising.

When it gets right down to it, what most of us want from cycling for weight loss is either to lose fat weight or keep it off. Cycling allows you to expend large amounts of calories either by riding for long periods of time or riding at high intensities. Let's take a look at both sides of this equation: what you eat and how much you exercise.

If you are interested in fat loss, you can reduce your fat intake to 20 to 30 percent of your total calories; reduce your body fat by exercising, especially at 60 to 80 percent maximum heart rate; reduce your total injested calories and increase your muscle mass.

Using your heart rate monitor along with smart eating and exercising is one of the keys to your success. Refer to the following chart, which shows you the ratio of fuels burned at various intensities:

Here are a few suggestions to smart weight management. Count fat grams, not just calories. Read labels and keep track of the number of fat grams you eat. Eat to feed your lean mass.

You lose weight cycling by using your heart monitor in your aerobic zones. To begin, stay in these moderate zones for at least 20 to 30 minutes a day. As your body adapts to 20 to 30 minutes per day, you'll notice how quickly the time passes and that you're eager to stay longer in the fat-burning zones. For weight loss purposes, the key is to extend the length of time that you are in the zones, not to go into the higher ones.

For fat to be released from fat cells, ride in low-intensity zones for progressively longer and longer periods of time. When 30 minutes seems easy, move on to the next phase of your training. If you can extend your workout to 45 minutes a day, you'll be burning fat calories. You'll also be giving your fat cells more time to release fat molecules and your bloodstream more time to carry them to your muscles where

Fat and Calorie Chart

Calories per day(grams)	20% fat (grams)	30% fat
1200	27	40
1300	29	43
1400	31	46
1500	33	50
1600	36	53
1700	38	56
1800	40	60
1900	42	63
2000	44	66
2100	47	70
2200	49	73
2300	51	76
2400	53	80
2500	56	83
2600	58	86
2700	60	90
2800	62	93
2900	64	96
3000	67	100

they will be readily metabolized. Your goal is to extend your workout to 50 or 60 minutes a day, 3 to 6 days a week. You'll find that by cycling in the lower zones, you'll also be rewarded with more than burning more fat. Rather, you will realize lower blood pressure, lower resting heart rate, reduced percentage of body fat, stabilized weight and lower LDL, or "bad" cholesterol.

Marie applied these lessons. She stopped using her heart rate monitor as a speedometer. She decided to shift her energy equation. For a month, she kept a food diary and found that she was snacking too much and on the wrong things. She added more fruit, subtracted some fat from her diet and spent more time in the lower zones, burning more calories and building endurance. Today, she's happy, her doctor is pleased with her lowered cholesterol and her self-image has changed from middle-aged couch potato to emerging athlete.

10. Can You Give Me a Sample Program to Lose Weight?

One of the keys to losing weight and keeping it off is the time factor. Short-term thinking doesn't work the way commitment to your plan and goals will. The goal of this 12-month program is to spend more time in the lower zones and gradually increase your frequency and intensity. Decide how many total workout minutes a week you want to do and divide those into the number of workouts per week (frequency) and the number of minutes in each zone (intensity). The following annualized chart below shows an example for you to preview a 12-month program using a heart rate monitor to manage your riding in the different heart zones.

Sample Cycle Training Program

Month		Zone 1	Zone 2	Zone 3	Zone 4	Zone 5	Total time riding and other training
1	WEEKLY TIME IN ZONE	60	60	0	0	0	120
2		100	100	20	0	0	220
3		100	150	50	0	0	300
4		100	140	100	0	0	340
5		100	160	160	10	0	430
6		100	175	200	20	0	495
7		100	190	210	30	0	530
8		100	200	250	30	0	580
9		100	200	260	40	0	600
10		100	200	300	40	0	640
11		100	200	350	50	0	700
12		100	200	400	60	0	760

TIP: BURN RATE ON THE BICYCLE

In the quest for the ideal heart zone in which to burn maximal amounts of fat? First, a basics review of fat burning facts:

1) Fat burns in every heart zone.

2) In every zone, a different ratio of fat to carbohydrates is burned.

3) The burn rate of the ride is key to weight loss.

4) Power output on the bike is proportional to the energy burn rate.

5) No additional fat is burned in riding intensities above the anaerobic threshold.

6) Oxygen and carbohydrates must be present for additional fat to burn.

When you start a ride, your muscles first start to contract and burn fuel. During this warm-up phase in the lower heart zones, the burn rate, as measured in calories per minute per power output, remains low. In the highest heart zones, you reach the highest burn rate, highest power output, highest total number of calories consumed and the highest absolute amount of fat and carbohydrates utilized.

The burn rate of caloric expenditure is what is key, yet currently impossible to measure without sophisticated equipment. The burn rate is the sum of burning two fuel sources: glycogen, or muscle carbohydrates, and fat. To maximize the amount of fat burned, you should ride at a heart rate intensity just below your anaerobic threshold. However, to maximize the burning of both carbohydrates and fat total calories burned, the higher the intensity, the more total calories burned.

The following graph represents a rider's ratio of nutrients used and quantity of total calories consumed when riding at a steady state power output.

Energy burn rate and nutrient proportion depend on five events:

1) Ratio of foods in your current diet

2) Time of your last meal

3) Workout intensity

4) Whether you eat during the ride

5) Your bicycle fitness level

Only a range of burn rates can be given because so many variables affect burn rate.

Burn Rates

Heart Zone	Name	Carbohydrates Burned (glycogen)	Fat Burned	Protein Burned
5	Redline Zone	85-90%	10-15%	1-5%
4	Threshold Zone	80-90%	10-20%	approximately 5%
3	Aerobic Zone	50-85%	40-60%	approximately 5%
2	Temperate Zone	25-50%	50-70%	approximately 5%
1	Healthy Heart Zone	10-25%	70-85%	approximately 5%

WORKOUTS

Indoor Training

Change of Heart
Fitness 50-70 percent

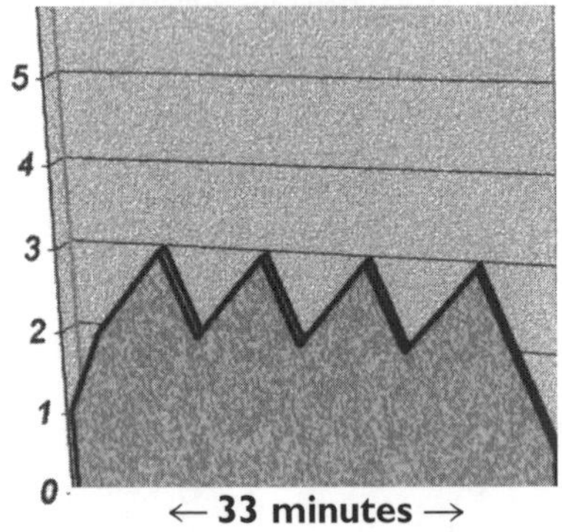

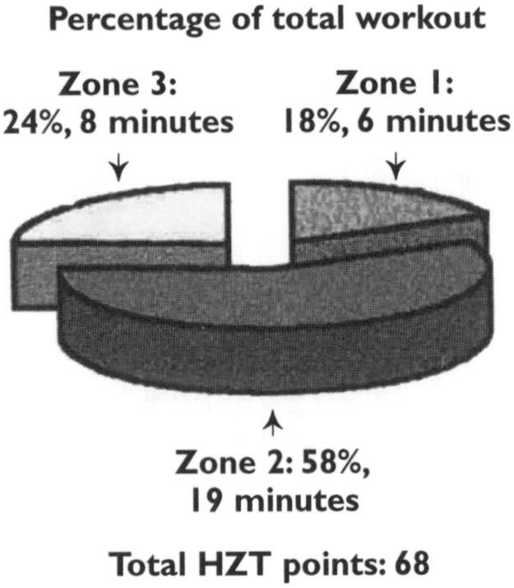

Percentage of total workout

Zone 3:
24%, 8 minutes

Zone 1:
18%, 6 minutes

← 33 minutes →

Zone 2: 58%,
19 minutes

Total HZT points: 68

This 33-minute workout is based on the concept that fat burning occurs up to the estimated anaerobic threshold, or what is sometimes called the "cross over point". This is the point at which, if you cross over, your body will not be burning any additional fat. The good news is the higher your anaerobic threshold number, the higher the "burn rate." This workout estimates your anaerobic threshold at about 70 percent of maximum heart rate, which is typical for a sedentary to moderately fit individual.

Purpose

The goal is to spend as much time at or just below your estimated anaerobic threshold in order to burn the most fat. By staying in these lower zones you'll also get the added benefits of lower blood pressure, lower resting heart rate, lower percentage of body fat, stabilized body weight and lower LDL ("bad") cholesterol. For fat to be freed from its fat cells, it needs low-intensity exercise for progressively longer and longer periods of time. Extend the length of time that you are riding. If you can extend your workout another 10 to 15 minutes you will be burning a third more total calories than before.

Workout Plan

Warm up in Zone 1 for 3 minutes. Increase cadence and heart rate to the bottom of Zone 2 over the next 2 minutes.

At 5 minutes into the workout you will begin a series of 2-minute intervals. From the bottom of Zone 2, add 10 beats and sustain for 2 minutes then increase your intensity (HR) to the bottom of Zone 3 and sustain for 2 minutes followed by a 2-minute easy pedal recovery back down to the bottom of Zone 2. Repeat this interval set 3 more times and then warm down to Zone 1.

Change of Heart

Elapsed Time in Minutes	Coaching notes	Zone	Your HR numbers	Duration
0–3	Warm up in Z1	1	_____	3 min.
3–5	Warm up to the bottom of Z2	2	_____	2 min.
5–27	Add 10 beats and sustain for 2 min., increase	2	_____	22 min.
	intensity (HR) to the bottom of Z3 and sus-	3	_____	
	tain for 2 min., easy pedal 2 min. (rec) to the	2	_____	
	bottom of Z2; repeat a total of 4 times. Your	2	_____	
	choice of cadence or resistance (R), standing	3	_____	
	or seated	2	_____	
		2	_____	
		3	_____	
27–30	Recover to the bottom of Z2	2	_____	3 min.
30–33	Warm down, easy pedal to Z1	1	_____	3 min.
	Total HZT Points 68			

30-20-10

Fitness 60-88 percent

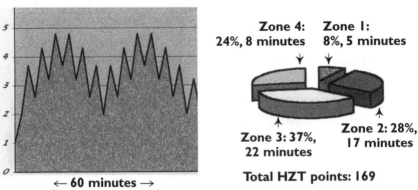

Percentage of total workout

Zone 4: 24%, 8 minutes
Zone 1: 8%, 5 minutes
Zone 3: 37%, 22 minutes
Zone 2: 28%, 17 minutes

Total HZT points: 169

← 60 minutes →

This 60-minute workout will give you a new view of exercise intensity with each interval and peak heart rate number (highest heart rate during a session). You will be climbing to the top of multiple heart rate summits, burning gobs of calories and increasing your muscular endurance.

Purpose

The 30-20-10 workout is designed to improve your ability to respond to stress and recovery. Like all interval training, it features going hard, recovering and going hard again. It is also a recovery heart rate test that allows you to measure your recovery fitness level by timing how quickly you recover. Try this workout once a month to measure your improvement – that is, to see if your recovery times get faster than the month before. If they do, your heart and sports-specific muscles are getting fitter.

Workout Plan

During this exercise session you will climb up a ladder of higher and higher heartbeats that increase in 30 bpm steps. The recovery between each step is "active," which means you back off the intensity and slow down the speed but continue to move. "Complete" recovery is when you stop motion and allow complete rest. During the workout you will increase exercise intensity by 30 bpm and then recover by decreasing heart rate 20 bpm before increasing and climbing another 30 bpm step.

Warm up to the bottom of Zone 2. Gradually increase your intensity or heart rate up 30 bpm until you reach your specific heart rate goal. When you reach the top immediately back off and allow yourself to recover for 20 beats using an "active" recovery. As soon as your heart

30-20-10

Elapsed Time in Minutes	Coaching notes	Zone	Your HR numbers	Duration
0–5	Warm up, easy pedal	1	_____	5 min.
5–8	Warm up, easy pedal, bottom Z2	2	_____	3 min.
8–20	Add 30 bpm, choice, sustain for 2 min.	3	_____	12 min.
	2 min. (rec) drop 20 beats, note (rec) time.	2	_____	
	Repeat a total of 3 times	4	_____	
		3	_____	
		4	_____	
		3	_____	
20–30	Add 20 bpm, choice, sustain for 2 min.	4	_____	10 min.
	2 min. (rec) drop 30 beats, note (rec) time.	3	_____	
	Repeat a total of 3 times	4	_____	
		2	_____	
		3	_____	
30–32	Easy pedal to the bottom of Z2 and sustain for 2 min.	2	_____	2 min.
32–44	Repeat 2 min. 30 bpm work interval and timed 20 beat 2 min. (rec). Repeat a total of 3 times	3	_____	12 min.
		2	_____	
		4	_____	
		3	_____	
		4	_____	
		3	_____	
44–58	Repeat 2 min. 20 bpm work interval and timed 30 beat 2 min. (rec). Repeat a total of 4 times	4	_____	14 min.
		3	_____	
		4	_____	
		2	_____	
		3	_____	
		2	_____	
		2	_____	
58–60	Warm down to the bottom of Z2		_____	2 min.
	Total HZT Points 169			

rate drops 20 beats note the amount of time and hold that heart rate number until the next work interval begins.

Attack again with a 30-bpm increase and then a 20-beat "timed" recovery.

At 20 minutes you will switch and do a 20-bpm work interval and a 30-beat recovery until minute 30, when the intervals switch again to a 30-bpm increase and 20-beat recovery.

At 44 minutes the work interval changes again to a 20-bpm increase and 30-beat recovery until the end of the workout and you warm down.

Afterburner

Fitness 60-85 percent

Percentage of total workout

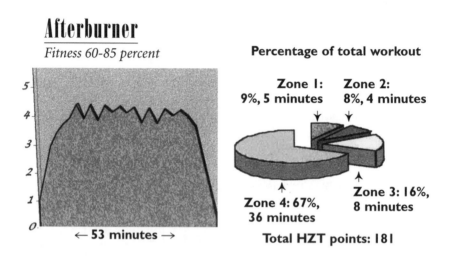

← 53 minutes →

Zone 1: 9%, 5 minutes

Zone 2: 8%, 4 minutes

Zone 3: 16%, 8 minutes

Zone 4: 67%, 36 minutes

Total HZT points: 181

This 53-minute workout is not only a fat burner but also a calorie burner. The workout is based on the premise that fat burning occurs up to the estimated anaerobic threshold (in this case, 85 percent, or the middle of Zone 4) or what is called the "cross over point." At this point, you don't burn any additional fat calories, but rather more calories from carbohydrate.

Purpose

The goal is to spend as much time as possible at or just below your anaerobic threshold. Our goal is to stay just below or at this cross over point in order to burn the most fat. If we cross over, the body's choice of additional fuel turns to pure carbohydrate as the muscles become anaerobic. You may change this workout to fit whatever you think your anaerobic threshold (AT) heart rate number is. Remember that your AT is a moving target; it changes with your fitness level. The fitter you become the higher it will become.

Workout Plan

Warm up in Zone 1 for 3 minutes. Increase cadence and heart rate to the bottom of Zone 2 for 2 minutes, then to the bottom of Zone 3 for 2 minutes.

Add 10 bpm for the next 2 minutes then 5 bpm for 2 minutes.

At 11 minutes into the workout, increase heart rate to the bottom of Zone 4 and sustain for 2 minutes. For the next 10 minutes you will be increasing your heart rate to the middle of Zone 4 for 2 minutes and dropping to the bottom of Zone 4 for 2 minutes. It is your choice of how you want to increase heart rate; seated, standing, cadence, resistance or a combination.

At minute 23 you will drop your heart rate only 5 beats from the middle of Zone 4 and sustain for 2 minutes, then increase again to the middle of Zone 4 for 2 minutes. Repeat this interval one more time.

At 31 minutes into the workout you will drop your heart rate to the bottom of Zone 4 for 2 minutes then increase it to the middle of Zone 4 for 2 minutes. Repeat this interval one more time.

At 39 minutes drop your heart rate 5 bpm for 2 minutes then increase 5 bpm for 2 minutes. Repeat this interval one more time.

At minute 45 drop your heart rate to the bottom of Zone 4 for 2 minutes then easy pedal recovery to the bottom of Zone 3 for 2 minutes, Zone 2 for 2 minutes and finally Zone 1 for 2 minutes.

Afterburner

Elapsed Time in Minutes	Coaching notes	Zone	Your HR numbers	Duration
0–3	Warm up in Z1	1	_____	3 min.
3–7	Increase HR to bottom of Z2 for 2 min. then	2	_____	2 min.
	bottom of Z3 for 2 min., choice	3	_____	2 min.
7–9	Add 10 bpm (R)	3	_____	2 min.
9–11	Add 5 bpm (R)	3	_____	2 min.
11–23	Increase HR to the bottom of Z4 for 2 min,	4	_____	12 min.
	increase HR to mid-point of Z4 for 2 min.,	4	_____	
	choice. Repeat a total of 3 times	4	_____	
		4	_____	
		4	_____	
		4	_____	
23–31	Drop HR 5 bpm from the mid-point of Z4 for	4	_____	8 min.
	2 min. then increase HR 5 bpm for 2 min.	4	_____	
	Repeat	4	_____	
		4	_____	
31–39	Drop HR to the bottom of Z4 for 2 min.,	4	_____	8 min.
	increase HR to the mid-point of Z4 for 2 min	4	_____	
	(R). Repeat	4	_____	
		4	_____	
39–45	Drop 5 bpm from the mid-point of Z4 for 2	4	_____	6 min.
	min. then increase HR 5 bpm for 2 min.	4	_____	
	Repeat	4	_____	
45–53	Drop HR to the bottom of Z4 for 2 min., easy	4	_____	8 min.
	pedal (rec) to the bottom of Z3 for 2 min.,	3	_____	
	then bottom of Z2 for 2 min. and Z1 for 2	2	_____	
	min.	1	_____	
	Total HZT Points 181			

Outdoor Training

Noodling

Here's your chance to stay in the saddle a little longer, work on some technique and stay under 65 percent of your maximum heart rate. This is easy riding and can also be used as a recovery ride to give your body a chance to rest.

Pick a distance depending on your fitness level, ranging from 5 miles to 50 miles, or ride for a certain amount of time, from 30 minutes to 3 hours. The goal is to keep your heart rate under 65 percent for most of the time. Try to pick a ride that is relatively flat. If you have hills use an easy gear and small chainring to spin your way to the top while staying seated. This is a "feel good" ride designed to keep you spinning along and smelling the roses. Simply work on body position, pedal stroke and tempo. Your legs should feel relaxed as noodles. Don't forget to relax your upper body too. Ride like a noodle, relaxing every muscle in your body and let your mind go. Do whatever you have to do to stay below 65 percent. Easier said than done!

5x5

This ride is very similar to the indoor ride in Chapter 2 called 5 x 2. The purpose is to teach your cycling-specific muscles and cardiovascular system to adapt to a changing workload every 5 minutes. It will be entirely your choice on how you want to increase your heart rate. Pick a course that is flat to moderately rolling hills with no traffic or stop signs. This ride will take approximately 60 to 70 minutes depending on warm-up and warm-down time.

Warm up adequately to your maximum heart rate minus 50 beats. If your maximum heart rate is 180 bpm that would be 130 bpm. Increase your heart rate 5 bpm every 5 minutes until you reach the highest heart rate you think you can sustain for 5 minutes. Your heart rate number may be anywhere from 75 to more than 90 percent of your maximum heart rate. You decide the highest percentage that you want to ride to and sustain for 5 minutes then decrease your heart rate 5 bpm every 5 minutes until you reach your original starting heart rate number (in this case, 130 bpm).

Finish the ride by warming down gradually.

Aerobic Time Trial

You will want to pick a flat 5-mile section of road with no stop signs or dogs. After an adequate warm up ride five miles at 75 percent of your maximum heart rate or the mid-point of Zone 3. Use the same gear, no shifting for the entire time trial. Record your time. The conditions need to be the same from one time trial test to the next. This includes the amount of rest since your last high intensity workout, the length and intensity of your warm up, the weather and road conditions and the gear you used in the previous test. As you become fitter, your time should decrease. This is a good test to do on the endurance spoke of the training wheel and retest as you progress to the other training spokes.

REFERENCES

Baker, Arnie, MD. *Smart Cycling,* New York, Fireside Book, 1997.

Blair, Steven, Ph.D., Jacobs, David R., Ph.D., Powell, Kenneth, MD, MPH. *Relationships Between Exercise or Physical Activity and Other Health Behaviors.* Public Health Reports, Journal of the U.S. Public Health Service, 100:2, 1985.

Brownell, K.D. *Obesity: Understanding and Treating in Serious, Prevalent, and Refractory Disorder.* Journal of Consult Clinical Psychology, 50:820–840, 1982.

Burke and Berning. *Training Nutrition,* Carmel, IN. Cooper 1996.

Butterfield, Gail and Gates, Joan, Hershey Foods Corporation. *Topic on Nutrition and Food Safety.* Fueling Activity, 1994.

Epstein, L.H., and Wing, R.R. *Aerobic Exercise and Weight.* Addict Behavior 5:371–388 (1980).

U.S. Department of Health and Human Services, *The Surgeon General's Report on Nutrition and Health,* Publication number 88:50211, Washington, D.C., 1994.

CHAPTER 6

High Performance Heart Cycling

John Saylor played college rugby. After serving in the U.S. Army in Vietnam, he knew he wanted to stay in shape. He continued running sans combat boots and for 20 years found it a meaningful way to stay fit. Realizing his joints were deteriorating, he looked for an alternative form of exercise and stumbled into an indoor cycling class in Seattle. He didn't have a heart rate monitor, so Sally loaned him one and that was all it took; he was hooked.

John's first experience was overwhelming. After almost 20 years of RPE training, he finally had a tool to guide his workout. He worked out, observing his heart rate numbers, comparing them with how he felt. He had very high heart rate numbers training on his studio bike, which made him think his heart might burst out of his chest. It didn't, of course.

What he was observing was the preservation of his maximum heart rate number. John had maintained a high maximum heart rate all these years by maintaining his fitness. As we learned from Paul Camerer's experience (see Chapter 4), maximum heart rate won't decline with age if you stay fit.

John's first heart cycling ride convinced him to buy a low-end monitor, only to regret it later as he learned more about training and wanted more features. He decided to learn everything he could about the application of heart zone technology to his training. He attended seminars, read books, asked questions and most of all, used himself as a fitness laboratory.

As he worked out using the Heart Cycling system, John found he was no longer exercising but training. After determining his maximum heart rate in class, his next step was to set his heart zones, which was easy. Then he set a training goal. He'd always wanted to complete the Seattle-to-Portland bike ride, fondly known as the STP, which covers 200 miles in two days. He set out by writing down his goal and promising himself a better heart rate monitor if he met his goal to finish the ride in two days.

John's goal was to extend the running life of his knees by cross-training using indoor cycling as his method. He went on to set and accomplish his outdoor cycling goal, using his monitor to keep him in his most effective heart zone. When he crossed the STP finish line, he felt elated. It took him 15 hours, all in heart zone 3 and below.

Then he went back to the goal-setting process. This time, the dream was to finish a triathlon, train with his monitor, follow the 10 Steps of Heart Cycling and most of all, to place in his age group. John had transformed himself from an exerciser to a trainer, from a fitness enthusiast to a cyclist.

—*Sally Edwards*

BEGINNING A TRAINING PLAN

In the preceding chapters, you've been completing the steps, building progressively on each to reach the next. You've learned to set your maximum heart rate, create your heart zones, write a goal, determine how fit you are and put that into the training wheel. You're now ready to write a training program that best fits you.

Let's go through a few basic ideas about the training plan. First, as with your 30-day training program, this is a plan you write. It's based on accepting that you are your own fitness laboratory and again recognizing your unique physiological responses to the training experience.

The personal trainer or coach's role should be to guide and motivate you, teach you how to design a program and help you psychologically more than physiologically. But you can do this yourself. Letting go of this personal power in any part of your life, including your fitness, just doesn't work.

Designing your own personal training program will teach you a new skill that will improve with practice, like riding a bike. Perhaps you started with training wheels and a beginner bike. You are now reading a book on how to train more effectively and efficiently. Congratulations! You have come a long way. What you will experience when you first write a training program is powerful. Write your training plan in pencil and be ready to make lots of changes and be flexible. Learn. Grow. Change.

Creating your riding program can also be a lot of fun! Looking back as you reach your milestones to become ever fitter, you'll find many layers of small successes. You also can apply the process to almost every other aspect of your day. The same planning process can help with your finances, personal life and job. Do this and watch yourself become more confident, self-empowered and fit.

STEP 7. WRITING YOUR TRAINING PLAN

First decide the amount of time needed to reach your riding goal. A weekly training plan is a week's time divided into individual days, with indoor workouts and outdoor rides. Establish the plan for a workable period of time, depending on your goal deadline and training wheel spokes involved.

Heart Cycling Training Plan

Beginning and Ending Week:_____Number of Weeks:_____

Quick Goal:_____Training Tree Limb:_____

Date	Day	Sports activities	Type of rides or workouts (interval or steady state)	Total min.	TIZ	TIZ	TIZ	TIZ	TIZ	HZ points
/ /	Monday									
/ /	Tuesday									
/ /	Wed.									
/ /	Thursday									
/ /	Friday									
/ /	Saturday									
/ /	Sunday									
Summary	Number of workouts:		Total minutes:							
			Total % by zone:		%	%	%	%	%	

You can photocopy the *Heart Cycling Training Plan* and put two to a page in a binder.

Understanding the Plan

If you're like most riders, you'd like to train less and get more out of every workout. That is what a training plan provides by taking the guesswork out of which workout to do and why. The plan is built around a system of training that integrates principles you've learned about how to be your own best trainer, yielding a shorter training time with more benefit. Better still, it's something you can easily accomplish.

Filling Out the Training Plan

The best way to fill out your heart cycling plan is to follow these steps in sequence:

1. Write in today's date.
2. If you anticipate a "rest" or recovery day, note it under "Sports activities."
3. Enter under "Workouts" activities that are already part of your training program, such as a group ride or indoor cycling class.
4. Note other classes or workouts such as stretching or weight training on their corresponding day.
5. Fill in the rest of the workouts under the "Sports activity" section.
6. Under "Workout type," enter the kind of workout in code:

    I = Intervals   S = short, M = medium, L = long
    SS = Steady state   B = Bottom of the zone , T = Top of the zone,
    Mid = Midpoint   Multiples = Multiple zones   A = Average heart rate

    You can use codes such as I/S, which would mean that the plan for the workout is short intervals; I/M, medium length intervals; SS/T if you are going to hold the heart rate steady at the ceiling or top of the zone; or Multiple/SS/T for multiple zones, steady state, top of the zone. Make up other codes that work for you.
7. Fill in the "Total minutes" section next. How many minutes do you have to train that day? If you can include what time of day you're training, you'll find it saves even more time.
8. Assign those minutes to zones. You should do most of your warmup and cool-down in Zone 1 or Zone 2, representing about 10 percent of your total riding time for each. For example, you might want to do all Zone 3 training in a 30-minute workout. In that case, plan for 6 minutes in Zone 2 for warm up and cool down and 24 minutes in Zone 3 for the main set of the workout.
9. Calculate the weight or value of the workout by multiplying zone number times minutes. This total is the number of Heart Zone Training Points earned for that day. One HZT point is equal to one minute in Zone 1. If you were to spend 20 minutes in Zone 4, you would record 80 HZT points.
10. Complete the summary section along the bottom of the Heart Cycling Plan to determine whether your planned training week matches your goals.

STEP 8: ANALYZING YOUR PLAN

After writing your first Heart Cycling training plan, think for a few minutes. Look at the workouts. Listen to your heart. Will this work? Do I have the time? Am I committed to accomplishing the goal? Do I believe in it?

If you notice your training plan causing you some discomfort, fix it now. People tend to write the ideal plan and then only accomplish half of it because they didn't build in a fudge factor. Interruptions and changes occur that you need to anticipate. There must be room for spontaneous events and changes in others' schedules that affect yours to reflect our imperfect world.

ADVANCED TRAINING MECHANISMS

Now that you have a basic plan, consider adding a few advanced training mechanisms. A training mechanism is the application of a training principle. The three advanced training mechanisms referred to as the Training Triad can take your training to a new level. As illustrated below, the triad is the application of threshold training, overload-adaptation training and specificity cross-training:

Threshold training

Overload-adaptation training   Specificity cross-training

THE TRAINING TRIAD

Threshold training is a powerful tool to add to your training toolbox. It relates to getting fitter by training at the heart rate point dividing aerobic and anaerobic metabolism. Muscles contract and use energy in two ways: aerobic metabolism and anaerobic metabolism.

Aerobic is derived from a Greek word that means "with oxygen." When you train aerobically, you are at a low enough intensity to provide plenty of oxygen through your respiratory delivery system to allow the muscles to contract without accumulating an oxygen debt. However, when you exercise too hard, you get shortness of breath. This inability to breathe in enough air is an indicator that you've crossed the threshold into anaerobic training.

The human muscle system is so well designed that when the muscles lack enough oxygen to meet their demands, they can continue to contract but use a different energy pathway called anaerobic metabolism. ("An" in Greek means "without.") Anaerobic metabolism thus functions "without enough oxygen."

You've discovered from your own training experience that you can't sustain an intensity level above your anaerobic threshold. It's a perfectly fine place to train for a short time, but then you have to take the intensity down, lower your training heart rate so you return to the lower three aerobic zones to recover. This type of anaerobic effort mixed with recovery is another way to describe interval training. Threshold training is one of the best mechanisms to use because it helps you get fitter fastest.

Overload-Adaptation Training

If you overload a muscle group or system, it responds first by getting tired or fatigued. When allowed to rest and recover, the muscle responds by adapting, or getting stronger. The overload-adaptation mechanism works only if you allow adequate recovery time following stress. A positive stress-recovery cycle will cause muscles to adapt positively by improving their work capacity, meaning you're fitter.

Negative adaptation due to inadequate recovery means the muscle or system responds by getting deconditioned, one of the results of overtraining. Overtraining is too much training load without enough recovery time. The following chart will help you understand the difference between over-reaching and its positive fitness improvements and overtraining with its negative deconditioning response:

Positive Training Effect
(over-reaching*)

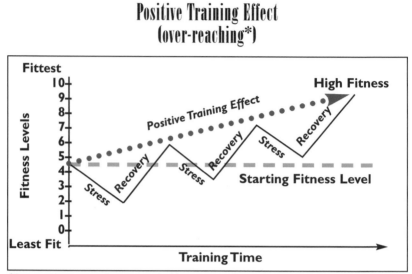

Over-reaching: a type of training marked by temporary fatigue from high training load which results in positive training effect.

Negative Training Effect
(over-training**)

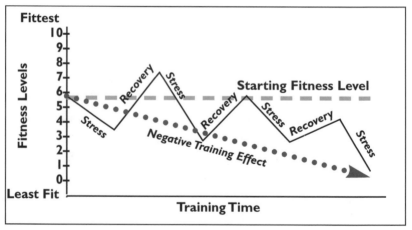

**Over-training: training in excess of what is healthy leading to a higher risk of injury, illness or staleness.*

Optimal Performance vs. Overtraining

Symptoms of overtraining vary and can only be broadly described. They appear to be associated with depressed immune function so that you are at risk for infection and sheer fatigue. They are most commonly associated with high ambient, delta, and resting heart rates plus slow recovery heart rates. These heart rate indicators are some of the best gauges to predict the overtraining syndrome. Other terms for overtraining are chronic fatigue syndrome, exercise-induced immune system dysfunction and overwork. A shorter group of descriptors uses the word "out": burned-out, stressed-out and trained-out.

To prevent overtraining, you must allow for adequate recovery, vary the training program and do multiple zone training workouts.

Over-reaching is an excellent training mechanism for high performance and improved conditioning. This progressive overload-adaptation cycle is planned to combine high training load or high Heart Zone Training Points with recovery workouts and rest.

Specificity Cross-Training

After finishing second in the 1981 Ironman in Hawaii, Sally Edwards coined the term cross-training in the first book written about triathlon training, aptly titled *Triathlon: A Triple Fitness Sport.* Her thesis—that you must cross-train in order to become your fittest—was criticized strongly at the time. Today most exercise scientists and coaches agree with her.

In contrast, specificity training is working in only the specific activity or event in which you plan to perform. The more specific the training program is to a given sport or activity, the greater the improvement in performance. Yet in the world outside the exercise laboratory, people cross-train to successfully improve their single-sport performance.

Since writing the book, Edwards has devised a new training mechanism synthesizing two concepts once considered antithetical. If you want to train for performance, as Jon Ackland writes in his book *The Power to Perform* (Reed Books, 1994), you must always include specificity cross-training.

Good examples of specificity cross-training come from swim training. Swimmers improve in their single events by learning the different swim strokes, not just the one stroke they use to race. Specificity cross-training works for cyclists who indoor cycle, then train for their racing season outside. It works for football players who study dancing to gain the agility they use on the field.

At-About-Around Your Anaerobic Threshold (AT)

The training mechanism called "At-About-Around AT" means:

At: at your specific anaerobic threshold heart rate number

About: train at or about that threshold heart rate number

Around: training at, about, and around that threshold heart rate number

This book offers several workouts and tests to determine your current anaerobic threshold heart rate. As you grow fitter, your training heart rates drop because you can do more exercise at a lower heart rate. Your anaerobic threshold heart rates go up, however, as more exercise stress is required to reach your anaerobic threshold. This is the very definition of fitness: to move your anaerobic threshold as close as you can to your maximum heart rate.

Two non-laboratory and basic workouts serve as field tests to give you an approximate anaerobic threshold heart rate number. To measure it precisely, invest in an exercise stress test that will determine your anaerobic threshold heart rate more precisely by collecting your expired air (measuring your oxygen capacity) or by collecting samples of your blood to measure the lactic acid concentrations.

Once you know your anaerobic threshold heart rate, training at-about-or-around it becomes a valuable addition to your weekly training plan.

CONCLUSION

For many of us, the hardest part of doing anything is simply getting started. John Saylor was lucky because he was committed to a base fitness level and had continued to run and stay relatively fit. Some of us have to start a little lower on the training spoke, but no matter where we start, the key is to start, write down some goals and dream a little about your goals.

Hundreds of books discuss how to write, set and keep goals. Technology and high-speed communication subjects us to reams of information on any subject we desire, and sometimes it's hard to sort out what's best for us. We believe that what keeps us on track and training on days we'd rather be elsewhere are goals—differentiating training from exercise, drawing us like magnets closer to our aspirations.

John's smart! He chose cycling to save his joints and learned how to train with a heart rate monitor. When he began his indoor cycling class to escape the wet Seattle weather, he was aware of the indoor cycling craze and figured the class would be a great way to meet new people and work on his cycling skills while waiting out the rain.

What John didn't realize was that indoor training complements outdoor cycling in a variety of ways. Most of his workouts were 50 minutes of interval training in multiple zones, emphasizing good cycling technique to get stronger, faster and fitter. John got a lot more than he expected: increased fitness in all zones; improved cycling technique; muscles and energy systems to support him across the finish line; a huge jump-start for the outdoor season and new cycling friends. Last but not least, he met his new best friend and coach, his heart rate monitor.

John reached his goal, taking his friends with him. He wound up bringing all his indoor friends with him on the Seattle-to-Portland bike ride, the STP, even though the last time some of them had ridden a real bike was when they were kids or covered a paper route. You can imagine how much fun they had.

That's what's powerful about training smart for high performance. You become committed and your passion inspires another who in turn motivates someone else on down the line.

WORKOUTS
Indoor Training

At, About, Around

Fitness 60-90 percent

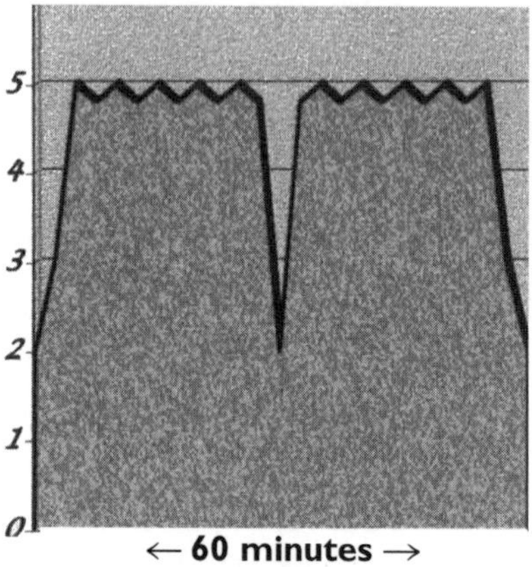

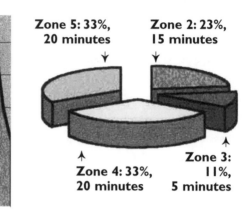

Percentage of total workout

Zone 5: 33%, 20 minutes
Zone 2: 23%, 15 minutes
Zone 4: 33%, 20 minutes
Zone 3: 11%, 5 minutes

← 60 minutes →

Total HZT points: 227

It is difficult to sustain your anaerobic threshold heart rate for longer than about 20 to 60 minutes in any single activity. (Remember anaerobic threshold heart rate [AT HR] is sport-specific). The closer you can race at or above your AT HR, the higher your achievable maximum sustainable HR (MS HR) and the higher your MS HR, the faster you can race.

Purpose

You can apply this 60-minute workout to almost any activity. It is not for the beginner. It is based on the principle that the AT HR number is an individual heart rate buried in the center of a very, very narrow heart rate window or zone. For this workout, the zone is five beats, with a top number or ceiling of your AT HR number and the bottom or floor of the workout zone five beats lower.

Workout Plan

This workout is 2 times 20 minutes. Warm up to the bottom of Zone 2 in the first five minutes then to the bottom of Zone 3 in the next 5 minutes. Use an easy spin, working on pedal stroke and cadence.

At 10 minutes into the workout, increase your heart rate to your estimated anaerobic threshold and sustain it for 2 minutes. The next two minutes you will drop your heart rate 5 bpm and sustain it for 2 minutes, then increase 5 bpm for 2 minutes. This interval is repeated for 20 minutes followed by a 6-minute recovery to the bottom of Zone 2.

The 20-minute interval is then repeated again by increasing heart rate to anaerobic threshold for 2 minutes, dropping 5 bpm for 2 minutes then a 2-minute increase in heart rate. Finish by warming down gradually to the bottom of Zone 2.

At, About, Around

Elapsed Time in Minutes	Coaching notes	Zone	Your HR numbers	Duration
0–5	Warm up to the bottom of Z2	2	_____	5 min.
5–10	Warm up to the bottom of Z3	3	_____	5 min.
10–30	Increase HR to estimated AT and sustain for 2 min., drop 5 bpm for 2 min. and continue to repeat for 20 min. period		_____	20 min.
30–36	Drop 30 bpm, easy spin		_____	6 min.
36–56	Increase HR to estimated AT and sustain for 2 min., drop 5 bpm for 2 min. and continue to repeat for 20 min. period		_____	20 min.
56–60	Gradually warm down to the bottom of Z2		_____	4 min.
	Total HZT Points 227 if AT is in Z4			

Winner's Circle

Fitness 60-90 percent

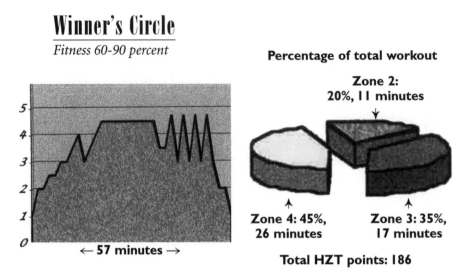

Percentage of total workout

**Zone 2:
20%, 11 minutes**

**Zone 4: 45%,
26 minutes**

**Zone 3: 35%,
17 minutes**

← 57 minutes →

Total HZT points: 186

This is a perfect 57-minute workout for those wanting to improve their pedal stroke, hence "Winner's Circle" emphasizing pedaling in circles. This is a great workout to build strength and muscular endurance for those long hill rides. You will also be identifying a heart rate number that you can sustain for an extended period of time. This should be close to, but just below, your anaerobic threshold. The goal is to pick a high heart rate number but not so high that you can't sustain it for the five-interval set. Anaerobic threshold is a moving number depending on your fitness level. As you get fitter, your anaerobic threshold number or heart rate should get higher. Typically this means you can go faster for longer

Purpose

There are four goals starting with isolated leg training. Isolated leg training (ILT) will help smooth out your pedal stroke and train your lifting muscles (hip flexors, hamstrings and glutes) to last longer. Pedal smooth and easy, concentrating on constant pedal pressure for 360 degrees of the stroke. It helps to think of scraping mud off the bottom of your shoes through the bottom of the stroke.

The second goal is gradually adding more revolutions to your stroke, keeping your spin smooth and relaxed and your upper body quiet and steady.

The third goal is to build leg strength and power by keeping the resistence heavy and increasing cadence. Reduce resistence if your knees hurt.

The fourth goal is training the aerobic system just below your anaerobic threshold, or "cross over" point. When picking this number, think of the highest number you can sustain, then ride just under that number. This will give you a heart rate number for measuring future workouts against. As you get fitter this heart rate number should go up, meaning you can ride at a higher intensity for a longer period of time. It also means your heart and lungs are getting stronger.

Workout Plan

Start with a 5-minute warm-up to the bottom of Zone 2.

Next, pedal at a cadence of between 50 rpm (5) and 60 rpm (6) training one leg at a time. Put your non-pedaling leg on a stool, box or just rest it in the pedal or off to the side. The key is to use only one leg at a time to build strength and smoothness. Do one minute on each side twice, then finish with both legs.

The next 7 minutes works on the pedal stroke by increasing the rpm every minute until a cadence of 120 is reached. Keep the pedal stroke round and the upper torso steady and quiet. A 1-minute recovery follows to the bottom of Zone 3.

Coming up is a 12-minute strength set working your way into Zone 4 and staying there. The rpm stays at 60 (6) for the first 45 seconds of each minute and increases to 80 (8) for the last 15 seconds. This interval is repeated 11 times with a two-minute easy pedal recovery back down to the bottom of Zone 3.

The last set is training "just below" your anaerobic threshold. Pick a number "just below" a heart rate you think can be held for a series of timed intervals. Start at 1 minute and continue up to 5 minutes with 1-minute recoveries in between. The goal is to hold this "just below" number on each interval. If you find this easy then either you haven't set the number high enough or you may have set the heart rate number too high.

Make sure you are fully rested when doing this workout and give yourself plenty of rest after.

Winner's Circle

Elapsed Time in Minutes	Coaching notes	Zone	Your HR numbers	Duration
0—5	Warm up to the bottom of Z2	2	_____	5 min.
5—10	Isolated leg training (ILT), right 1 min, left 1 min. x (2), finish with both legs 1 min. 80 rpm (8)	3	_____	5 min.
10—17	60 rpm (6) for 1 min., working on pedal stroke, 70 rpm (7) for 1 min., 80 rpm (8) for 1 min., increasing 10 rpm each min. to 120 rpm (12)	2 3 4	_____ _____	7 min.
17—18	(Rec) to the bottom of Z3	3	_____	1 min.
18—30	(R) hard effort, 60 rpm (6) for 45 sec., last 15 sec. increase to 80 rpm (8), x (12) top of Z3 for the first min. then Z4 for remaining 11 min.	3 4	_____	12 min.
30—32	Easy pedal (rec) to the bottom of Z3	3	_____	2 min.
32—33	*Just below Anaerobic threshold (AT) with (R), 80rpm (8), seated		_____	*1 min.
33—34	Easy pedal to the mid-point of Z3 (75%)	3	_____	1 min.
34—36	*Just below (AT), (R), 80 rpm, seated		_____	*2 min.
36—37	Easy pedal to the mid-point of Z3 (75%)	3	_____	1 min.
37—40	*Just below (AT), (R), 80 rpm, seated		_____	*3 min.
40—41	Easy pedal to the mid-point of Z3 (75%)	3	_____	1 min.
41—45	*Just below (AT), (R), 80 rpm, seated/standing		_____	*4 min.
45—46	Easy pedal to the mid-point of Z3 (75%)	3	_____	1 min.
46—51	*Just below (AT), (R), 80 rpm, seated/standing		_____	*5 min.
51—53	Warm down to bottom of Z3	3	_____	2 min.
53—57	Bottom of Z2 *1, 2, 3, 4, 5 min. ladder	2	_____	4 min.
	Total HZT Points 179			

Red Shift
Fitness 50-95 percent

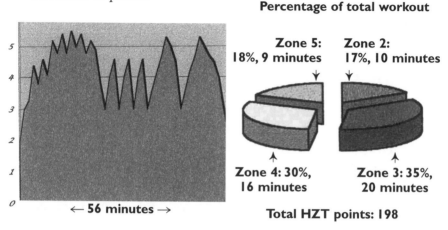

Percentage of total workout

Zone 5: 18%, 9 minutes	Zone 2: 17%, 10 minutes

Zone 4: 30%, 16 minutes	Zone 3: 35%, 20 minutes

← 56 minutes →

Total HZT points: 198

A quick look at the chart above tells you this 55-minute workout is intense. Think of it as a series of four hills: the first hill is a 12-minute "pyramid climb" taking you up into the "ozone" layer of Zone 5; the second set of hills is a series of three, one-minute sprints ranging from easy to heavy resistance or easy to hard gearing with brief recoveries; and the last two hills are the finale, using moderate to heavy resistance, fast hammers (spins) and changing body positions to simulate climbing. About half of this workout is above 80 percent of your maximum heart rate so make sure you get plenty of rest, recovery and water afterwards.

Purpose

Pyramid climbs are great for improving your muscular endurance and power. Each work interval as you go up the ladder should be as fast a sprint as you can sustain for the period of time required. This will stress your muscles with speed and strength work while improving your lactate clearance systems on the recoveries. Over 90 percent of the 12-minute pyramid climb will be spent in Zone 4 and Zone 5 building your anaerobic power and capacity and raising your anaerobic threshold. The following series of hills re-emphasizes the strength work and helps your nervous system adapt to patterns you often experience on the road or during competition.

Workout Plan

Begin with a 10-minute warm up, gradually increasing your heart rate to the bottom of Zone 3.

Beginning at 10 minutes into the workout is a series of sprint/recovery intervals, called Hill No. 1. The first 30-second sprint should take you close or into Zone 4, then do a 30-second easy pedal recovery. The next sprint is 60 seconds followed by a 30-second recovery, then a 90-second sprint followed by a 30-second recovery and so on up the pyramid, increasing the work interval by 30 seconds each time and leaving the recoveries at 30 seconds. A 2-minute sprint is the top of the pyramid with a 30-second recovery, then back down to a 90-second sprint and so on back down decreasing the sprints by 30 seconds each time. A three-minute recovery to the bottom of Zone 3 precedes the next hill set.

Hill No. 2 consists of three identical intervals. Twenty-five minutes into the workout you begin a 30-second sprint of easy to moderate resistance at the bottom of Zone 4, remaining in a seated position. The next 30 seconds is standing with moderate to heavy resistance to the mid-point of Zone 4 (85 percent of max HR) followed by a 2-minute recovery to the bottom of Zone 3. Repeat this interval two more times.

After a 2-minute recovery to the bottom of Zone 3, Hill No. 3 begins by increasing your heart rate 10 bpm in 1 minute. This should put you about in the middle of Zone 3 (75 percent). Between 36 and 39 minutes into the workout you will be increasing your heart rate 10 bpm every minute. At 39 minutes you should be well into Zone 5 or at least holding the bottom of Zone 5 (90 percent) for another minute. At 40 minutes you get a well-earned two-minute recovery to the bottom of Zone 3.

Repeat the above interval for Hill No. 4, finishing at the bottom of Zone 5 (49 minutes).

The warm-down begins with a controlled recovery to the bottom of Zone 4 for two minutes, then Zone 3 and finishing at the bottom of Zone 2. Make sure you spend at least 10 to 15 minutes stretching after you get off the bike and drink a bottle of water!

Red Shift

Elapsed Time in Minutes	Coaching notes	Zone	Your HR numbers	Duration
0–5	Warm up to bottom of Z2	2	_____	5 min.
5–10	Increase HR to top of Z3	3	_____	5 min.
10–22	Hill #1 Pyramid Climb	4	_____	12 min.
	30 sec. sprint / 30 sec. (rec) (30/30),	4	_____	
	60/30, 90/30, 120/30, 90/30, 60/30, 30/30	5	_____	
		5	_____	
22–25	(Rec) bottom of Z3	3	_____	3 min.
25–34	Hill #2 30 sec. sprint, moderate (R) Z4, fol-	4	_____	9 min.
	lowed by 30 sec. sprint, heavy (R) mid-point	3	_____	
	of Z4 (85%), 2 min. (rec) bottom of Z3,			
	Repeat a total of 3 times.			
34–42	Hill #3 add 10 bpm to the bottom of Z3, 2	3	_____	8 min.
	min. From mid-point of Z3 add 10 bpm, mod-	4	_____	
	erate (R) 1min.	4	_____	
	Add 10 bpm, fast spin, 1 min.	5	_____	
	Add 10 bpm, heavy (R), 1 min.	5	_____	
	sustain 90%, standing, 1 min.	3	_____	
	2-min. (rec) bottom of Z3			
42–50	Hill #4, repeat Hill #3		_____	8 min.
50–55	5-minute warm down, bottom of Z2	2	_____	5 min.
	Total HZT Points 210			

Outdoor Training

The Anaerobic Threshold Ride

First, let's get a clear idea of what anaerobic threshold really means. There is lots of confusion about the concept of anaerobic training. Basically, during any training you are riding at an intensity level that requires your body to utilize fuels—a combination of carbohydrates, fats and proteins. For most, when you are in the aerobic intensity levels (Zones 1, 2 and 3) as measured with your heart rate monitor, you have sufficient oxygen and are producing lactic acid but not in enough quantity to limit your exercise time. There is a heart rate point that can be measured when you shift your fuels and the metabolic process from aerobic to anaerobic. This is called the "cross over point," where there is insufficient oxygen to sustain the exercise intensity and there is too much lactic acid production, so it builds up in the working muscles and causes the muscle to fatigue. The rate of lactate accumulation will depend on how high above this threshold the intensity is and how effective the body is at clearing blood lactate.

To measure blood lactate accurately, you need access to a gas exchange analyzer or a lactate analyzer. Given that those aren't readily available, there is a way to estimate your anaerobic threshold heart rate, which we affectionately call the 2x20 ride. This ride can also be done indoors as the 2x20 Anaerobic test in chapter 4. This is a strenuous ride and not for the faint of heart.

A FOUR-POINT GUIDE TO IMPROVING YOUR RACING

Point 1. Heart rate lower during the race

- Started out too fast at the beginning of the event
- Overtrained
- Poor tapering
- Insufficient off-season recovery
- Too high a maximum sustainable heart rate (bonked, blew up, hit the wall)
- Too much competition in training and racing
- Insufficient base or endurance training
- Monotony in training program

Point 2. Heart rate higher during the race

- Insufficient warmup
- Training periods did not include enough speed or interval workouts and rides
- Cardiac drift phenomenon occurred from dehydration
- Overtrained: tired, too much training volume, too much training intensity
- Inappropriate amount of general strength training

After you are warmed up adequately, set your HR monitor so you can get an accurate reading of average heart rate. Then, time trial a steady state heart rate for 20 minutes. This heart rate needs to be the highest heart rate you think you sustain for the 20-minute period. You will need to pick your route carefully, making sure you have no stop signs. Focus on your heart rate monitor during the entire time. Mount it on your handlebars so you have a clear view during the ride.

This workout is only for the very fit cyclist. It isn't easy because for most of us it's a Zone 4 threshold ride. This is an ideal training ride once a month to see if your average heart rate improves—that is, if it slowly goes up. The closer your anaerobic threshold heart rate is to your maximum heart rate, the fitter you are. Make sure you are fully rested before doing this ride and take an easy recovery ride or a day off the next day.

• Lifestyle problems: travel, lack of sleep, irregular eating patterns, family commitments, insufficient rest, emotional challenges, too much stress from work, life events and insufficient successes in achieving goals.

Point 3. Heart rate fluctuation
• Chest strap too loose
• Insufficient conductivity (dry skin or electrodes not moist)
• Cross talk from another participant's monitor
• Interference from other sources
• Rare heart rate abnormality. Stop exercising and see a physician immediately

Point 4. Heart rate normal
• Training program works—training load is appropriate
• Excellent planning for the peak training spokes in the Training Wheel
• The energy was right—it was a "good day"

Need for Speed

Sprinting is not something most cyclists practice because they see no need for it. In practicality we use it more than we think. How about those bursts of speed to hold your place in traffic or make it through the intersection before the light turns red. Not to mention the less than friendly dogs that come raging out of yards; your best defense is quick acceleration.

Interval training helps you ride faster and develops your aerobic and anaerobic capacity. The emphasis of this ride is on acceleration and leg speed. Your heart rate will vary according to the effort and length of the interval. The idea is to give it your best effort, which will be as hard as you can go followed by enough time for a complete recovery.

Warm up for at least 15 to 30 minutes or even add this interval set to the middle or end of an existing ride. Do five to eight sprints of up to 30 seconds each with a full recovery (bottom of Zone 2). Use gears that you won't completely spin out in. Choose to do some of the sprints standing focusing on good form and technique. After several weeks of incorporating these sprints into your rides you will notice a significant improvement in your top-end speed and your ability to hold that intensity longer.

The Heat Is On

Power and speed are related like identical twins in a family. To the outsider they may look totally alike, but in reality they are distinctly different. The speed twin is great sprinting at high rpm in any gear and can hold that redline effort for short periods of time. "Quick" would be his middle name. On the other hand the power twin is all about strength, pace and perseverance. A triple chain ring or a "granny" gear is not in their vocabulary. Head winds and hills are nothing more than appetizers to him.

So why as a cyclist do you care about power or speed? You may not unless you want to go faster, cover more ground and not be dropped by your friends on the hills. The following ride will help you develop more power making you a better all-around cyclist.

Warm up for at least 15 to 30 minutes. Choose a course that is flat to rolling terrain. You will be using a lower cadence and bigger gears during this ride so beware if you have knee problems. This may not be the ride for you. Listen to your body and increase the cadence and use easier gearing if needed.

Ride along at 40 rpm in your big chain ring and in the middle of your back sprocket. In other words, use some hard gearing. Stay seated and accelerate as hard as you can for 10 seconds, recover by spinning in a lower gear until you have reached the bottom of Zone 2. Repeat five to eight times.

Developing power can also be accomplished by riding in rolling terrain and charging up short hills in the saddle without shifting down or letting your cadence drop. You can even try to increase your cadence. Watch your heart rate increase, especially if you try to increase your cadence. As you develop more power you will notice your heart rate is lower for the same effort. That is exactly what you want; a lower heart rate for the same power output.

On longer hills, shift to a harder gear halfway up, stand and power over the top. As you get stronger and stronger, don't forget to wait for your friends.

REFERENCES

Ackland, Jon, with Brett Reid. *The Power to Perform: A Comprehensive Guide to Training and Racing for Endurance Athletes,* Auckland, NZ: Reed Books, 1994.

Wilmore, Jack, and David Costill. *Physiology of Sport and Exercise,* Champion: Human Kinetics, 1994.

Duane Reed doing a standing sprint, sometimes called a standing run.

CHAPTER 7

Cycling Environments

My friend Bev and I were headed for a Dallas orphanage affiliated with Bev's church. She'd asked me to help her train a group of orphan children who lived there for an Ironkids triathlon. As we approached the campus auditorium where she was to speak, we noticed a stack of eight kids' bikes rusting and abandoned outside the door.

In her speech, Bev told the children, ages four to 18, that all 300 of them could train to swim, bike and run to become triathlon winners—but not on abused, abandoned bikes. She went on to discuss the benefits of training and reminded them that all finishers would be winners. We were happy when about half the children raised their hands to volunteer to enter the first triathlon. To celebrate, Bev and I went for a ride.

I borrowed Bev's spare road bike and we began what turned out to be one of those days. We had a flat; neither one of us had brought a repair kit. It turned cold, but we hadn't dressed for a change in weather and didn't have extra clothes. When it got dark, we had no lights. We simply hadn't taken the time to check the basics and we suffered the consequences.

As we returned, making the best of our situation, I thought back to the faces of the orphan children, each of whom I emotionally wanted to adopt. Remembering what we'd told them about being prepared and how to take care so the elements didn't damage their bikes, I realized what had happened. By not preparing we'd allowed ourselves to become victims of our environment, with about as little control as the orphans had over their family circumstances.

—Sally Edwards

Some conditions in our lives we can control. Some control us. The best we can hope to achieve is to manage them both. Environment is one of those factors in our lives that we are best at managing and not controlling. Here are a few conditions you can readily manage.

Bike Fit

Working to achieve your optimal bike fit not only makes you a better cyclist but also keeps your heart rate lower as you go faster. Finding the right bike fit takes experience and guidance from a bike fit specialist.

Fitting a bicycle depends on a number of factors. When you have it right, you'll immediately know the difference in both comfort and performance. You'll simply love riding your bike when it's a good match.

Starting with the right frame size and geometry is paramount to choosing outdoor bikes. Before you select the frame, decide what type of riding you prefer. Road and mountain bike frames are based on function; downhill bikes differ from time trial or criterium bikes. All-around bikes are the first choice for a beginner, but as you evolve, investigate special bikes for special purposes.

As you learned in Chapter 3, studio bikes are all the same size, and to compensate for different sized riders the components, not the frame, are adjustable. Spend the time to make adjustments to get a better fit. Tinker with your bike fit until you find what truly works. Make minor changes until you have a finely-tuned bike fit.

Here's a general checklist of changes you can make easily:

Bike and Equipment Adjustments

Seat height	Seat fore and aft position	Seat angle
Foot/pedal rotation angle	Handlebar stem height	Stem extension
Handlebar shape	Handlebar width	Handlebar angle
Brake levers	Toe clips and straps or clipless pedals	Tubes and tires
Saddle	Wheels	Pedals
Shoes	Proper apparel	Helmets

You can ride longer and faster at lower heart rates, sparing your fuels, if you make the work easier with proper bike and gear fit.

Fuel

Chapter 5 discussed how what, when and the way you eat can greatly affect your performance. Which fuels you burn and how quickly they are metabolized are directly affected by your exercise intensity and your training heart zones. To summarize, four factors influence fuel usage:

• The ratio of carbohydrates, proteins, and fats in your normal diet
• What you eat before and during the ride
• How hard you are riding
• How long you ride

Manipulating these four variables is a management skill that you can use to improve your performance.

In one of the most extensive research projects ever conducted on high performance athletes, Sally Edwards, in 1985, took part in an endurance research project at Temple University in Philadelphia. Researchers measured her body fat, aerobic capacity, threshold points, metabolic rates and heart rates. They wired her body and installed blood testing devices. She was asked to simulate swimming for an hour with an arm crank, then hop on a stationary bike for five hours, followed by three hours on the treadmill. During the test, technicians scraped off sweat, measured the amount and type of calories consumed, drew blood and analyzed it for its chemical composition, measured quality and quantity of her urine, counted calories expended, determined oxygen consumed and analyzed hydration.

Researchers concluded—not surprisingly—that they needed to do more research with more controls since athletes are highly individual, especially in the fuel ratios they burn. While Sally chose and metabolized carbohydrates at a high rate, other subjects who were fat-burning athletes preferentially chose foods higher in fat and burned a higher ratio of fat to carbohydrates.

Proper balanced nutrition is a manageable variable in efficient and performance-oriented cycling. You need to eat what you can effectively metabolize, understanding that the conditions under which you eat will also affect your performance. Finally, the heart zone in which you ride is key to the ratio and total amount of calories burned.

Jet Lag

Some cyclists travel extensively. The result of traveling, especially by jet, is a disruption of their normal sleep and training patterns. For airplane travelers, this disruption is caused by changes in time zones and sleeping patterns. For those who travel into high altitudes, physiological responses when riding are affected by the low partial pressure of oxygen forcing the heart to pump harder and faster and the lungs to work harder for the same riding effort. Travel from higher altitudes to lower ones causes little noticeable effect on heart rate and lung capacity.

Everyone responds to the effects of travel differently. Your heart rate monitor is one of the best tools to measure those effects on yourself. You'll note this change when you ride after a particularly difficult travel schedule or any other similar stress. For most cyclists the best way to deal with jet lag is to arrive days in advance of an event, allowing time to adjust to its effects.

Rest and Recovery

The higher your heart zone training, the more rest and sleep your body needs. Again, your monitor will tell you when you aren't allowing adequate rest and recovery between workouts. If you have a choice between getting a full night's rest or training more, choose sleep so that your body can restore itself, repair and recover. If you forego sleep, your next workouts may be of less benefit to you and you'll sacrifice positive training improvements.

The quality of your sleep also affects your ability to get fitter and enjoy your workouts. Many studies show that sleep disruptions impair the benefits you gain from sleep.

Adequate recovery from riding also is critical. Measuring your ambient heart rate is an excellent assessment to insure you allow enough time between rides to recover sufficiently. Other potentially helpful recovery techniques include massage, saunas and whirlpool baths; stretching; meditation or prayer; listening to music; and spending quality time with friends and loved ones.

Illness and Injury

Most illnesses such as colds and flu involve weakening your body's immune system. You can erode your immune system in various ways; one frequently experienced by cyclists is called the "too high, too hot" syndrome. Riding in too high a heart zone for too long a period of time causes the immune system to compromise.

Illnesses and injuries are a double negative. They not only force you into periods of sustained inactivity, they cause you to suffer a lost opportunity of rides that lead to improvements. You are then forced into a rebuilding phase to return to your pre-illness riding levels.

Injuries are caused mainly by either traumatic experience or overtraining. Too long, too hot burnout usually results from inadequate rest and response to your body's messages of weakness. Most often, overtraining is expressed by pain, lack of sleep or decrease in your riding capacity. Athletes will say, "I'm training harder than ever and getting slower. What's wrong?" This usually means their anaerobic threshold has been suppressed by training for too long in Zones 4 and 5.

If you experience chronic or persistent pain when you ride, stop or change your riding. It takes careful attention to train through an injury, although it's possible if you cross train or change your training pattern substantially.

Stress

You have significant control over other manageable phenomena, such as rapid weight loss and inadequate nutrition and hydration. Stress from other parts of your life—whether personal, financial, spiritual or professional—impact your riding and your performance, yet can be managed to a degree. All of these stresses have a cardiac response that is measurable on your heart rate monitor.

Resting or awakening heart rate is one of the best ways for you to assess the impact of stress. If your heart rate exceeds its average by more than five beats per minute, either drop your training heart zone by at least one level and shorten the training time, or cancel the workout for the day. Rest and recovery will make you fitter than one more training ride.

Some riders always have an excuse for poor performance. Sometimes everything just goes wrong: hot day, storm and freezing cold, then hot again, hills, wrong gears, too little water, no food, got lost, wind, flat tire, no pump, glasses fogged, wrong glasses, wrong clothes, no night light, sunburn, and/or scratched paint on frame. All of these external conditions, especially those not anticipated, affect heart rate. Your anxiety goes up, or maybe depression sets in, or you respond with anger, and as a result, enthusiasm evaporates.

You can see the benefits of preparation and maintenance in managing stress and improving riding conditions. To promote trouble-free riding, try to:
• Clean your bike
• Make regular bike tune-ups
• Lighten your bike
• Improve your bike equipment

- Adjust your bike to fit you
- Change your bike position
- Match your bike frame to your riding events
- Replace your headlight batteries regularly
- Carry a map when you ride in a new area
- Use sunscreen
- Check tire pressure before riding
- Carry spare tubes
- Carry two water bottles
- Carry saddle bag with your identification, money for telephone call, and all tools for changing a flat tire or to deal with mechanical problems

NATURAL ENVIRONMENT

The natural environment can be your best friend or your worst enemy. Tailwinds are gifts from the heavens, but headwinds can quickly turn an exhilarating ride into a grind. Crosswinds can keep your hands vice-gripped on your handlebars.

Wind is a part of the cycling experience. You learn how to be low and narrow into the wind and tall and wide like a sail when the wind is at your back. The best way to handle wind is to prepare for it mentally. In a strong headwind you can say to yourself, "this is good, the wind is my friend, it's making me stronger and better." One open-water swimmer likens it to swimming in seaweed: You can't get angry at the seaweed or the wind or they will overcome you. As with all challenges, your success is in how you handle them.

Heat is rarely a cyclist's friend, even if you have acclimatized and stay properly hydrated. Nearly all record-breaking endurance performances have been set under cool conditions. Hot environments and a high rate of internal heat production from muscle metabolism doubles thermal stress. The cardiovascular system is trying to meet the demands by shunting blood from the organs and supplying it to the skin, while simultaneously trying to supply oxygen to the working muscles. In mild air temperature conditions, body temperature is more easily regulated, and heat is dissipated mostly by sweat evaporation as more blood oxygen is directed to the muscles. Heart rate goes up in hot ambient conditions.

According to *The Physician and Sports Medicine,* "acclimatization typically requires 10–14 days in the warmer environment, and 75 percent of the adaptation is believed to have occurred within 5 days" (Sparlings and Millard-Stafford, July 1999).

If you're not used to heat, your initial rides should be shorter and at a lower heart rate intensity (Zone 2 to 3), building to longer rides and higher intensity over subsequent days and weeks. In order to minimize body heat storage and enhance sweat evaporation, wear shoes and breatheable clothing that wicks away perspiration.

Staying properly hydrated is important because dehydration retards acclimatization and increases demands on your cardiovascular system. Fluid ingestion during cycling in the heat reduces body temperature, dehydration and cardiovascular strain, increases performance and decreases average heart rate.

The general recommendation suggests that the rate of fluid ingestion during prolonged exercise should attempt to match fluid losses from sweating, or about 5 to 10 ounces every 15 minutes. The typical bike water bottle will hold roughly 24 ounces, so one water bottle will last an average of about 30 to 45 minutes. Remember, higher intensities and higher environmental temperatures require a higher fluid intake.

Sweat-loss rate may give the best approximation of individual fluid requirements. Sweat loss is easily estimated by measuring the difference between pre- and post-exercise body weight. For every pound lost, you need one to two cups of fluid. A mere two percent decrease in body weight from water loss can negatively impact performance.

Historically, plain water was thought to be the ideal fluid to drink during riding. However, recent studies indicate that 6 to 8 percent carbohydrate-electrolyte sports drinks are well tolerated during exercise in the heat and improve endurance. However, solutions greater than 12 percent carbohydrate, such as fruit juices and soft drinks, may cause gastrointestinal distress and impair warm-weather performance.

Drinking a lot of water (hyperhydration) before cycling in hot weather is another recommended strategy. The current guideline is to ingest 15 to 20 ounces of fluid two hours before competition; the rationale is that gastric emptying is enhanced when the stomach is full.

After cycling in heat, sodium replacement may maximize rehydration. Sodium is more important for fluid restoration after exercise than during it. Recovery requires both higher fluid volume replacement and higher sodium content.

Eight Natural Environment Recommendations

- Stay low and narrow into the wind. Be willing to grind it out. Stay positive.
- Initial rides in heat should be short and at lower intensities, as it takes 10 to 14 days to acclimatize to heat.
- Choose clothing that breathes and wicks away perspiration.
- Ingest at least one liter or 34 ounces of a 6 to 8 percent carbohydrate-electrolyte-drink every hour to maintain hydration and increase performance during long rides.
- Stay fully hydrated to improve acclimatization.
- Drink more fluids when cycling at higher intensities and higher temperatures.
- After cycling in heat, replace sodium to maximize rehydration.
- The fitter you are, the quicker you will adjust to heat. Get fitter.

Rain

It's only fair that two cyclists from Seattle write about rain. Rain is inevitable if you are a cyclist, a matter of when, not if. The rule of the ride is to be prepared.

Buy a breatheable rain jacket that repels water while allowing body heat to dissipate and sweat to evaporate. Check with your local bike shop or the Internet and become familiar with the latest inclement weather apparel. Consider wearing performance fabric cycling tights or rain pants to keep your legs dry and your knees warm.

Most cyclists wouldn't choose to start a ride in the rain unless it was a race or sponsored event, so most of the time, rain happens at some point during your ride, which means thinking ahead. Conditions can change quickly for the worse so you will need to use your best judgment in determining whether it's safe to continue.

Since water creates a slick surface, rain can make the road slippery for turning and braking. Give yourself more time to maneuver and stop. Watch out for puddles that can grab your wheel, reducing control. What looks like a puddle can be a 10-inch-deep pothole. Slow down and be more cautious, realizing that your brakes may not work as well. If the road is very slick, you can underinflate your tires slightly to get more surface area and traction.

As visibility decreases drastically for both you and motorists, you should wear brightly colored clothing so you can be seen. Dark glasses should be replaced with clear or amber lenses.

Keep your core body temperature up, as rain can bring cooler temperatures. If you become wet either from rain or sweat, your body temperature can drop quickly and your ride can become not only miserable but dangerous.

During RAMROD (Ride Around Mount Rainier in One Day) in 1998, a thunderstorm hit near the top of an 8-mile climb up a steep mountain pass. Mountain thunderstorms can be one of the scariest things on the planet. You are helpless and exposed to their awesome power. As Sally Reed neared the top of the climb, the air was thick and energized with electricity. Lightning bolts and cracking thunder merged in a giant din. The support crew waited anxiously 10 minutes away with rain gear, but by then, she didn't care about getting wet; she just wanted to get off the mountain!

By the time Sally reached the top, put on her rain gear and started her descent, her body temperature had dropped dangerously and she'd begun to shiver uncontrollably. If it hadn't been for planning and a great support crew waiting with dry clothes and a warm car, her RAMROD experience would have been over.

Always keep in mind that cycling weather can be unpredictable, so prepare for all likely conditions and most importantly, use common sense.

Rain Tips

• Use clear or amber-colored lenses.
• Allow extra time for slowing down, stopping and braking.
• Watch out for standing water and puddles.
• If you have to draft, ride off to the side to avoid the "rooster tail" and mud.
• Maintain core body temperature by dressing properly and stopping often to warm up.
• Wear bright yellow or orange-colored clothing for visibility.
• Underinflate tires for more traction.

After the ride, wipe down your bike, lubricate the chain, and use a water-dispersing spray on all cables, housings and pivot points of the brake and gear systems. Make sure no water has gotten inside your frame.

Altitude

At altitude increases, the oxygen percentage remains relatively the same, while the barometric pressure changes. You find yourself breathing more rapidly in order to get more oxygen. Maximum heart rates are reduced about one beat for every 1000 feet of ascending elevation.

Athletes who have trained at sea level experience higher heart rates at higher elevation. As elevation increases, performance decreases. The good news is that thin air provides less resistance.

Altitude Tips

• Dehydration occurs rapidly at high altitude so drink more than normal.
• Give yourself time to adapt. Take it easy for the first few days if possible.
• Avoid caffeine and alcohol as they lead to dehydration.
• If you have symptoms of altitude sickness such as headache and nausea, descend quickly.

Temperature and Humidity

As temperature and humidity increase, so does your heart rate. On the average, heart rate increases one beat higher for every two to three degrees temperature increase above 70 degrees Fahrenheit. Your ability to generate power with the exception of short sprints will also be reduced. Cold weather also diminishes power output and heart rate.

WORKOUTS

Indoor Training

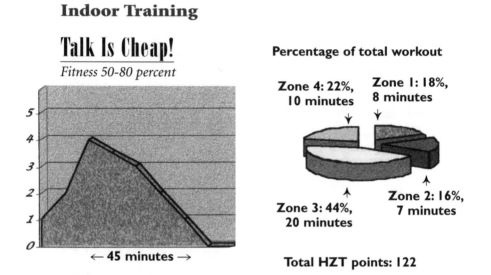

Talk Is Cheap!

Fitness 50-80 percent

← 45 minutes →

Percentage of total workout

Zone 4: 22%, 10 minutes

Zone 1: 18%, 8 minutes

Zone 3: 44%, 20 minutes

Zone 2: 16%, 7 minutes

Total HZT points: 122

This is one of those fun yet challenging workouts. You get a lot of bang for your investment time of 45 minutes. The whole idea is to train around your "talk threshold heart rate" or TTHR. Training at your TTHR is typically within the aerobic zone (Zone 3). This may be a new concept so let's explain it to you in the next paragraph. Training at your TTHR results in huge fitness gains in small amounts of time. This is a great workout for making fitness deposits into your health and emotional wellbeing.

Purpose

Your talk threshold or TTHR is a very narrow range of heartbeats around the intensity level at which it is difficult to talk easily. At this point, you will begin to feel that the training intensity is hard, strained or difficult. If you were following a feeling of perceived exertion, you might give this a rating of 7 or 8. The TT heart rate is near your anaerobic threshold heart rate. It is your subjective feeling about when you hit your TTHR point. It will be a different heart rate for each person. As you get fitter, TTHR changes and increases.

Workout Plan

Warm up for 5 minutes in Zone 1 and 5 minutes in Zone 2. Pedal with little resistance and easy gearing.

Gradually increase intensity until you reach the heart rate that is 5 bpm above your TTHR (in this workout example, that heart rate would be the bottom of Zone 4). Sustain this 5+ bpm above TTHR for 10 minutes. Use cadence, resistance (R) or a combination to sustain this heart rate. You may choose to alternate standing and seated positions.

Next, drop down 5 bpm to your estimated TTHR and sustain for 10 minutes. Again, your choice of sustaining this heart rate.

Drop another 5 bpm below your TTHR and sustain for 10 minutes (your choice).

Drop 10 bpm and sustain for 5 minutes using cadence and little resistance, then drop to the bottom of Zone 2 for 2 minutes and finish in Zone 1 for 3 minutes.

Talk Is Cheap!

Elapsed Time in Minutes	Coaching notes	Zone	Your HR numbers	Duration
0–5	Warm up, easy pedal, Z1	1	_____	5 min.
5–10	Increase HR with cadence to top of Z2	2	_____	5 min.
10–20	Increase HR to 5 bpm above estimated TTHR and sustain, choice		_____	10 min.
20–30	Drop HR to TTHR and sustain, choice		_____	10 min.
30–40	Drop HR to 5 bpm below TTHR and sustain, choice		_____	10 min.
40–42	Drop HR to bottom of Z2, easy pedal	2	_____	2 min.
42–45	Drop HR to Z1, warm down, easy pedal	1	_____	3 min.
	Total HZT Points 122			

The Zipper

Fitness 60-85 percent

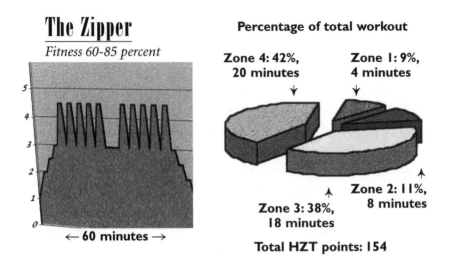

Percentage of total workout

Zone 4: 42%, 20 minutes

Zone 1: 9%, 4 minutes

Zone 2: 11%, 8 minutes

Zone 3: 38%, 18 minutes

← 60 minutes →

Total HZT points: 154

This is one of those workouts that demands the pedal to the metal. For those who want a red line experience, push the intensity to 90 percent instead of 85 percent or mix it up. If you have that masochistic sense of feeling it in every cell, here's where you will be in your own element. You can do this workout with some fellow lactic hedonists and push yourself even harder. You can also choose a lower intensity, such as 80 percent.

Purpose

The purpose of the workout is lactate tolerance training if you choose the 85 percent and above intensity level. You are trying to build up your body's ability to remove lactate during the session by exercising at a very high intensity. This is truly a workout that offers delayed gratification. Tomorrow, you may be tired and sore so prepare for a low intensity training day after this one. You will also wonder why just a few intervals at a high intensity are so fatiguing. All lactate tolerance training sessions stress you as they help you become a fitter cyclist.

Workout Plan

This 50-minute workout is a series of 10 repeats performed at 85 or 90 percent of your true cycling maximum heart rate. The workout is broken into two sets of five intervals with a short recovery between each and a longer rest between sets. Start by warming up to the bottom of Zone 3 in the first 9 minutes.

The first set of five intervals begins at 9 minutes into the workout. It is a 2-minute hard effort to the mid-point of Zone 4, followed by a 1-minute recovery to the bottom of Zone 3. Repeat 4 more times followed by a 4-minute recovery to the bottom of Zone 3.

Repeat the next five interval sets beginning at minute 28.

Warm down gradually from Zone 3 to Zone 1 for a total of 50 minutes. You decide what the goal is on each work interval. You may want to sprint, stand and climb with heavy resistance, or mix it up. Add some variety by changing positions on the bike and recruiting different muscles. If 10 intervals are too difficult in the beginning, start with five. Be sure to keep your recovery "active" in order to help remove the lactates in your blood. With each high intensity surge, be prepared to accelerate into the "ozone" layer of your training thresholds.

The Zipper

Elapsed Time in Minutes	Coaching notes	Zone	Your HR numbers	Duration
0–2	Warm up, easy pedal	1	_____	2 min.
2–7	Warm up, easy pedal steadily to mid-point of Z2	2	_____	5 min.
7–9	Increase HR with cadence to bottom of Z3	3	_____	2 min.
9–24	First set, increase HR to mid-point of Z4 (85%) and sustain for 2 min. (choice) followed by a 1 min. (rec) to the bottom of Z3. Repeat a total of 5 times	4	_____	15 min.
24–28	Easy pedal to bottom of Z3 and sustain	3	_____	4 min.
28–43	Second set; repeat work/recovery interval a total of 5 times. Vary body position, cadence and (R)	4	_____	15 min.
43–50	Warm down by gradually decreasing HR	3	_____	7 min.
		2	_____	
		1	_____	
	Total HZT Points 154			

Ladder to Success

Fitness 60-80 percent

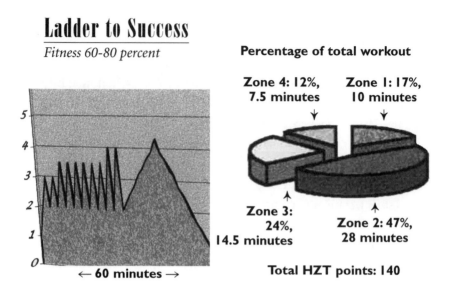

Percentage of total workout

Zone 4: 12%, 7.5 minutes

Zone 1: 17%, 10 minutes

Zone 3: 24%, 14.5 minutes

Zone 2: 47%, 28 minutes

← 60 minutes →

Total HZT points: 140

This 60-minute workout is a series of sprints, hill climbs and a fast-paced pyramid climb into Zone 4 and back down with a challenging controlled recovery.

Purpose

The goal of this workout is to increase your leg speed and muscular power and train your body to adjust to an increasing workload. The 30-second interval sprints will test how quickly you can raise your heart rate and how quickly you can recover. These bursts of speed followed by ample recovery are designed to make you fitter. The heavy resistance intervals are meant to simulate a series of six hills, each one a little steeper and a little longer. This will not only test your muscular strength and endurance but your mental toughness to hang in there. The pyramid climb teaches your cycling-specific systems to adapt to constantly increasing workloads every 30 seconds forcing your cardiovascular system to get stronger. The most challenging part may be controlling your recovery heart rate. Your body will be thinking it is time to recover and relax and you will have to control and focus on just five-beat increments every minute, and no more. Easier said than done! This one may take some practice. To make this a performance workout and more challenging, increase each zone to the next highest zone. The HZT points then go from 140 to 190. About half of the time will be spent in Zone 3 and over a third of the workout will be spent in Zone 4.

Workout Plan

Warm-up for 5 minutes in Zone 1 with an easy pedal. Increase cadence and intensity to the bottom of Zone 2 for 5 minutes.

At 10 minutes into the workout the sprint series begins. This is an interval set of (5) 30-second sprints with 30-second recoveries. The sprints may be done with moderate to heavy resistance or less resistance and fast cadence. This sprint set will take you to the mid-point of

LADDER TO SUCCESS

Elapsed Time in Minutes	Coaching notes	Zone	Your HR numbers	Duration
0–5	Warm-up, easy pedal	1	_____	5 min.
5–10	Increase HR with cadence, bottom of Z2	2	_____	5 min.
10–20	(5) 30-second sprints with 30-sec. (rec),	3	_____	10 min.
	Sprints start at bottom of Z3 and go to the mid-point of Z3 (75%), (rec) to the bottom of Z2 (60%)	2		
20–32	A series of (4) hills with heavy (R) to the mid-point of Z3 (75%). 1 min. (R), seated to mid-point of Z3 with a 2-min. (rec) to the bottom of Z2. Repeat a total of 4 times.	3	_____	12 min.
		2		
32–43	Hill #1, 4 min., standing, heavy (R), rpm above 60 (6+), to bottom of Z4, 2-min. (rec) to the bottom of Z2. Hill #2, 3 min., standing, heavy (R), rpm above 60 (6+), bottom of Z4, 2 min. (rec), bottom of Z2.	4	_____	11 min.
		2		
43–47	Pyramid climb from the bottom of Z2 into Z4. Increase HR with (R) 5 bpm every 30-sec., steady tempo/cadence.	2	_____	4 min.
		3	_____	
		4	_____	
47–60	Drop HR 5 bpm every min. Mental focus! Control (rec).	4	_____	13 min.
		3	_____	
		2	_____	
		1	_____	
	Total HZT Points 140			

Zone 3 (75 percent) with recoveries to the bottom of Zone 2 (60 percent). Don't be surprised if you don't recover the full 30 beats. As you get fitter, the number of recovery beats will increase.

Twenty minutes into the workout you will start a 23-minute interval set simulating a series of six hills. Each successive hill is steeper and longer followed by 2 minutes of recovery to the bottom of Zone 2. Recruit different muscle groups by alternating standing and seated positions. Throw in "jumps" or "hovers" for variety (Chapter 3, Interval Training Tips).

The final set is a pyramid climb starting at the bottom of Zone 2 and holding a steady tempo, using resistance to add 5 bpm every 30 seconds (R) until you reach the top of the pyramid at 47 minutes. The recovery back down the pyramid is 5 bpm every minute. Focus on your heart rate monitor and stay within the 5-beat window as you decrease intensity. You may start your recovery or decent by decreasing resistance and slowly adding cadence so your heart rate doesn't drop too quickly. Easy pedal down to the bottom of Zone 2 and then warm-down into Zone 1.

Note: For a performance workout, increase each interval by one zone and add another 50 HZT points for a total of 190.

Outdoor Training

Criss-Cross Zone 3

This 70-minute ride takes you on a tour through three zones, leaving you feeling energized and smiling from all those endorphins. The goal is not to go into Zone 4, even on the hills. You might want to pick a riding route through relatively flat to moderately rolling terrain. The idea is to spin your way up any hills using easy gearing and staying in the saddle. Select gears that keep your cadence between 70 and 90 rpm. This is a great opportunity to work on your pedal stroke and body position. Relax, enjoy the scenery and spin your way along. You may choose not to use the big chain ring. If that is the case, you may

Listening to Your Emotional Heart

Heart rate monitors give you continuous biofeedback information as to the relative level of your exercise intensity. There's no guesswork involved. It provides information immediately and without the complications of manual measurement.

A monitor is the link between the heart and mind. That may be its most powerful use. When we have information about what's going on inside, we can mentally respond to it.

Using a monitor is a way of opening our heart muscle by giving it a voice. The language that it speaks is numbers—how many heartbeats per minute. When you listen to your heart, you will find more joy and be more successful in your training. That is because a heart rate monitor is a bridge between the mental and the emotional states.

There are days that I don't want to train even though it's in my ride plan. I struggle like everyone to get to the club or get on my mountain bike and find every excuse not to do so. This is stressful. My ambient heart rate numbers for the day show that stress by increasing. My athletic heart says go ride, while at the same time my emotional heart wants the freedom to skip training.

My monitor records the stress that occurs during this debate between these two hearts—the athletic heart talking to the emotional heart. Usually on these days, I follow my emotional, intuitive heart and I ditch the ride. It's usually the right decision. The next day, I usually realize that I needed a day of rest. Beware not to further stress your heart muscle by worring or feeling guilt about missing a ride or workout. Turn it to your advantage and thank your heart for communicating with you that it, too, needs a complete recovery day.

find yourself pedaling at a slightly higher rpm than 90. Stay away from big gears on the hills and pedal on the downhills to maintain your heart rate.

Warm up for 10 to 20 minutes, gradually working your way up to the bottom of Zone 3. Slowly increase your heart rate to the top of Zone 3 and hold it there for 15 minutes, then recover down to the bottom of Zone 3 for 5 minutes. Repeat; 15 minutes to the top of Zone 3 and 5-minute recovery to the bottom of Zone 3. Warm-down for 10 minutes with easy pedaling in Zone 2 and Zone 1.

THE FIVE EMOTIONAL HEART ZONES
By Dan Rudd, Ph.D.

Emotional heart zone training is a way to listen to your heart by becoming aware of your emotional state and consciously shifting to a healthier zone, particularly if you happen to be in a toxic emotional zone. Just as the body is designed to heal itself, the emotions can be used to guide us from a condition of stress and disease to a state of peace, health and compassion.

The field of psychoneuroimmunology (psycho = mind, neuro = body's nervous system, immunology = the body's natural ability to defend and heal itself) teaches us about the connection between our thoughts and what happens in our bodies. Our emotions and perceptions of what is happening in our world cause our heart and brain to send messages that stimulate physiological responses in our body. Our emotional states trigger reactions in our body that affect heart rate, blood chemistry and the activity of every cell in the body.

Emotional heart zone training is designed to help you stay conscious of what emotional zone you are in. Many people get "stuck" in a particular emotional zone without conscious awareness. When we are agitated, angry or stressed, the stress hormones continue to flood our bodies like a chemical bath. We need to know how to turn them off.

There are five emotional heart zones. As they are being described, notice which of these zones is most familiar to you and where you tend to spend your time.

Zone No.	Zone description	Zone benefit
5	Red Zone—Out of control, frantic, total panic, disconnected, emergency	Toxic
4	Distress Zone—Worried, anxious, angry, scattered, fearful, reactive	Cautious, alert
3	Performance Zone—Focused, positive stress, fulfillment, completion	Achievment
2	Productive Zone—High concentration, effective, energetic, prolific	Results
1	Safe Zone—Meditative, relaxed, regenerative, comfortable, peaceful	Energized

Zone 1. Safe Zone

The Safe Zone is where we go to recharge our batteries, calm ourselves, get peaceful, refocus our energy. The Safe Zone is very personal and it is important for you to design your own safe place. For some, Zone 1 will have a prayerful or meditative focus. For others, certain music or sounds of nature will create a peaceful inner feeling. A visual memory of a beautiful place or a remembrance of a special moment or thoughts of compassion toward a loved one may put your heart at peace. Just as exercise is one of the best things for your physical heart, a well-developed safe zone is the greatest gift you can give to your emotional heart.

Zone 2. Productive Zone

The Productive Zone is where you may spend much of your time at home, work or play. In this zone, you are getting things done and feeling pretty good. You are relatively peaceful and focused, going about your day-to-day responsibilities. In Zone 2, you have complete access to your emotions and your thoughts.

Zone 3. Performance Zone

The Performance Zone has all of the features of Zone 2 except it is characterized by greater focus, concentration, positive intensity and accomplishment. You would probably be in Zone 3 when you are doing something you really love, whether it be work, play or relationships.

Zone 4. Distress Zone

The Distress Zone is a state where the bad stuff starts to happen. It is characterized by feelings of fear, worry, anger, anxiety, depression, guilt and helplessness. This is where the stress response is triggered and physiological changes begin to affect heart rate, blood chemistry and activity in all the cells and organs within the body. The ability to think clearly declines and the emotions begin to take over. In Zone 4 we become much less productive in our work and much more destructive in our relationships.

Zone 5. Red Zone

The Red Zone is a place you never want to go. This is out of control behavior, raw emotion with no rational thought. It is characterized by aggression, violence and hysteria. This is where abusive and destructive behavior happens. It is highly toxic to the person in Zone 5, as well as anyone else nearby.

To put your heart back into your life, we all need to train and condition both our physical and our emotional hearts. Learning to use your emotional and physical heart zones together leads to more energy and less stress in your life.

Dan Rudd, Ph.D., is the president of Blitz, Business Leadership In The Zone. Together with Sally Edwards, he teaches organizations and companies how to put the heart back in. For further information on how they use heart rate monitors in this corporate training program or to learn more about the company's new book, More Energy, Less Stress, *go to its Web site, at www.blitztraining.com.*

Rock 'n' Roll

You can make this ride as long and as tough as you want. The idea is to repeat work and rest intervals every 15 seconds for 5 minutes. "Rock" for 15 seconds, then easy "roll" for 15 seconds. Rest and recover for 5 minutes then repeat the work/rest, rock 'n' roll interval again. Repeat this 5-minute interval as many times as you want. You may choose to do your 15-second work or "rock" interval at any intensity above 70 percent. Your rest or roll heart rate should increase in recovery beats the fitter you become. The only requirement is to keep your cadence high. If you are giving an all-out effort for 15 seconds your heart rate will be in Zone 4 and Zone 5. You will be doing most of the interval set above your anaerobic threshold. Rock 'n roll will help your pedaling efficiency and leg speed at whatever intensity you choose.

Saturday Night Fever

As you crawl out of bed Sunday morning to meet your riding partners, have you ever questioned why you did what you did Saturday night, or better yet, why you didn't do what you should have done Saturday night?

This speed interval can be incorporated into your ride when you are ready to focus on the task at hand: speed work!

The basic way to develop fast, smooth leg speed is to spin easy to moderate gears at a high rpm or cadence. Choose a relatively flat section of road. After a 15- to 30-minute warm-up start with your normal riding cadence. That could be anywhere from 75 to 95 rpm. Gradually increase your cadence until your legs lose coordination and you are bouncing on the saddle. Ease off about 5 rpm and sustain for 5 to 15 seconds. Repeat several times. This is not a high intensity heart rate interval. Most of these repeats will be in Zone 3 and 4. After a few times your maximum cadence and smoothness will be much better. You can also stay in easy gears on the downhills letting gravity help turn your legs.

Stay in the small chainring in front and move to bigger gears in the back, increasing your cadence to 120 rpm and trying to sustain for 1 minute. Focus on relaxing, keeping your upper body quiet and arms loose. All the motion happens in your legs. Keep your head still and think "smooth and fast." Your legs should be a blur just like in the cartoons. As you develop your leg speed and get smoother and more efficient your heart rate should be lower during these intervals.

REFERENCES

Below, P.R., Mora-Rodriquez, R., Gonzalez-Alonzo, J., et. al. *Fluid and Carbohydrate Ingestion Independently Improve Performance during One Hour of Intense Exercise.* Medical Science Sports Exercise, 1995. 27 (2): 200–210.

Kregel, K.C., Wall PT, et. al. *Effects of Ingesting Carbohydrate Beverages during Exercise in the Heat.* Medical Science Sports Exercise, 1986. 18 (5): 568–575.

Millard-Stafford, M., Sparling, P.B., Rosskopf, L.B., et. al. *Carbohydrate-Electrolyte Replacement Improves Distance-Running Performance in the Heat.* Medical Science Sports Exercise, 1992. 24 (8): 934–940.

Tools of the Trade

Heart Bra

Coded Transmitter Belt

Heart Rate Monitors

Bike Computer

CHAPTER 8

Tools for Heart Cycling

I used a heart rate monitor in my first triathlon without knowing how, beyond the training we had done in Heart Cycling class. I knew nothing about thresholds or cardiac drift. I just looked at the numbers and hoped my heart wouldn't blow up. During the bike leg of my first Danskin Triathlon, I correlated the numbers with what I had seen on a spin bike, but during the swim and run the numbers didn't have much meaning. My training partners were all in the same boat. Before the race, Sally Edwards gave us a hard time about being "club triathletes" because we trained indoors in a 50-meter pool, on spin bikes in an air-conditioned studio and on treadmills with towels and water bottles handy.

I realized after this, my first race, that I needed to know more about what the numbers on my monitor were telling me. I decided to test my anaerobic threshold heart rates in the swimming pool, on the track and on the bike. I definitely wanted to do better next year and knew my heart rate monitor was going to be the key.

With a big hug and a signed book from Sally, I was armed for my year of training. What Sally didn't know was that she gave me the best racing advice and motivation possible. Inside the front cover she wrote, "Read this and win your age group!" I immediately thought, "she thinks I can do it." She believed in me more than I did. It's a common theme in life and in races. We have people who believe in us and inspire us to do what we think are extraordinary feats.

I wrote a race plan for my second Danskin, laying out my goals. I planned to know my split times and average heart rate numbers for each leg. My anaerobic threshold heart rate had gone up about five beats in each event and I knew exactly what heart rate I could sustain. I didn't win like Sally said, but I also didn't read all of her book! Second place was just the motivation I needed for the next year, along with turning 50 and "aging up."

For the third Danskin Triathlon, I convinced my riding partners to start seriously using their monitors and when they got faster, so did I. It's amazing how that works! This time I mounted my monitor on my handlebars along with a second one on my wrist. I stared at the monitor almost every moment of the bike and run.

This continuous information made all the difference in the race. It gave me the confidence to push hard, knowing that I had trained at these heart rate numbers and my heart wasn't going to blow up. A half-mile before the finish line, as Lynn Brooks (20-time Ironman finisher) passed me, I looked down and my heart rate had dropped. At that moment, second place just didn't sound good to me so I did what I had heard Sally Edwards say so many times: "You reach down deep, throw away your heart rate monitor and run with your emotional heart." That finish line never looked so good! No, I didn't catch Lynn, but I knew I had given it my best shot. If that meant second place, it was okay. I still didn't know how my good friend and nemesis Sue had done because she had started in the wave five minutes ahead of me. Third place might be looking good and that was hard for me to accept.

When the age-group winners were announced I heard my name over the loud speaker. It wasn't third place; it wasn't second place…. It was first! How could that be? Lynn clearly passed me, unless I was seeing things (strange things happen at high heart rates). I found out that both Lynn and Sue were in the wave before me. If Lynn hadn't provided me with that last half-mile of motivation, it may well have been another second place for me.

When I help my friends train using heart rate monitors, I joke about giving away all my training secrets. The most important secret is that there are no secrets. We hope you will use the information we provide to successfully cross your own personal finish line.

—Sally Reed

THE HEART RATE MONITOR, THE NUMBER ONE TOOL

Your heart rate monitor is more than your friend, coach and tool. It's difficult to describe what it can do emotionally and physically to help you do your best. It's a hard-working, durable device that keeps on ticking, storing data and giving you a continuous information about for the most important muscle in your body, your heart

In a tool chest of key sports performance equipment, the heart rate monitor would occupy an established place. To interpret this important muscle in relation to so many other events, activities, and cycles within the body, it must possess some special power.

Here is a description of some of those key powers:

Motivation. For a boost of energy to keep you training, turn to your monitor for motivation to complete a workout or improve a training session. Strap it around your handlebars or wrist and it's like taking a hit of energy. When you drift above a set ceiling or floor, the alarm sounds to let you know. Conversely, when you lose focus and slow down, it sounds the alarm to tell you to pick it up. It keeps you fresh by objectively assessing your performance.

Biofeedback. Because the monitor reads your heart's frequency of contraction, the data it provides are more precise than perceived exertion. The delicate range of heartbeats surrounding the anaerobic threshold heart rate zone can be measured with much greater accuracy using a monitor.

Braking. If you're one of those high achievers who loves to train in high zones, you can use your monitor for getting faster by having it slow you down or hold you back. This is useful when you must conserve your energy supply to finish a final climb with energy left to do it well.

Computing. High-end monitors feature accessory software and download capability, allowing you to use them with your computer to interpret data on a more sophisticated level. Some software programs also have analysis capabilities; others include training programs to fit your current fitness level.

Diagnosis. Undertraining, overtraining, and overreaching are all phases of training that can result in different outcomes to your overall plan. You can use a monitor to assess your body's response to a dosage of exercise. For example, awakening heart numbers as well as ambient and delta heart rate values all have direct application to diagnosing the current status of your working muscle groups. Changes in these values are critical in evaluating your ability to train for improvement.

Quantification. The Heart Zone Training system uses the monitor as a prescription tool to recommend the quantity of training. This system is explained in more detail in Chapter 9. In an ideal world, the best quantification tool would be a power meter that measures energy output on a bike. Since technology has not yet furnished this tool for the mass market, a heart rate monitor is the best tool we have today.

Workings of a Heart Rate Monitor

Today's portable and wireless heart rate monitors measure the number of beats the heart contracts in one minute. Extremely accurate compared with laboratory quality devices, they are relatively inexpensive and readily available. Basically, a heart rate monitor measures exercise intensity or metabolic demand.

A heart watch or heart rate monitor consists of three different parts. A washable, adjustable elastic band circles your upper torso at chest level to attach the transmitter to the front or back area of the body. The signal detection unit or electrodes form part of the transmitter device. A plastic casing holds two separate rubber electrodes, which must touch the skin to operate. The electrodes detect the electric potential of each heartbeat and pass this electrical current through signal, noise and data processing. The transmitter unit also contains a copper-coiled radio-like transmitter and a battery that powers the signal transmission to the receiver. Transmission power is predetermined; most monitors project unidirectionally for 32 to 36 inches from the transmitter.

The watch-like device is the receiver. It displays the heart rate as a number on either a dot matrix or other screen. Inside this unit is an application-specific integrated circuit masked with prescribed actions that coordinate the inner workings of the monitor, including the external buttons used to program it.

Four Basic Types of Heart Rate Monitors

Four types of heart rate monitors are available, differentiated by the features they display. Cost and features are directly related, so the more you spend, generally the more monitor you get. Pricing is highly variable based on the many factors. The four monitor types are continuous read monitors, zone monitors, downloadable, and bike monitors.

Continuous read monitors have no external buttons. The only display on the face of the receiver is heart rate. They tend to be small, accurate and strong. Their retail price range is $50-$99 U.S.

Zone monitors allow you to program custom information into the monitors, such as heart zones and time functions. Features vary greatly, but basically these provide the user with the ability to set a minimum of one ceiling, or top, and one floor, or bottom, of one heart zone. Most include a function that tells users they are within or outside this training zone by either a sound or a flashing display. More sophisticated zone monitors include time functions such as a wristwatch, stopwatch, elapsed time and some memory for recall, such as time within the programmed zone. The range of retail prices for zone monitors is $100-$200.

Downloadable monitors come in two types: manual and computer downloadable. In one, the monitor does not directly interact with the computer. Instead, the monitor will play back heart rate data that can be recorded manually or entered into a software program developed by a number of different software companies. Computer downloadable monitors directly upload data to the computer from one or multiple workouts. This data is transmitted by either sonic (sound waves), infrared or with an interface box that attaches to the monitor and extracts the stored heart rate data. Downloadable monitors range in price depending on whether the software and interface systems are included with the monitor; they generally sell for $150-$400.

THE BIKE MONITOR

A bike monitor is a combination of a bike computer, heart rate monitor and altimeter. The merging of these three technologies results in a powerful new information tool. Bike monitors simultaneously and continuously provide you with three or more data streams to use to manage your training and racing. Different manufacturers market different versions of the bike monitor, but most are downloadable into a computer or mobile Internet device.

A bike monitor can provide you with more essential data to learn about your fitness and measure your progress. For many serious cyclists, the attraction is the power of having a personal bike laboratory by having a training tool like a bike monitor.

Because heart rate monitor features and models change, no feature chart is included with this text. Rather, some features are more appropriate for some users. Organized by user and features, the following chart should help you to make an informed decision about which monitor to use for indoor cycling or outdoor riding:

STEP 9: LOGGING YOUR WORKOUTS

As you start to practice the habits of the 10 Steps to Heart Cycling you may find that keeping a diary of your rides can be one of the most enjoyable parts of training because it's a chance to record the event. As you record information about your ride, the process and the words can become motivational. It gives you a way to compare your riding plan from Step 7 with the actual rides in Step 9. By recording these quantifying characteristics, you'll be able to maximize your workouts and rides and fine-tune your riding program, as well as eliminate certain rides and workouts that don't help you achieve your goals.

You'll quickly discover you like to record certain information. It might be average heart rate because it's useful for measuring improvement—or just because you like numbers.

It takes less than a minute a day to fill out a log sheet, but thein-

Heart Rate Monitor Buyers' Guide

Type of cyclist / Monitor Features:	Indoor	Outdoor		
		Basic	Fitness	Advanced
1. Continuous-Read Monitor:				
Heart rate	♡	♡	♡	♡
Time of day			♡	♡
Water resistant	♡	♡	♡	♡
2. Zone Monitors:				
Programmable zone(s)	♡		♡	♡
Peak heart rate	♡		♡	♡
Stop watch	♡	♡	♡	♡
Time within zone	♡		♡	♡
Time above/below zone			♡	♡
Out-of-zone alarm			♡	♡
Average heart rate	♡		♡	♡
Wake-up alarm				♡
Maximum heart rate	♡		♡	♡
Countdown timer				♡
Back-light			♡	♡
Calorie counter			♡	♡
3. Downloadable Monitors				
Manually downloadable	♡		♡	♡
Direct computer download	♡			♡
4. Bike Monitors				
Cycle functions: speed, cadence	♡		♡	♡
Altitude			♡	♡
Heart Rate	♡	♡	♡	♡
Manually downloadable	♡			♡
Direct computer download	♡			♡

formation you record can be used for a lifetime. Furthermore, a well-kept log is far superior to relying on sheer memory when you want to recall a training period leading up to achieving a goal. Share your log with others and ask them for their support and evaluation

If you've never kept a log, now is the time. You can photocopy the blank page provided or order your own *Heart Rate Monitor Logbook for Outdoor and Indoor Cyclists* by contacting **www.velogear.com** or **www.heartzones.com.**

DATE	SPORT ACTIVITY	ACTIVITY		TIME IN ZONE				
		DISTANCE	TIME	ZONE 1	ZONE 2	ZONE 3	ZONE 4	ZONE 5
Weekly Summary								
Year-to-Date Summary								

Notes:

Key Workout Type	Average Heart Rate	Rating A to F or 1 to 10	Strength training time	Stretching time	% Fat / Body Weight	A.M. heart rate	Altitude changes	Total HZT points

Notes:

DATE	SPORT ACTIVITY	DISTANCE	TIME	TIME IN ZONE				
				ZONE 1	ZONE 2	ZONE 3	ZONE 4	ZONE 5
3/15	Swim	100	30min	3min	15min	12min	—	—
3/16	Run	8mi.	1:30	—	10min	60min	—	—
	Swim	100	30min	3min	15min	12min	—	—
3/17	Rest Day							
3/18	Bike	18mi	1:15	—	9min	41min	25min	6min
3/19	Run	5mi	45min	9min	12min	28min	—	—
3/20	Bike	20mi	1:15	—	15min	60min	—	—
3/21	Run	6mi	55min	—	15min	30min	10min	—
Weekly Summary	Swim	2500	1:30	9min	45min	42min	—	—
	Bike	38mi	2:30	—	24min	1:21	25min	6min
	Run	19mi	3:10	10min	37min	1:58	10min	—
Year-to-Date Summary	Swim	8500	12:30	42min	6:45	8:42	—	—
	Bike	380mi	20:30	—	8:45	14:00	8:00	6:00
	Run	190mi	30:10	4:30	6:45	10:58	10:30	—

Notes: I am really enjoying this training period. The feeling of getting fitter is wonderful!

Key Workout Type	Average Heart Rate	Rating A to F or 1 to 10	Strength training time	Stretching time	% Fat/ Body Weight	A.M. heart rate	Altitude changes	Total HIT points
Interval	157	B	15min	20min	27%	63	1000'	125
					154 lb			
Interval	149	A	0	15min	27%	61	1500'	170
					155 lb			
Interval	149	A	0	15min	28%	62	0	75
Endurance	125				155 lb			115
88		A-	15min	10min	28%	62	500'	230
Steady	152				155 lb			
State								
	165							
Speed	175	A	0	10min	27%	62	0	75
Endurance	125				154 lb			115
Hills	151bpm	A-	30min	70min	155 lb	62	3854'	970
		B						26,222

Notes: *Happy with consistency. Followed my training plan. Earned a B+, which keeps me motivated. Weight is steady.*

WORKOUTS

Indoor Training

Fast Lane
Fitness 60-83 percent

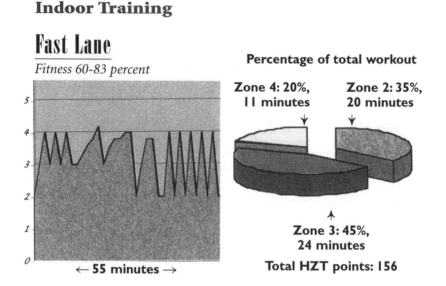

Percentage of total workout

Zone 4: 20%, **Zone 2: 35%,**
11 minutes **20 minutes**

Zone 3: 45%,
24 minutes

Total HZT points: 156

← 55 minutes →

Life may be lived in the "Fast Lane!" For most cyclists, this is where we want to be; getting faster and stronger, looking back just long enough to appreciate where we started and how far our training has brought us. Just thinking about this workout makes your legs want to go fast.

Purpose

This 55-minute workout is designed to enhance the functional capacity of the heart, lungs and vascular and skeletal systems. Almost half the workout is in Zone 3, which is the transition zone into the two performance zones, 4 and 5. Zone 3 is where performance-training effects begin and tremendous physiological changes occur.

You will push yourself through the aerobic zone and into the threshold zone, briefly getting a taste of training with less oxygen and increasing the blood lactate in your cycling-specific muscles. Your time spent in Zone 3 will feel great because you will have released both emotionally and physically some of your stored-up toxins.

Training in Zone 3 also builds resistance to fatigue and increases cardiovascular efficiency. It is a zone that teaches the metabolic pathways to spare carbohydrates and metabolize fatty acids. You may become addicted to this workout, not just because it's fun but because of the mood-altering endorphins that are so profuse in Zone 3 and Zone 4.

These opiate-like stress reducers can increase up to five-fold from the resting state as a result of exercise. Labeled the "exercise high," this state of euphoria can result in mood improvement and is implicated in increased pain tolerance, reduction in anxiety, tension, stress and improved appetite control. The beauty is these benefits continue for hours after the workout is said and done!

Fast Lane

Elapsed Time in Minutes	Coaching notes	Zone	Your HR numbers	Duration
0–10	Warm up gradually to the bottom of Z2	2	_____	10 min.
10–16	From the bottom of Z2 add 30 beats to the mid-point of Z3 in 1 min., recover down to the bottom of Z2 in 1 min. Repeat a total of 3 times	3 2	_____	6 min.
16–21	From the bottom of Z2 add 5 beats each min. for 5 min. using (R) and 80 rpm (8)	3 4	_____ _____	5 min.
21–24	(Rec) to the bottom of Z2	2	_____	3 min.
24–29	5 min. interval, 10 sec. "on," 10 sec. "off," alternate standing and seated.	3 4	_____ _____	5 min.
29–32	(Rec) to the bottom of Z2	2	_____	3 min.
32–38	6 min. interval, 30 sec. "on," 30 sec. "off" Super Spin (120 rpm)	3 2	_____ _____	6 min. 4 min.
38–42	(Rec) to the bottom of Z2	2	_____	
42–51	From the bottom of Z2 increase HR to the bottom of Z4 in 1 min. All-out effort. (rec) down to Z2 in 1 min. Repeat a total of 5 times	4 2	_____ _____	9 min.
51–55	Gradually warm down into Z2 and Z1	2 1	_____ _____	4 min.
	Total HZT Points 156			

*For a performance workout increase by one zone

Workout Plan

Begin with a gradual 10-minute warm-up to the bottom of Zone 2.

At 10 minutes into the workout the first 6-minute interval set begins. From the bottom of Zone 2, increase heart rate 30 beats to the mid-point of Zone 3 in 1 minute. That means a hard effort, pedaling at 100 rpm. Recover down 30 beats to the bottom of Zone 2 in 1 minute. Repeat this 30-beat interval 2 more times.

At 16 minutes, increase heart rate to the bottom of Zone 3 holding 80 rpm, increasing heart rate 5 bpm every minute for a total of 5 minutes, using (R) and holding cadence steady at 80 rpm. Add resistance or gearing to increase heart rate. Stay seated. Recover back down to the bottom of Zone 2 for 3 minutes.

At minute 24 begin a 5-minute interval set from the bottom of Zone 2 to the bottom of Zone 4 using a 10-second interval of hard effort and resistance followed by a 10 second easy recovery with no resistance. Alternate standing and seated. This tough interval set is followed by a 3-minute recovery to the bottom of Zone 2.

At 32 minutes, a 4-minute interval set begins from the bottom of Zone 3 to the top of Zone 3. Alternate 30 seconds on, (fast spin 120 rpm) with 30 seconds off (easy pedal recovery). You may choose standing or seated. A soft pedal recovery follows to the bottom of Zone 2 for 4 minutes.

At 41 minutes into the workout, increase heart rate from the bottom of Zone 2 to the bottom of Zone 4 in 1 minute followed by a 1-minute recovery to the bottom of Zone 2. Repeat this interval a total of 5 times. In order to increase your heart rate this many beats in a short amount of time you will need to add resistance and cadence. You may even choose to stand and use your body weight and leg power to sprint to the bottom of Zone 4. Finish by warming down into Zones 2 and 1.

Pumped

Fitness 60-90 percent

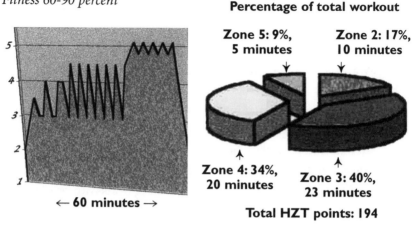

Percentage of total workout

Zone 5: 9%, 5 minutes

Zone 2: 17%, 10 minutes

Zone 4: 34%, 20 minutes

Zone 3: 40%, 23 minutes

← 60 minutes →

Total HZT points: 194

This 60-minute workout consists of five tough interval sets, each working on a specific cycling skill and training effect. Ten minutes of anaerobic threshold training at the end when the muscles are fatigued simulates racing and tests you, not only physically, but also mentally. Over 40 percent of the workout is in Zone 4 and Zone 5, suggesting a good 48-hour recovery period before your next high, heart cycling ride.

Purpose

The first two interval sets are designed to build leg strength and work on a steady tempo or cadence. You will want to remain seated using heavy resistance to attain the desired heart rate. Concentrate on using your hamstrings on the isolated leg training as you pull up and over on the pedal stroke, keeping constant pressure on the pedals and eliminating any dead spot at the top of the stroke. Pedal in circles making the stroke round. The next two interval sets will add power, working on fast starts with heavy resistance in both a seated and standing position. The last interval set is training your anaerobic threshold and lactate clearance systems, getting you ready for race day performance. Your goal is to improve your maximum sustainable heart rate. It is the fastest heart rate that you can sustain for a given distance or time without having your performance suffer. Racing at your maximum sustainable heart rate will improve your performance in any athletic event. Researchers have discovered that maximum sustainable heart rate is one of the best predictors of your racing performance.

Workout Plan

Warm up to the bottom of Zone 2 with an easy pedal and relaxed body position.

Beginning at 5 minutes into the workout, increase heart rate 10 bpm by holding a steady 90-rpm and increasing the resistance or gearing.

At 8 minutes increase the heart rate to the bottom of Zone 3 with resistance, holding a steady 90-rpm cadence.

At 11 minutes increase heart rate 10 more beats with resistance or gearing sustaining 90 rpm for 3 minutes.

Beginning at minute 14 reduce cadence to 60 rpm, adding enough resistance to sustain your heart rate at the bottom of Zone 3 using your right leg only. Concentrate on a round pedal stroke using your hamstrings to pull up and over the backside of the pedal stroke. Every 2 minutes, change legs until minute 24 to26, when you return to pedaling with both legs keeping the rpm at 60.

At minute 26 begin a 2 minute super spin (120+rpm) followed by a 1 minute soft pedal recovery to the bottom of Zone 3.

Minute 37 begins a 5-minute interval set with 1 minute of heavy resistance, standing and pedaling at 60 rpm followed by 1 minute of easy spin, seated, at 90 rpm. Your heart rate will be at the mid-point of Zone 4 with the recovery down to the bottom of Zone 3. Repeat this interval two more times.

At minute 42, sprint to your anaerobic threshold and sustain that heart rate for 1 minute, followed by 1 minute of 5 bpm above anaerobic threshold then a 1 minute drop back down 5 bpm to anaerobic threshold. Repeat this interval 4 more times (add 5 bpm above AT for 1 minute then drop back to AT for 1 minute).

At minute 52, drop your heart rate to the bottom of Zone 4 and sustain for 2 minutes, followed by another 2-minute drop in heart rate to the bottom of Zone 3 then a final drop in heart rate to the bottom of Zone 2 for the remaining 2 minutes of the workout.

Pumped

Elapsed Time in Minutes	Coaching notes	Zone	Your HR numbers	Duration
0–5	Warm up to the bottom of Z2, easy spin	2	_____	5 min.
5–8	Increase HR 10 bpm, 90 rpm (9)	2	_____	3 min.
8–14	Increase HR to the bottom of Z3 and sustain	3	_____	3 min.
	for 3 min. then increase HR 10 more beats for 3 min.	3	_____	3 min.
14–24	Isolated Leg Training (ILT), every 2 min. change	3	_____	10 min.
	legs, 60 rpm (6) beginning at the bottom of Z3	3	_____	
	and increasing HR gradually by adding (R) until the bottom of Z4	4	_____	
24–26	Pedal with both legs 60 rpm, mid-point of Z4	4	_____	2 min.
26–28	Super Spin (120+ rpm) (12), sustain bottom of Z4	4	_____	2 min.
28–29	Easy pedal recovery to the bottom of Z3	3	_____	1 min.
29–37	1 min. fast start to the mid-point of Z4 from a	4	_____	6 min.
	slow easy pedal, heavy (R), hard effort, seated, followed by a 1 min. easy pedal (rec) to the bottom of Z3. Repeat a total of 4 times	3	_____	
37–42	Heavy (R) standing, 60 rpm (6), increase HR to	4	_____	5 min.
	the mid-point of Z4, sustain for 1 min. then soft	3	_____	
	pedal (rec), seated to the bottom of Z3, 90 rpm (9). Repeat a total of 3 times	4		
42–43	Increase HR to anaerobic threshold and sustain for 1 min.	4	_____	1 min.
43–52	Increase HR to 5 bpm above anaerobic threshold and sustain for 1 min. Decrease HR 5 bpm for 1 min. Repeat a total of 5 times	4/5	_____	9 min.
52–54	Decrease HR to the bottom of Z4	4	_____	2 min.
54–60	Decrease HR to the bottom of Z3 for 2 min.,	3	_____	2 min.
	then warm-down to the bottom of Z2 for 4 min.	2	_____	2 min.
	Total HZT Points 194			

Seattle Ridge
Fitness 60-95 percent

Percentage of total workout

Zone 5: 20%,
12 minutes

Zone 2: 13%,
8 minutes

Zone 4: 47%,
28 minutes

Zone 3: 20%,
12 minutes

Total HZT points: 224

← 60 minutes →

This Seattle Ridge is not in Seattle; it's in Sun Valley, Idaho. For this 60-minute indoor cycle workout you are going to feel like you have pedaled the ridges and valleys of Baldy Mountain at 7000 feet of altitude. The air is thin at that elevation, yet you feel like you are on the top of the world. Your legs and lungs won't forget this one.

Purpose

Almost 70 percent of this workout is in Zone 4 and Zone 5 and that means anaerobic interval training to improve your fitness level. It's designed to make you faster, fitter and stronger. This is an intense workout that trains your cycling-specific muscles to be capable of driving your anaerobic threshold higher toward maximum heart rate. The 20- and 40-beat intervals can be done with leg speed or strength. Vary body position simulating hill climbs. You may choose to raise your front wheel 4 to 6 inches and support it off the ground to get a more realistic climbing angle for the hills. Plan on taking at least 48 hours off from cycling after this one to give your cycling-specific muscles a chance to rest. Do an easy Zone 2 or 3 cross-training recovery workout the next day or cross train.

Workout Plan

This is a series of five interval sets mostly in Zone 4 (80 percent to 90 percent). Warm up in Zone 2 for 5 minutes. Increase heart rate to Zone 3 from 5 to 7 minutes with easy, smooth pedaling, keeping your legs loose and relaxed. From 7 to 10 minutes, increase your heart rate 10 beats or to the middle of Zone 3. Ten minutes into the workout you will increase your heart rate to the bottom of Zone 4 and maintain for 2 minutes. Keep a fast spin, saving the resistance for the hills coming up.

Beginning at minute 12 you have 3 sets of 2-minute hill climbs to the middle of Zone 4 with 1-minute recoveries to the bottom of Zone 4 (this is about a 10-beat interval). The work to recovery ratio is 2:1. Be careful you don't go below Zone 4 on your 1-minute recovery. The idea is to visualize three moderate hills while working on your leg strength.

Twenty-one minutes into the workout you begin a series of (3) 20-beat intervals from the bottom of Zone 4 to the bottom of Zone 5 and back down. Each work interval is 2 minutes and the recoveries are 1 minute. Again, work on leg strength by adding resistance while keeping your tempo (cadence) steady. Gradually work your way to the bottom of Zone 5 in the 2-minute period then take the resistance off, spinning your legs fast on the 1-minute recoveries.

The next series of hills are (3) 40-beat intervals from the bottom of Zone 3 to the top of Zone 4. The work interval is 2 minutes and the recovery is 2 minutes. These intervals are all-out efforts. Sprint your way to the top of Zone 4 and sustain for 2 minutes. Try to get there as quickly as possible, then level off and sustain until the 2 minutes is over, then recover back down to the bottom of Zone 3 with easy pedaling.

If fatigue hasn't set in, it will soon. The hardest part is always left for last. At 42 minutes you begin a slow climb to your peak heart rate (highest heart rate number for the session) followed by 10 minutes of anaerobic threshold training. From 42 to 44 minutes sustain your heart rate at the bottom of Zone 4. Add 10 beats to your heart rate from minute 44 to 46. You may want to stand at this point to increase your heart rate and recruit different muscles. From minute 46 to 48 increase your heart rate to the bottom of Zone 5, mentally preparing yourself to sprint from minute 48 to 49. Here is your chance to go for your peak heart rate.

At minute 49, drop your heart rate down to the bottom of Zone 5 for 1 minute and sustain it. Drop another 5 beats from 50 to 51 minutes.

This is when it gets tough. Your body and mind want to recover but instead you increase your heart rate 5 beats back to the bottom of Zone 5 for 1 minute then drop 5 beats for 1 minute. Repeat one more time.

At 55 minutes, drop 10 beats, at 56 minutes, drop 10 more beats for 2 minutes, then your final drop is into Zone 2 for a warm-down.

Seattle Ridge

Elapsed Time in Minutes	Coaching notes	Zone	Your HR numbers	Duration
0–5	Warm up to the bottom of Z2	2	_____	5 min.
5–10	Increase HR gradually to the mid-point of Z3 using rpm's.	3	_____	5 min.
10–14	(10-beat interval). Increase HR to the bottom of Z4 for 2 min., steady tempo, increase with (R). Increase HR to the mid-point of Z4 (85%) for 2 min., steady tempo, increase with (R). Seated	4 4	_____ _____	4 min.
14–21	(Rec) to the bottom of Z4 for 1 min., easy pedal, increase HR to mid-point of Z4 for 2 min. using (R), steady tempo. Repeat	4 4	_____ _____	7 min.
21–30	(20-beat interval). Increase HR from the bottom of Z4 to the bottom of Z5 in 2 min., using (R), steady tempo. Recover to the bottom of Z4 in 1 min., easy spin. Repeat a total of 3 times	5 4	_____ _____	9 min.
30–42	(40-beat interval). Increase HR to the bottom of Z5 in 2 min., sprint with (R). (Rec) to the bottom of Zone 3 in 2 min., easy pedal. Repeat a total of 3 times	5 3	_____ _____	12 min.
42–44	Increase HR to the bottom of Z4, choice	4	_____	2 min.
44–46	Increase HR 10 beats to mid-point of Z4	4	_____	2 min.
46–48	Increase HR to the bottom of Z5, choice	5	_____	2 min.
48–49	All out sprint for "Peak HR"	5	_____	1 min.
49–55	Drop to the bottom of Z5 for 1 min., drop 5 bpm for 1 min., add 5 bpm for 1 min., choice. Repeat (drop 5 bpm and add 5 bpm interval) a total of 3 times	5 4	_____ _____	6 min.
55–60	Drop 10 beats every min., warm down		_____	5 min.
	Total HZT Points 224			

Outdoor Training

S.O.S.

"Spin," optimal power and sprint (SOS) are the three intervals to remember for this ride. It's really maximum sustainable power we are talking about, but we'll call it optimal power for ease of remembering what to do on the ride. These three interval sets can be worked into most any ride you are doing. For the first interval spin you will want to be completely warmed up and have picked a nice long, flat stretch in the road. The purpose is to work on your pedal stroke by increasing your cadence 10 rpm every 10 seconds starting with 70 rpm and finishing at 110 rpm. Start in an easy gear (small chain ring) and keep your pedal stroke smooth and round. Pedal circles rather than squares, concentrating on scraping mud off the bottom of your shoe as the pedal goes around at the bottom of the stroke. Recover to the bottom of Zone 2 and immediately begin another set. Repeat five times total.

Cyclists train to develop "power" and to sustain a high power output. This next interval set will help to do just that. Again, you will need a fairly flat stretch of road where you can ride for at least 10 minutes without interruptions or hills. Choose the biggest gear you can ride in at 110 rpm. Sustain this cadence and gearing for 1 minute followed by a 1-minute recovery. Repeat one more time. As you get fitter, work your way up to sustaining this interval for 3 minutes with a 3-minute recovery and then repeat. This will take you well into Zone 4 if it is done right. As you get fitter you will also notice your recovery heart rate dropping faster because your heart is getting stronger. You will also be able to push a bigger gear at the same cadence which means your muscles are getting stronger.

The third interval is a "sprint." These sprints are all done in a standing position, which will help your balance and confidence. Look for another 10 minute flat stretch in the road. In an easy gear, bring your speed up to 10 to 20 miles per hour. Come out of the saddle in a standing position for 10 seconds at a high cadence or pedal speed, then sit down and recover for 10 seconds. Repeat as many times as you can, building toward a total of 5 minutes. Finish by recovering down to Zone 2 with an easy pedal. This interval set will get your HR well into Zone 4.

Remember, SOS is a ride to improve your overall fitness.

Sign Here! Press Hard!

This is a fun game to play and one that my friend Duane loves to include when things get a little slow. He will pick out a sign anywhere from 200 to 300 yards away and challenge anyone to beat him to it. Ready, set, go! It's the pedal to the metal and a fun way to work on your sprints and fast starts. If you are just a "little" competitive you will want to make the game the best three out of five sprints. Duane always catches me off guard on the first one and I like to think I get smarter and faster on the next ones. Just make sure the signs aren't stop signs and give yourself plenty of recovery between sprints. Plan on seeing some big heart rate numbers on this one especially if the sprints are longer than 300 yards.

How to Buy a Heart Rate Monitor

When buying a monitor, you'll find a long list of features that you should consider aside from the three basic types discussed earlier. Since more than two dozen manufacturers worldwide produce heart rate monitors, it's impossible to list the features and the models of each. This short list of features, however, can make a difference in keeping you riding with your heart:

Heart zones. Allows you to program at least one heart zone's ceiling and floor and provides an audible signal or visual display telling you if you are within, above or below that range. Advanced features include time in zone, which after finishing the ride gives you the amount of time you spent within, above or below the zone you programmed. More advanced monitors provide multiple heart zones.

Watch. Shows you the time of day. Usually includes an alarm function.

Percentage of maximum heart rate. Displays at what percentage of your maximum heart rate you are performing at that moment.

Memory. Stores information throughout the ride for later review or downloading. Also known as recall function.

Hill Sprints

Hills are our friends. They, like head winds, make us stronger! It's all a matter of attitude and what your training goals are. If you want to be stronger, then sooner or later hills will be in the plan. You can expect your heart rate to go well into Zone 4 even Zone 5 if you are giving it your best effort. It also will depend on the length of the hill. The longer the hill for these sprints, the higher the heart rate.

Find a gradual hill 200 to 400 yards long. Spin halfway up then shift into the big chainring and sprint over the top. Try two to five repeats with complete recovery between efforts. Over time as you get stronger shift to harder gears in the back and stay with your big chainring in the front. Always try to finish your last repeat strong as if you were sprinting for the finish line.

Stopwatch. Records the elapsed time during your ride. May provide lap functions that include heart rate with the lap.

Average heart rate. When you start your stopwatch, records the time and heart rate to later provide you with your average during that time period.

Computer interfaceable. Monitors that download heart rate data through several different transmission methods to enable manipulation by computer software for advanced information.

Almost all monitors today are water-resistant, mount easily on your handlebars and offer backlighting. The technology for heart rate monitors is rapidly changing. Some models display calories burned, provide fitness testing, fitness analysis and improvement, and help you determine your training heart zones on a daily basis.

This may seem like a lot of features to consider, but the basic continuous-read model can work well for the beginning cyclist. This monitor has no buttons, no programs, no time of day or alarms. It just tells you your heart rate for a low purchase price. Buying one with too many features can be so overwhelming that you don't use it, making it less useful than the simplest type.

Heart Rate Monitor Myths

A heart rate monitor is not the Holy Grail, although some athletes live, breathe and swear by theirs. They never work out without one, and if they were forced to train without it, their symptoms would be similar to those of addicts in withdrawal.

Below are a few problems that might be helpful for you to recognize as you use a monitor so you can maximize its effectiveness.

Inconsistency. Your heart rate has a great deal of beat-to-beat as well as minute-to-minute variability because it's controlled as much by the involuntary nervous system as by the volitional one. Day-to-day variability is also sizeable, influenced by environmental factors such as stress, ambient temperatures, altitude, hydration, sleep patterns, nutrition and training intensities. If you see variations in your heart rate numbers, don't be surprised. It's not the monitor, it's you.

Research. Exercise scientists and coaches generally agree that training with a heart monitor improves performance, but verifying research is lacking. The term "going naked" or intentionally shunning the use of a monitor has become popular in a number of sports by athletes who insist they perform equally well without the technology as with it.

Laboratory versus the real world. Exercise physiologists agree that oxygen utilization (VO_2) is directly related to heart rate, but they disagree about relying on that same relationship when athletes perform in competitive situations versus the results they can report in laboratory settings. It appears that heart rates in performance far exceed those predictable from laboratory testing, especially at intensities above 85 percent of maximum heart rate. Some are thus led to ask whether heart rate is a valid measurement tool for exercise intensity.

Comprehension. In advanced models of heart rate monitors and their companion software programs, the programming of the hardware and understanding of the software is beyond the scope of most coaches and athletes. Reading the accompanying manuals for many of the monitors is likewise difficult and laborious. Many have found themselves seriously afflicted by information overload from downloaded monitor information. For those who can interpret the data correctly, the final step—how to use the data to change the training dosage—may also pose a challenge.

Response time. Heart rate monitors use complicated algorithms, or mathematical equations, to determine the number that's displayed on the face of the watch-like device. There is a certain lag time in both the heart's response to a change in exercise intensity and the monitor's algorithmic calculation of that number. For example, if you were warmed up and sprinted 100 yards on your bike, you might be breathing at maximum respiratory and heart rate, but your monitor would not read that absolute number because of the lag time in both heart rate and the nature of how heart rate monitors collect and process the heart rate numbers.

Group training. Have you ever tried to do your workout with a training partner and a couple of heart rate monitors? Have you noticed that at first it's a struggle to decide whose heart rate and whose pace to follow? That's because in group training situations, it's hard to do your own workout and not the group's. This is most often true in cycling. If you're riding in a group and you don't feel comfortable riding in close proximity to others who are riding fast, using a heart rate monitor has limited application. When riding in a pack in a race, bike handling skills and drafting to maintain bike speed are more important than staying at the right heart rate.

Fixation. Some riders stare more at their heart rate monitors than they do at road conditions or obstacles such as cars. In a recent Danskin race, one racer staring at her bike monitor hit a parked car due to monitor fixation. Common sense should tell you that knowing your heart rate numbers is less important than riding safely on your bike.

CHAPTER 9

Putting It All Together

Training is, as you've heard repeatedly, an individual process. You'll now apply this principle as you journey through the 10 steps to training with your heart monitor. On one level the 10 steps are quite simple; on another level it takes you into the individual process of riding at your best.

Richard Epstine was captivated by this potential. A 48-year-old mathematically minded man, Richard struggles constantly with the limits of time. He only has 30 minutes a day to ride and squeezes the most out of every training heartbeat. He's completed more than 1000 Heart Zone training sessions, all on an indoor cycle, with a manually downloadable heart rate monitor.

What's significant isn't Richard's ability to persist and keep track of five years of workouts with his monitor, and remain totally motivated, but that with only 30 minutes of daily workout—2.5 hours of training time a week—he's getting fitter. Furthermore, Richard can measure and prove it using his monitor.

At first I questioned whether such improvement was possible with such a low time investment, but after seeing the graphs and analyzing his data, I'm convinced Richard's fitness levels are progressively improving. His intensive recording and analysis occasionally astonish me, but for Richard it works. Using his monitor makes him happy. He's excited about writing goals, tracking changes and sharing his work with others. Recently, he outlined a new hypothesis he'll test for a year. His goal for this year is to prove that the heart zones are progressive. He believes that by training entirely in heart zone 3 through heart zone 5, he will get the benefits of living in heart zone 1 through heart zone 5. I look forward to monitoring his results.

—Sally Edwards

REVIEW OF THE 10 STEPS TO HEART ZONE TRAINING FOR CYCLING

Richard prefers keeping records in pencil and placing them in binders. Others record them in the companion log that accompanies this book, *The Heart Rate Monitor Logbook for Outdoor and Indoor Cyclists.* We also have provided you with a free CD-ROM interactive software program to automate your recordkeeping. All these options will help motivate your training.

Let's now extract from earlier chapters the information to assemble your cycle training program. You've already done the work; this is just where you'll assemble it. You might want to resist this and skip this section; please don't. Finish the brief process of putting together the 10 Steps. If you feel it takes too much time, consider that it takes more time not to complete the worksheet. Invest the effort now and it will pay off in improved fitness and a sense of accomplishment.

Step 1. Determining your maximum heart rate

Chapter 1, page 8, bpm _____.

Step 2. Setting your heart zones

Chapter 2, page 29.

Zone number	Percentage of maximum heart rate	Your Heart Zones
Zone 5. Redline Zone	90–100%	- bpm
Zone 4. Threshold Zone	80–90%	- bpm
Zone 3. Aerobic Zone	70–80%	- bpm
Zone 2. Temperate Zone	60–70%	- bpm
Zone 1. Healthy Heart Zone	50–60%	- bpm

Step 3. Choosing your goals

Chapter 2, page 37.

Goal-writing is an important step because if you haven't set a clear destination, it's very hard to get there! Most of us ride and train to accomplish something new. Review your goals and again list them briefly here.

Short-term goals: _____

Long-term goals: _____

Step 4. Determining your weekly riding times

Chapter 3, page 54.

To get fit, you need to ride in different zones on different rides. Some days your ride will be high intensity, high heart zone rides. Others will be recovery days. It's this variability, this commitment to taking the monotony out of your rides that's going to stimulate your increased fitness.

Take the time you have committed to riding and put it into the different heart zones:

Sample Training Program

Month	Zone 1 Healthy Heart	Zone 2 Temperate	Zone 3 Aerobic	Zone 4 Threshold	Zone 5 Redline	Total Workout Time
		WEEKLY TIME IN ZONE				
1	30	30	0	0	0	60
2	55	65	0	0	0	120
3	40	120	20	0	0	180
4	30	140	30	0	0	200
5	20	160	50	0	0	230
6	15	175	80	0	0	270
7	0	190	90	0	0	280
8	0	185	105	0	0	290
9	0	180	120	0	0	300
10	0	175	140	0	0	315
11	0	165	165	0	0	330
12	0	180	180	0	0	360

Step 5. Determining your training spokes

Chapter 3, page 62.

Have you filled out your Training Wheel?

Step 6. Determining your current cycle fitness level

Chapter 4, page 83.

Here is where you determine how fit you are now. You can find your current fitness level by taking some training rides and measuring a few parameters.

STEP 7. Writing a training plan

Chapter 6, page 127.

Make a plan to accomplish the goals you set in Step 3. Your success will bring a sense of accomplishment and improved self-esteem.

STEP 8. Analyzing your training plan

Chapter 6, page 130.

Is your plan realistic? If so, it will keep you on your bike, motivated and getting faster.

STEP 9. Logging your workouts

Chapter 8, page 178.

All the tools for recording your workout are provided here. You'll author a book about yourself and riding your bike, filling it with a year's worth of riding information and impressions of your growth and development as an athlete.

STEP 10. Assessing your fitness

Chapter 4, page 83.

You've now come full circle. One of your early steps was to determine how fit you were on your bike. If your training program is working, it's easy to measure with a heart rate monitor and possibly a bike computer. Repeat the fitness assessments listed in Chapter 4 and apply your monitor and your body in your own personal exercise laboratory. We're interested in your progress. It's easy to reach us through one of our Web sites: www.HeartZone.com or www.HeartCycling.com.

RIDING INTO THE FUTURE

Isn't there always one last thing? Think about the possibility of riding and staying fit the rest of your life. The road to sustainable wellness is right here, in the form of your individual plans.

Think about riding into the future as a long-term commitment. For competitive riders, this is called an annualized approach. For a fitness rider, it's called riding forever, one year at a time. In this approach, you take a full year and divide it into its different logical parts. For most riders, this is based on the seasons—in the cold months we tend to train more indoors and in the warmer periods we ride more outside. Group rides and races are based on the seasons of the year, so building your training on a seasonal annualized system makes the most sense.

An annualized approach provides for different phases, blocks or periods of training—building your base, strengthening, getting faster for longer rides and then enjoying a recovery phase on the bike. It's for you to decide how many phases are in your training system.

Annualized training adds variety to your training. As we've discussed, variety stimulates improvement, so the more you can include in your training program—different bike modes, indoor/outdoor, new routes, changing partners, food options—the more these changes can lead to enhanced fitness. They provide a positive stimulus and a positive response that leads to the all-so-important training effect.

Exercise scientist and researcher Darvin McBrayer of Baylor University coined the term "functional wellness" to describe the ability to function on a higher level of health. To Darvin, that means increasing your metabolic rates, the number of calories you are burning just being. In assessing you he would measure your blood chemistry to see if your stress byproducts are at healthy levels. Ultimately, whether you are a beginner or a competitive rider, isn't this the true goal—to live a happier and healthier life with more energy and less stress?

The road to this paragraph may seem like a long one because you've learned so much. You understand a new and different way of riding that involves the emotional and physical parts of training. You have all the tools you need to take your heart, your most important muscle, on an incredible life journey on your bike. When you put your two hearts together—the heart that pumps blood and the heart that enhances the joy of riding—you've found the road to lifetime wellness. That's the road to ride.

TEN COMMON HEART MONITOR CONCERNS AND MISTAKES

Everyone makes mistakes, so it's always helpful to learn from those made by others. Here are Sally Edwards's responses to common concerns about heart monitors to help you in your training:

1. My heart rate monitor is broken; it's always displaying too high a number.

I hear this from those who love to train in the high, hard heart zones—cyclists who only know how to hammer on their bike, constantly pushing the pace and who are unfamiliar with recovery riding. Most of the time I find that the heart rate monitor works fine; the human needs to slow down to get fitter and faster.

2. The longer I ride at the same speed, the higher my heart rate soars.

This common phenomenon is called cardiac drift (Chapter 4). When you ride, especially in the heat, dehydration decreases your blood volume, increasing your heart rate unless you drink fluids to stay hydrated.

3. When I first start to ride, my heart rate jumps above 150 bpm but I don't perceive that I am riding at that heart rate.

This is difficult to explain. I often ride with others who share that experience and the only thing I can say is that your monitor is correct. Eliminate mechanical problems with the monitors such as too loose a chest strap. Riding too close to others so that the monitors "cross talk" can sometimes add the heart rate number of the person next to you to that of your own heart.

4. Sometimes I can't get a reading.

Usually this is caused by a problem with your transmission range. The monitor and chest strap must be within 32 inches of each other for the connection to be strong enough to sense. If you use aero' bars and your monitor is on your wrist more than 32 inches from your chest, it will go blank because the monitor is too far from the chest strap.

5. I can't push the right buttons for the right functions.

We all get frustrated with learning how to program our heart rate monitor. The answer is to spend the time to read your owner's manual and memorize your monitor's functions. For the most complicated monitors, it can take up to three hours of reading the booklets and practicing with the monitor to learn the proper use of the buttons. Be patient.

6. I want to get only my average

People ask, "I know my average heart rate during my training interval, but the reading includes my warm-up and warm-down heart rates, so how do I get my average without having it distorted by these lower values?"

My suggestion is that you wear a sports watch on your wrist and bike or heart rate monitor on your handlebars. Use the sports watch to measure elapsed time; start the stopwatch function on the monitor when you begin the main part of your workout. Since the monitor is averaging every heartbeat, it records only when the stopwatch is running, giving you only the data you want. If this is too much trouble, maybe it's time to invest in a higher-end monitor that allows you to see separate averages for your warm-up, cool-down and intervals.

7. Is using my heart rate monitor the same as measuring power output?

It would be valuable to know how many watts of power you generate when you ride. To do this, you need a special gauge, sometimes mounted inside the rear hub of your wheel. These are expensive, around $600–$1000. However, a heart rate monitor, particularly if it's a bike monitor (altitude, heart rate, distance and speed) can furnish most of the information that you need to quantify your training experience.

8. I bought a monitor that's too difficult for me to figure out.

Most people find that there are certain features on a monitor that they appreciate. The problem is that when you buy one for the first time, you don't know what those will be. Most of us want to wear our monitor as a watch, but it wasn't until recently that manufacturers reduced the size and electronics to make monitors comfortable for all-day wear and cosmetic appeal. Try to learn all of the features on your monitor and see if you can't increase your understanding of its functions. Also remember that you don't have to immediately master features you might not need right away.

9. I notice a great deal of daily variation in my heart rate.

Your heart rate monitor is telling you about your physical and emotional stress at the moment. Your heart rate varies a great deal as your body subtly responds to ambient changes. If you take medication, if you are in different climates, if you change altitude or diet or sleep patterns, these will all affect your heart rate.

10. I download information from my monitor to my computer, but I don't know what it means.

You certainly aren't alone. Sometimes computer software is difficult to understand. Engineers tend to create software based on what a piece of hardware can do, regardless of whether the user needs that information. Keep track of the information that's important and significant to accomplishing your goals. Period.

WORKOUTS

Indoor Training

Lancelot

Fitness 60-75 percent

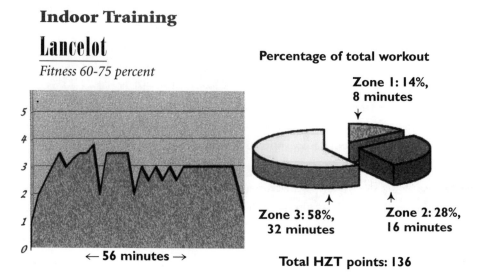

Percentage of total workout

Zone 1: 14%, 8 minutes

Zone 3: 58%, 32 minutes

Zone 2: 28%, 16 minutes

← 56 minutes →

Total HZT points: 136

This 56-minute workout is named after one of the greatest cyclists ever, Lance Armstrong. His amazing comeback from cancer and his determination to beat the odds have provided inspiration for so many people. Lance is one in a million physiologically but we average folks can still take advantage of his training techniques and realize great success in reaching our goals and overcoming challenges.

Purpose

There are four major training goals in this ride. The first is building muscular strength and endurance with low rpm and moderate to heavy resistance or gearing. The second goal is developing power using power starts from a standing position to simulate a quick start or jump. These are done from a slow "spin" with heavy resistance or using a big gear. The third goal is anaerobic threshold training, picking the highest heart rate you can sustain for a 12-minute period. The higher the number you can sustain typically the fitter you are. The fourth is neurological training for your legs, or training to spin fast. It's also an opportunity to work on your pedal stroke. This is one of those workouts that can be increased a zone to make it even more challenging for the fittest athlete. If you decide to increase the intervals by a zone, your total HZT points jump from 136 to almost 200.

Workout Plan

The first 10 minutes is a warm up to the bottom of Zone 2 with an easy pedal.

At 10 minutes into the workout, the strength and endurance training begins with an increase in heart rate by 10 beats to the mid-point of Zone 2 using resistance or gearing. Maintain a steady tempo rpm of 55-60 rpm (5–6) for the entire interval set. Increase heart rate 10 more beats at minute 12 and minute 14, taking you to the middle of Zone 3 (75 percent). Recover to the bottom of Zone 2 for 2 minutes.

Eighteen minutes into the workout begin the second interval set of power starts. These are done from a standing, sprinting position and consist of 10 seconds of hard effort in a big gear or heavy resistance followed by 20 seconds of easy pedaling with no resistance or an easy gear. Alternate lead leg on each start. This is repeated for a total of 14 times followed by a 3-minute recovery to the bottom of Zone 2. You may choose to sit on the recoveries or alternate positions. This entire interval set is done in Zone 3. If you find 14 times are too much, then do as many as you can.

Forty-four minutes into the workout the third interval set begins with anaerobic threshold training. You may choose any heart rate you think you can sustain for 12 minutes. Remember, the fitter you are typically the higher your anaerobic threshold is as a percentage of maximum heart rate. As a guideline, a sedentary person's anaerobic threshold may be anywhere from 60 percent to 70 percent of their maximum heart rate. A fit person's anaerobic threshold may be anywhere from 70 percent to 85 percent of their maximum heart rate and a super-fit person may be as high as 85 percent to 95 percent of their maximum heart rate. You need to decide where you think you are and give it your best effort. Any time you are testing your anaerobic threshold, make sure you are fully rested and hydrated. This should be your first and perhaps only workout for the day. Drink plenty of water during and after this workout and give your body 24 to 48 hours to fully recover. Mentally, you will want to stop after this anaerobic threshold interval but…you have one more and this one is important.

The fourth interval is "spin ups" and these will help remove the lactic acid you may have built up in your muscles during the anaerobic threshold interval. Beginning at 44 minutes into the workout from the bottom of Zone 3 with an rpm of 70 (7), gradually increase rpm over 30 seconds until you are pedaling at 120 rpm (12). Follow with an easy pedaling recovery for 30 seconds. Repeat a total of 3 times.

At 47 minutes switch to alternating legs, doing a 30-second spin up with the left leg to 120 rpm, recover for 30 seconds then switch to the right leg. Repeat a total of 4 times. Adjust resistance or gearing to maintain your heart rate in Zone 3.

Warm-down into Zone 2 and 1 with easy pedaling.

Lancelot

Elapsed Time in Minutes	Coaching notes	Zone	Your HR numbers	Duration
0–5	Warm up in Z1	1	_____	5 min.
5–10	Easy spin to the bottom of Z2	2	_____	5 min.
10–16	Increase HR 10 beats every 2 min. with (R), steady tempo 50–60 rpm (5–6)	2 3	_____	6 min.
16–18	Sustain bottom of Z3	3	_____	2 min.
18–26	Standing power starts. 10 sec. heavy (R) all out from a slow spin with 20 sec. easy pedal (rec). Repeat a total of 14 times	3	_____	8 min.
26–29	Easy pedal (rec) to the bottom of Z2	2	_____	3 min.
29–41	Anaerobic threshold training. Highest sustainable HR		_____	12 min.
41–44	Easy pedal (rec) to the bottom of Z2	2	_____	3 min.
44–47	Spin ups from 70 rpm (7) to 120 rpm (12) in 30 sec. with a 30 sec. (rec). Repeat a total of 3 times	2-3	_____	3 min.
47–51	Spin ups with isolated leg training. 30 sec. spin up with left leg, 30 sec. (rec) then switch right leg spin up 30 sec. with a 30 sec. (rec). Repeat a total of 4 times	3	_____	4 min.
51–56	Warm down with easy pedal to Z2 then Z1	2 1	_____ _____	5 min.
	Total HZT Points 136			

Note: For a performance workout, increase each interval by one zone.

Happy Feet
Fitness 60-95 percent

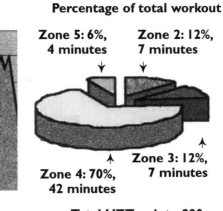

Percentage of total workout

Zone 5: 6%,   **Zone 2: 12%,**
4 minutes   **7 minutes**

Zone 3: 12%,
7 minutes

Zone 4: 70%,
42 minutes

← **60 minutes** →

Total HZT points: 220

Happy Feet, a song by the band "8-1/2 Souvenirs," was inspired by a CD with the same name. It's a play on words because this workout is meant to be fun yet challenging. When we "play" as adults and as kids, we disassociate the hard work from the performance or activity we are engaged in. In this 60-minute workout, time will literally fly and your feet will be anything but bored! As they say, "be happy!" It's all a matter of perspective.

Purpose

This workout has a lot of variety and opportunity to use your imagination. It's a good mind/body challenge because you are mentally focusing on incremental heart rate changes while your imagination transports you outdoors to steep hills and fast descents.

Your goal will be to raise your heart rate using a smooth, fast spin, concentrating on a quiet upper body and streamlined position. The heavy resistance hill climbs should be done with at least 60-rpm. The hills are for muscular strength and endurance and can be done in a standing or seated position. The sprint intervals can be done two ways: with high cadence and low resistance working on leg speed, or with a lower cadence and heavy resistance (bigger gear) developing strength and power.

Workout Plan

Begin with a 7-minute warm-up to the bottom of Zone 3 followed by a 3-minute 10-beat increase to the mid-point of Zone 3.

Minutes 10 through 15 work on leg speed and pedal stroke by increasing heart rate 5 beats every minute using cadence. Only add enough resistance to maintain a smooth pedal stroke and keep the hips from rocking. This will take your heart rate near the top of Zone 4. Decrease heartrate to the bottom of Zone 4 for 1 minute with easy pedaling.

The next 10-minute interval uses leg strength and a steady tempo to climb 5 beats every minute on your way into Zone 5 followed by a 5-beat drop in heart rate every minute to the bottom of Zone 4.

Twenty-six minutes into the workout you begin a series of five hill climbs. The first three hills are all done in Zone 4. From the bottom of Zone 4, heart rate is increased 5 beats with cadence and sustained for 2 minutes followed by a 1 minute, 10-beat, heavy resistance climb. Drop heart rate back to the bottom of Zone 4.

Next, visualize a 2-minute gradual hill that you spin up followed by a steep 1-minute section right before the top and an easy 1-minute pedal down the backside. This hill interval is repeated 2 more times.

The next two hills are the opposite of the first three. The hill is steep in the beginning and then flattens out toward the top. At 38 minutes into the workout, from the bottom of Zone 4, increase heart rate 10 beats in 1 minute using heavy resistance or gearing and a cadence of no less than 60 rpm. This is a steep, 1-minute section followed by 1 minute of fast spin, increasing the heart rate another 5 beats on your way over the top of the hill. Drop heart rate back down to the bottom of Zone 4 in 1 minute. Repeat this interval one more time and recover down to the bottom of Zone 3 for 2 minutes.

After a 2-minute recovery at the bottom of Zone 3 you begin a series of 30-second sprints and recoveries. These sprints are all done in Zones 4 and 5. The sprint interval is 10 minutes long and is very tough at the end when your legs are "dead" from the hill climbs. Hang in there if you can and you'll reap the benefits down the road. From the bottom of Zone 3 begin 30 seconds on (sprint) and 30 seconds off (recovery). Use a high cadence in the beginning and slowly start adding resistance or changing to a harder gear as you work your way up in intensity for this 10-minute interval.

Warm down gradually in an easy gear with very little resistance for 5 to 7 minutes.

Happy Feet!

Elapsed Time in Minutes	Coaching notes	Zone	Your HR numbers	Duration
0–7	Warm up gradually to the bottom of Z3	3	_____	7 min.
7–10	Increase HR 10 beats	3	_____	3 min.
10–15	From mid-point of Z3 increase HR 5 beats every	3	_____	5 min.
	min. by increasing cadence (rpm). Add (R) as	4	_____	
	needed			
15–16	Drop to the bottom of Z4 for 1 min.	4	_____	1 min.
16–26	From the bottom of Z4 add 5 beats every min.	4	_____	10 min.
	using (R). Steady tempo. Once you reach Z5	5	_____	
	drop 5 beats every min. to the bottom of Z4	4	_____	
26–38	A series of 3 hills. From the bottom of Z4 add	4	_____	12 min.
	5 beats with cadence for 2 min. then add 10	4	_____	
	beats with heavy (R) for 1 min. Drop HR down	4	_____	
	to bottom of Z4 for 1 min. Repeat 2 more			
	times			
38–43	Two hills. From the bottom of Z4 add 10 beats	4	_____	5 min.
	with heavy (R) for 1 min. then 5 more beats	4	_____	
	with fast cadence for 1 min., drop HR down to	4	_____	
	the bottom of Z4 for 1 min. Repeat			
43–45	(Rec) to the bottom of Z3 for 2 min.	3	_____	2 min.
45–53	(8) 30 second sprints with 30 second	3	_____	8 min.
	(rec) from the bottom of Z3 gradually increasing	5	_____	
	to the bottom of Z5			
53–60	Gradual warm down to the bottom of Z2	2	_____	7 min.
	Total HZT Points 220			

A Positive Spin

Fitness 60-85 percent

Percentage of total workout

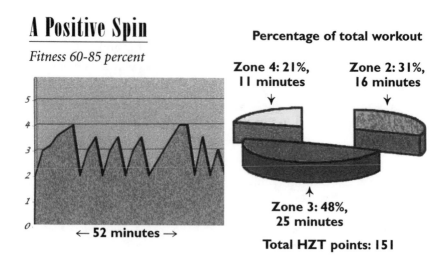

Zone 4: 21%, 11 minutes

Zone 2: 31%, 16 minutes

← 52 minutes →

Zone 3: 48%, 25 minutes

Total HZT points: 151

Being optimistic is a learned attitude and by starting the day thinking positively, we are more likely to be positive as the day progresses. This is good advice for our training, too. Approaching our workouts with a positive mental attitude and positive self-talk builds self-confidence and self-confidence breeds a winning attitude and success. Practicing positive self-talk helps keep a positive attitude when the going gets tough and your perseverance needs bolstering.

Purpose

This 52-minute workout provides the opportunity to practice positive self-talk, visualize your goals and put on a "positive spin" and "grin." There is a winning integration of strength, power and leg-speed intervals. The idea is to finish this workout feeling good about your effort and even better about yourself.

Workout Plan

Warm up to the bottom of Zone 2 for 5 minutes. Increase your heart rate gradually over the next 5 minutes to the bottom of Zone 3.

Ten minutes into the workout begin the first of (5) interval sets. This 12-minute pyramid climb begins at the bottom of Zone 3 (70 percent) and reaches the mid-point of Zone 4 (85 percent). From the bottom of Zone 3 the interval begins with a 30-second sprint and a

30-second recovery (1:1) followed by a 60-second sprint and a 30-second recovery (2:1). Next is a 90-second sprint with a 30-second recovery (3:1) and then the top of the pyramid with a 120-second sprint and 30 second recovery (4:1). Starting back down the ladder, the next interval is a 90-second sprint with a 30-second recovery then a 60-second sprint with a 30-second recovery, and finally a 30-second sprint with 30-second recovery. Finish with easy pedaling to the bottom of Zone 3 for 3 minutes.

Twenty-five minutes into the workout the second interval set begins. This is a series of (3) 1-minute sprints beginning with light and moving to moderate resistance, keeping the intensity at or below the mid-point of Zone 3 (75 percent). A 2-minute recovery follows to the bottom of Zone 2. Repeat a total of 3 times.

The third interval set begins 34 minutes into the workout. This set begins at the bottom of Zone 2 and peaks at the bottom of Zone 4. From the bottom of Zone 2, increase your heart rate to the mid-point of Zone 2 for 2 minutes with cadence. Then from the mid-point of Zone 2 increase your heart rate 10 more beats for 1 minute using moderate resistance and cadence. Increase another 10 bpm for 1 minute using a fast pedal and then a final 10-beat increase using heavy resistance and standing if needed. Sustain this heart rate for another minute then recover back down in intensity to the bottom of Zone 2 for 2 minutes.

The fourth interval set begins at 42 minutes with isolated leg training. Staying in the upper half of Zone 3, pedal with your right leg only using a cadence of 60 rpm (6) for 2 minutes then switch to your left leg for 2 minutes. Concentrate on pedaling with a smooth and round pedal stroke, adding just enough resistance to stay between 75 percent and 80 percent of maximum heart rate.

Finish the workout with a 3-minute spin-up starting at 60 rpm and increasing 10 rpm every 10 seconds until your reach 140-rpm (14) then decrease 10 rpm every 10 seconds until you reach 60 rpm.

Warm down into Zone 2.

A Positive Spin

Elapsed Time in Minutes	Coaching notes	Zone	Your HR numbers	Duration
0–5	Warm up to bottom of Z2	2	_____	5 min.
5–10	Increase HR to bottom of Z3	3	_____	5 min.
10–22	Pyramid climb (70%–85%) 30 sec. sprint/30	3	_____	12 min.
	sec (rec) (30/30), 60/30, 90/30, 120/30,	3	_____	
	90/30, 60/30, 30/30	4	_____	
		4	_____	
22–25	Recover (rec) to the bottom of Z2	2	_____	3 min.
25–34	3 min. (30 sec. fast pedal, bottom Z3 followed	3	_____	9 min.
	by 30 sec. moderate to heavy (R) to mid-point	2	_____	
	of Z3, 2 min. (rec) bottom of Z2). Repeat a			
	total of 3 times			
34–42	Add 10 bpm to the bottom of Z2, 2 min.	2	_____	8 min.
	From mid-point of Z3 add 10 bpm, moderate	3	_____	
	(R), 1 min. Add 10 bpm, fast pedal, 1 min.	3	_____	
	Add 10 bpm, heavy (R), 1 min. sustain 80%	4	_____	
	standing, 1 min. followed by a 2-min. (rec)	4	_____	
	bottom of Z2	2	_____	
42–46	ILT, 2 min. each leg. 60 rpm (6), heavy (R)	3	_____	4 min.
46–47	Easy pedal both legs	2	_____	1 min.
47–50	Spin ups 60-rpm (6) to 140-rpm (14) and	3	_____	3 min.
	back down. Increase 10 rpm every 10 seconds	2	_____	
50–52	Warm down bottom of Z2	2	_____	2 min.
	Total HZT Points 151			

Outdoor Training

Doublemint

Double your pleasure, double your fun! That's what this ride is all about. You are going to decide from the following list what you will "double" during your ride, then go out and try to do it!

Double:

• Resting HR (use this number "doubled" to warm up in for 15 to 20 minutes) as long as it's no more than 70 percent of maximum

heart rate
- Duration of the ride (if you normally ride 30 minutes double it and so on)
- Number of friends you ride with
- Cadence on hills. Instead of 60 rpm, try spinning your way up at 120 rpm
- Stand twice as long as you sit on hills or sit twice as long as you stand
- Pick a ride that has twice as many hills as you normally do
- Drink water twice as often as normal for you
- Hold 60 rpm at 60 percent of maximum heart rate for 6 minutes (6's). Try doubling the minutes, try doubling the rpm or both
- Hold 70 rpm at 70 percent of maximum heart rate for 7 minutes (7's). Try doubling the minutes, try doubling the rpm or both
- Hold 80 rpm at 80 percent of maximum heart rate for 8 minutes (8's). Try doubling the minutes (not for the beginner!)
- Hold 90 rpm at 90 percent of maximum heart rate for 9 minutes (9's). Try doubling the minutes (not for beginners).
- Maintain 85 to 90 percent effort in the biggest gear you can for 2 minutes, recover for 2 minutes, then double the minutes and recovery (4 & 4), then double the minutes again (8 & 8)
- 5 power starts…do 10
- 5 Spin ups…do 10
- Spend twice as much time in Zone 3 as all the other zones put together.
- Do 30-second sprints with 1 minute recoveries. Double it to 1-minute sprints, 2-minute recoveries. Double it to 2-minute sprints, 4-minute recoveries, repeat as many times as you can
- Find a "doubles" partner
- Make your rest/recovery time twice as much as your effort or work interval time
- If you do all of these you can afford to make two bakery stops as opposed to one!
- The idea is to be creative. Come up with your own "doubles" and challenge yourself!

Heart Zone Training is a universal training method that you can incorporate into any cardiovascular workout discipline. The system described here applies to cross country skiing, conditioning for team and individual sports—basketball, soccer, volleyball, bowling, football—inline skating, tennis, golf and most other activities.

Judy Stansbury and Deve Swain (www.HeartPhysicalEducation.com) read Sally Edwards's original heart rate monitor book and decided to universally apply it to their area of interest, school children. They've designed school-based programs for children to study in health classes, physical education classes and fitness courses. This new approach to a school-based application has gotten kids excited about exercise and technology, about themselves and their self-esteem because it's an individual approach to learning.

Horse training is being revolutionized through application of Heart Zone Training to equine fitness. Endurance, race and performance horses are being conditioned using heart rate monitor technology. Mike Nunnan of Pursuit Performance in Australia has trained thoroughbred horses that are winning the big prize purses in cash and breeding rights. Mike shares this information in his book Heart Rate Training for Horses and on his website: www.PursuitPerformance.co.au.

Heart Zone Training is international. The technology, finally more affordable, is sold in virtually every country. Seminars and conferences attended by both exercise scientists and fitness

"S" Squared

The goal is to improve your speed and your shifting at the same time. Your heart rate should range between Zone 2 and Zone 4 depending on how many shifts you make and how long you go.

Pick a section of road where you can pedal easily in your big chain ring and your easiest gear in back. Jump or accelerate quickly. Shift to a harder gear every 50 to 100 yards as you begin to spin out the gear. Aim for two to three shifts without losing speed. Finish in your hardest gear then recover to the bottom of Zone 2. Repeat four times during a ride to build sprint endurance as well as shifting technique.

enthusiasts are being held in countries like Switzerland and South Africa to inform the world about the heart rate monitor's applications as a stress monitor, fat-burning monitor and physical performance monitor.

Psychotherapists are applying Heart Zone Training to help clients become happier and solve their problems. Dan Rudd, Ph.D. writes in his forthcoming book More Energy, Less Stress: A Ten Week Program to Health and Fitness that "a heart rate monitor gives you the tool to be more loving with yourself through care of your physical and emotional heart". Learn from Dan's Web site, www.BlitzTraining.com.

Most Olympic athletes train with a heart monitor. Almost all high-level cyclists train with biofeedback data provided by their monitor to them or their coaches. Six-time Ironman triathlete Mark Allen, who admits to overdependence on his monitor, says "I've used the monitor in almost every running and cycling workout over the past eight years, and I love it." Five-time Tour de France winner Miguel Induráin used his monitor in each of his training workouts; his coaches downloaded the data every single day.

Although the monitor itself is only a tool, its application is powerful. Heart Zone Training works with any heart rate monitor, any model, for any sport or activity, every time you use it.

The Spoke n' Word

As the spokes spin faster the words become fewer! The temptation is to do this interval set at too high an intensity in the beginning by using hard gears. Pick easier gearing and think of this as a long, steady climb where talking will be at a minimum and focusing at a maximum. This interval set is between 20 and 30 minutes and you can repeat the set twice. Heart rate will range between Zone 2 and Zone 4 depending on gearing.

Warm up for 15 to 30 minutes and begin the interval set at approximately 90 rpm. Use the same gear for both the work interval and the rest interval. Small chainring on the front and your choice on the back. Increase rpm to 100 for 1 minute then rest for 1 minute by decreasing rpm to 90. Repeat interval 10 to 15 times. You may choose to use a harder gear and increase rpm from 100 to 110. The work and rest intervals may also change to 2 minutes each.

Riding with both your emotional and physical heart leads to improved performance.

Appendix A

HEART CYCLING WORKOUTS

Max HR	50—70%	60—80%	60—90%			
Workout	Healthy Heart	Fitness	Performance	HZT Points	Total Minutes	Page
Change of Heart	X			68	33	
Criss Cross Z1 & Z2	X			31	20	
Recovery Intervals	X			64	30	
Peak-a-boo	X	X		84	30	
Talk Is Cheap	X	X		84	30	
5 x 2	X	X		122	45	
Lancelot	X	X		69	33	
Heartbeat		X		149	50	
Ladder to Success		X		136	56	
30 Beat Interval		X		62	30	
A Positive Spin		X		151	52	
Fast Lane		X		156	55	
Criss Cross Z2 & Z3		X		119	45	
The Zipper		X	X	154	50	
Tailwind		X	X	209	62	
Afterburner		X	X	181	53	
Seattle Ridge			X	224	60	
Spentervals			X	183	53	
Red Shift			X	198	55	
At, About, Around			X	227	60	
Winner's Circle			X	186	57	
Happy Feet			X	223	60	
Pumped			X	194	58	
30-20-10			X	169	60	
2 x 20			X	242	65	
Top Spin			X	194	60	

Appendix B

OUTDOOR TRAINING

Workout	50—70% of max Healthy Heart	60—80% of max HR Fitness	60—90 % of max HR Performance	Page
The ObservationTrip	X	X		22
Steady State Pace Ride	X	X		22
Noodling	X			123
Doublemint	X	X	X	212
Steady Eddy	X	X		77
Aerobic Time Trial	X	X		124
Criss Cross Zone 3		X		164
Saturday Night Fever		X		170
The Recovery Interval Ride		X	X	22
S.O.S.		X	X	192
Crusin'		X	X	77
Paceline Ride		X	X	96
The Pyramid Scheme		X	X	98
5 x 5		X	X	123
Need for Speed		X	X	146
The Heat Is On		X	X	146
S Squared		X	X	214
The Spoke n' Word		X	X	215
Rock 'n' Roll		X	X	170
Distance Improvement Ride		X	X	77
Biggest Number Ride		X		45
The All-out Trip		X		196
Maximum Heart Rate Hill Sprints		X		48
The All-out Time Trial		X		95
Anaerobic Threshold Ride		X		143
Sign Here, Press Hard		X		194
Hill Sprints		X		48

Appendix C

HEART ZONE TRAINING POINT SYSTEM

The Heart Zone Training point system is truly one of the first times an athlete, coach or trainer can quantify workload. By using a heart rate monitor, it is now relatively easy to measure individual training load.

The Heart Zone Training point system uses the quantification of frequency as the number of workouts per week, intensity as measured by numerical heart zones and time in each zone to determine daily, weekly and monthly points.

Heart zones have weight. The higher the heart zone the heavier the exercise stress. To determine your weekly heart zone training points or training load, simply multiply the number of workouts per week (frequency) times the number of the zone (intensity) times the number of minutes (time).

F x I x T = Training load

Example: 6 workouts x Zone 3 x 30 minutes = 540 Heart Zone Training points

What is the maximum number of points? What is a healthy number of points? What is the ideal number of points? The answer is, it is totally individual and it depends. Each person has an individual workload threshold or a quantifiable amount of exercise they can sustain. Heart zone training points may range from 300 points a week to more than 3000. Higher points don't mean you are a better athlete, or faster or fitter, but that your tolerance of exercise quantity is higher. Workload thresholds vary greatly among individuals. Sally Edwards trained more than 3000 points a week prior to her 15th Ironman while others trained at lower points. Some athletes trained at higher points than that.

Athletes can use Heart Zone Training Points to predict when they will be at their peak performance level or when they are training to the point of injury or overtraining. By calculating training load accurately, you will get better results with your training. It is your responsibility to train at different weekly point levels to determine just how much, how hard and how long you as an individual can train.

Appendix D

COMPARING ADVANTAGES AND
DISADVANTAGES OF
INDOOR AND OUTDOOR CYCLING

INDOOR CYCLING		OUTDOOR CYCLING	
POSITIVES	NEGATIVES	POSITIVES	NEGATIVES
Uses the same muscles as outdoor	Program fee	Muscular strength and endurance	Cost of bike and equipment
Similar body position, no flat tires	Bike fit and anaerobic	Interval training, aerobic technique	Equipment failure, flat tires
Interval training, aerobic and anaerobic	Difficult for de-conditioned	Easy on joints	Traffic, roads, potholes
No sun or wind	Cost of trainer for home	Fresh air, scenery	Rain and wind
Multiple zones	Can be boring at times	Social	Bugs
Social		Coed	Dogs
Music		Balance and bicycle handling skills	Crashing, bills, safety
Most bang for the buck		Sunshine	Heat, sunburn
Sweat a lot	Sweat on the floor or carpet	Fun	
Coed		Drafting	
Non-competitive		Adventure	

Appendix E

SYNOPSIS OF ACSM REPORT

Summary "The Recommended Quantity and Quality of Exercise for Developing and Maintaining Cardiorespiratory and Muscular Fitness and Flexibility in Healthy Adults." Volume 30, Number 6, June 1998.

This pronouncement was written for the American College of Sports Medicine by Michael L. Pollock, Ph.D., FACSM, Glenn A. Gaesser, Ph.D., FACSM, Janus D. Butcher, M.D., FACSM, Jean-Pierre

Despres, Ph.D., Rod K. Dishman, Ph.D., FACSM, Barry A. Franklin, Ph.D., FACSM, and Carol Ewing Garber, Ph.D., FACSM.

The combination of frequency, intensity and duration of chronic exercise has been found to be effective for producing a training effect. The interaction of these factors provides the overload stimulus. In general, the lower the stimulus the lower the training effect, and the greater the stimulus the greater the effect. As a result of specificity of training and the need for maintaining muscular strength and endurance and flexibility of the major muscle groups, a well-rounded training program including aerobic and resistance training and flexibility exercises is recommended. Although age in itself is not a limiting factor to exercise training, a more gradual approach in applying the prescription at older ages seems prudent. It has also been shown that aerobic endurance training of fewer than two days a week at less than 40-50 percent of VO_2R, and less than 10 minutes, is generally not a sufficient stimulus for developing and maintaining fitness in healthy adults. Even so, many health benefits from physical activity can be achieved at lower intensities of exercise if frequency and duration of training are increased appropriately. In this regard, physical activity can be accumulated through the day in shorter bouts of 10-minute durations.

In the interpretation of this position, it must be recognized that the recommendations should be used in the context of participants' needs, goals and initial abilities. In this regard, a sliding scale as to the amount of time allotted and intensity of effort should be carefully gauged for the cardiorespiratory, muscular strength and endurance, and flexibility components of the program. An appropriate warm-up and cool-down period that would include flexibility exercise is also recommended. The important factor is to design a program for the individual to provide the proper amount of physical activity to attain maximal benefit at the lowest risk. Emphasis should be placed on factors that result in permanent lifestyle change and encourage a lifetime of physical activity.

Appendix F
HISTORY AND THE FUTURE OF HEART RATE MONITORS

Monitoring the heart has been a common practice for thousands of years. The early Chinese physicians first used the technique for diagnosing health. Accurate measurements of heart rate manually—called manual pulse palpation—are less reliable and accurate. For purposes of training, testing and biofeedback research, accuracy is extremely important in heart rate monitoring.

Monitoring your heart with a heart rate monitor first began in 1978 when Tunturi, a Scandinavian equipment manufacturer, released the "Pulser," developed by Polar Electro Oy. This primitive grandparent to today's sleek, small watch- like monitors was hardwired from the chest strap to the wrist monitor. It was big and bulky, but it worked.

Five years later, Polar introduced to the world the first wireless monitor called the PE 2000. Manufactured in Hong Kong by Dayton Industries and developed in the Department of Electronics at the University of Oulu, these early monitors were targeted for coaches, athletes and researchers to enhance their knowledge, skills and performances. The use of the medically accurate and fragile Holter monitors or portable but unwieldy electrocardiogram (ECG) apparatus was impractical. Today, the use of heart rate monitors has been expanded and used for health, fitness and wellness applied in dozens of ways such as:

• Physical and health education classes in the school
• Training of racing and performance horses and veterinarians
• Weight management
• Health professionals: doctors and physical therapists
• Cardiac rehabilitation
• Stress management
• Athletic clubs: imbedded in exercise equipment
• Corporate fitness and training

• Sports disciplines: running, triathlon, basketball, tennis and cycling
• General fitness training

This slow growth of heart rate monitor training, known today as heart zone training, is in part due to the complexity of the technology. Interestingly, the first consumer monitor was also one of the most complex to program and use. Because of its complex electronics and functions, acceptance of heart rate monitors was extremely slow. It took nearly a decade for an easy-to-use consumer friendly monitor to appear on the market.

This first wireless heart rate monitors were microcomputers like the Polar Sports Tester PE 2000. It was hard to program, bulky, but accurate. By 1989, Polar introduced in Europe the Sports Tester PE 3000 and the first computer downloadable monitor. It was equipped with a computer interface that transmitted via magnetic fields. The retail price was nearly $500 and few were bought in the USA because of its high price and complicated functions. Both models were extremely accurate and reliable. This monitor was in competition with other manufacturers who had now developed early technology such as the Exersentry (Respironics Ltd., Hong Kong), Pacer 2000 H (Sportronic AG, Switzerland) and Monark 1 (Monark-Crescent, Sweden) and the Seiko 1 (Seiko, Japan).

Simultaneously, monitors that measured blood flow using photoelectric sensors and not the electrical activity of the heart muscle were growing in popularity. These early pulse monitors were easy to use and less expensive but not as accurate as electrode sensors measuring the electrical activity of the heart.

In the early 1990s two factors affected the market and the developing technologies: increased competition and falling prices. As new technologies and features developed with new manufacturers such as Cardiosport, Sports Instruments, Cat Eye, Nike, Sensor Dynamics, Reebok, and Acumen, so the popularity of using a heart rate monitor increased.

Convergence was the buzzword of electronics in the last decade of the century. It means that different technologies come together, converge, and become available in one product. It happened to heart rate monitors as well. The sports watch, the heart rate monitor, the stopwatch, the bike computer and the computer all combined into one piece of sports equipment: the Polar CycloVantage. It had all of the functions of a bike computer—speed, cadence, time, distance as well as being downloadable into a computer interface. Latter convergence has resulted in the bike monitor, which also includes altitude and is manufactured by Specialized and others.

But what the market wanted was not more technology or features and functions; it was demanding lower prices and simplicity. Consumers wanted plug-and-play, easy-to-use heart rate monitors and watches. The first buttonless, read-only heart rate monitors hit the market in 1992, and they came from multiple manufacturers each with prices under $100 for the first time. Finally, the market started to simmer. A broad range of consumer applications and acceptance of the technology grew.

Polar's innovation in heart rate monitoring continues today to lead the field in technology. By 1995, the company introduced the Vantage NV, which included more firsts such as coded transmission. Each monitor had its own unique signal eliminating interference known as cross talk. This model also included R-to-R recording, which measures the time between each individual heart beat. The Vantage NV came with more sophisticated Windows analysis software. Recently, the Finnish-based company has added even more technology and features in different models that are designed to help individuals with measurement and motivation as follows:
• Caloric expenditure estimations
• Training zone estimates
• Estimations of fitness improvements
• Estimations of oxygen consumption

Here are just a few of the innovative technologies that were first introduced by Polar Electro Oy, Finland.

Polar Electro Oy's Innovations in Heart Rate Technology

1977 The first battery-operated fingertip pulsemeter

1978 Polar's first heart rate monitor: Tunturi Pulser

1983 The first wireless heart rate monitor–Sport Tester PE 2000

1984 The first heart rate monitor that downloads into a computer

1985 The first computer software that works with a personal heart rate monitor

1986 The first heart rate analysis software for the PC

1987 First heart rate monitor that calculates time in zone

1990 The first wireless bike computer and heart rate monitor: The Cyclovantage

1991 Windows based software analysis for the PC and Vantage series

1992 The first integrated one piece transmitter unit

1991-1993 The introduction by Polar of low-priced heart rate monitors: Favor and Edge models

1994 Nightvision in heart rate monitors

1995 First monitor with coded transmission: Vantage NV

1995 First heart rate monitor with R-R recording and analysis: Vantage NV

1997 First heart rate monitor to use R-R recordings to estimate training zones and calorie consumption: SmartEdge

1999 First heart rate monitor to estimate oxygen consumption and fitness improvement.

What does the future hold for heart rate monitor manufacturing? Here are several predictions for the next decade:

• New advances by Polar and other manufacturers continue to drive new product innovation and technology

• Market forces will continue to drive down price, resulting in fewer manufacturers

• New applications for heart rate technology within other technologies

• Development of human wearable heart rate monitors that use Blue-

tooth technology
- Plug-and-play features that make using a monitor easier
- Price competition and new manufacturers
- Performance monitors that use a new sensor technology eliminating the need for a chest strap
- Single appliance monitors that include all bio-information: blood pressure, cholesterol, heart rate, body composition, and more

What does the future hold for heart zone training, the application of heart rate monitoring? Here are several predictions for the next decade:
- Manufacturers become more involved in the application of their products
- Enhanced applications such as heart zone training used for diagnosing diseases, helping the aging population, use for individuals with special needs
- Mass and universal acceptance of the technology for both its cosmetic appeal and its functional use
- Development of powerful monitors that measure psychological stress and its commiserate biofeedback power
- Web-based applications for heart rate used by all applications
- Enhanced software that powers both client and server applications
- Sport-specific applications and monitors for tennis, rowing, aerobics and step, walking and other unique events

The future looks promising. Just 20 years ago cartoon character Dick Tracy was seen with a watch telephone on his wrist. Today, Finland's Nokia is manufacturing a wrist telephone. Just 20 years ago, wristwatch heart rate monitoring and heart zone training began. Today, Finland's Polar, headquartered in the same city as Nokia, is manufacturing leading edge heart rate monitor technology. Can the two converge with a digital, wireless, telephone heart rate monitor that communicates with you via the Internet? Probably.

GLOSSARY

Ambient heart rate The number of beats per minute your heart contracts when you are awake but in a sedentary and stationary position.

Average heart rate The mean heart rate during an exercise period.

Bottom of the Zone The floor or lower limit of a heart zone.

Cardiac Pertaining to the heart.

Cardiac Cycle The period of time between two consecutive heart beats.

Cardiac Drift The rise in heart rate during exercise that occurs as a result of loss of blood volume principally from dehydration. Also known as cardiovascular drift.

Cardiac Output The amount or volume of blood pumped by the heart per minute. Cardiac output is equal to heart rate times stroke volume.

Exercise heart rate The number of beats per minute you are experiencing during a workout.

Heart rate The number of beats or contraction cycles your heart makes per minute, measured by the electrical impulses emitted by the heart during this process.

Heart rate function The different type of features that a heart rate monitor provides, such as time of day, training zones, stopwatch and others.

Heart rate monitor An electronic device that measures the electrical activity of the heart and displays it.

Heart zones A range of heartbeats, usually 10 percent of your individual maximum sport-specific heart rate. There are 5 different heart zones.

Karvonen Formula An arithmetic formula to determine maximum heart rate based on using both the maximum and the resting heart rates to determine training zones.

Limits The dividing lines of a heart zone—the top of a limit is the ceiling and the bottom of a limit is its floor.

Maximum heart rate (MaxHR) The greatest number of beats per minute possible for your heart; this number is highly individualized and varies with fitness, age, gender and other factors.

Peak heart rate The highest heart rate number reached during any one-workout period.

Palpate Applying touch to feel for a medical diagnosis as in palpating an artery in order to manually count heart rate.

Pulse The regular throbbing felt in the arteries. Caused by the contractions of the heart, strictly speaking. This is not the same as electrically-measured heart rate.

Recovery heart rate The difference in the heart rate after a set post exercise rest interval such as 2 minutes.

Resting heart rate The number of heartbeats per minute when the body is at complete rest, usually determined upon waking, but before arising.

Target heart rate A heart zone that is variable and set for the specific workout.

Threshold heart rate The heart rate number at a crossover point between different exercise intensities. For example, anaerobic threshold heart rate is the heart rate at the crossover from aerobic to anaerobic metabolism.

Top of the Zone The ceiling or upper limit of a heart zone.

Zone Weight The mathematical value of a zone that is used to determine training load such as the Aerobic Zone is zone number 3 or a zone weight of 3.

Zone Size The dimensions of a heart zone, all heart zones have a size of 10 percent of the maximum heart rate.

GLOSSARY OF TERMS: INDOOR AND OUTDOOR CYCLING

Cadence The tempo or the beat of the movement measured in revolutions per minute.

Easy Pedal An easy cadence with easy resistance

RPM Revolutions per minute

Spin (and Spinning) Fast cadence; also a type of indoor cycling trademarked by MadDog Athletics.

Superspin Training at an rpm above 120.

Tempo The cadence or the speed of the revolutions per minute.

HEART RATE TRAINING TERMS

Adaptation The process of physiological change, which occurs when the body responds to the stresses of training loads.

Aerobic With or in the presence of oxygen; an exercise program at a low enough intensity to keep you and your muscles from running out of oxygen.

Aerobic capacity The ability of the body to remove oxygen from the air and transfer it through the lungs and blood to the working muscles.

Anaerobic Without oxygen; exercise characterized by short-spurt, high-intensity activities where the muscles briefly operate at an oxygen deficit.

Anaerobic threshold The point at which your body is producing more lactic acid than can be metabolized, also known as the "lactate threshold."

ATP Adenosine triphosphatase which is a source of energy in muscle contractions.

Base A training term for the fitness level required to exercise for a relatively extended duration without tiring.

Bonk A point of fatigue in which necessary fuels are spent and an individual is limited in his or her ability to continue to maintain an exercise intensity. Also known as hitting the wall.

Carbohydrates Organic compounds that, when broken down, become a main energy source for muscular work.

Crossover point The heart rate where your metabolism shifts fuels, such as from burning fats to carbohydrates.

Endorphins Natural chemicals similar to opiates released into the bloodstream by the brain that result in the feeling of happiness from training.

Fats Concentrated sources of energy for muscular work. They are compounds containing glycerol and fatty acids and may be saturated or unsaturated.

Functional Capacity The ability to do normal daily activities especially work, also known as fitness capacity.

Gas Analyzer A device that measures the volume, concentration and content of inspired and expired atmospheric air.

Intensity The degree of energy, difficulty or strength, as relates to a workout.

Interval The duration of a given intensity of training. Used in training to mean a set of stress and recovery sessions.

Inter-Recovery A way of doing intervals such that recovery is between workout sessions, usually between workout days.

Intra-Recovery A way of doing intervals such that recovery is within one workout session rather than between workouts.

Lactate Analyzer A monitoring device that measures blood lactate levels.

Lactic acid This product of the body's metabolic processes is created during all of the heart rate zones and is shuttled away from the skeletal muscles to different parts of the body where it is oxidized.

Lung function The relative ability to efficiently inspire and expire air.

Metabolism The chemical changes in the body's cells by which energy is provided for vital processes.

Mitochondria Strings of carrier molecules within the cell; they act like tiny energy factories, taking fuel and uniting it with oxygen for muscular combustion in muscles.

Overreaching A way of training that results in positive muscle fatigue.

Overuse Training too hard, to the point of stress or injury.

Oxygen Consumption The amount of oxygen utilized by the body during exercise. Maximum oxygen consumption is aerobic power or cardiorespiratory endurance capacity.

Periodization Varying the amount of training load over time to prevent monotony and overtraining yet result in a positive training effect.

Pick Ups A type of training that includes several quick burst of speed.

Repeats Repetition of the same set of exercises or training events

Redlining Spending time doing high intensity, hot training sessions mostly in heart zone 5.

RPE Rating of perceived exertion. A way of giving a numerical value based on the perception of the effort.

Steady State A heart rate or training rate that is sub-maximal and maintained at a constant intensity, speed or rate of work.

Strength The maximum force or tension that a muscle can produce against resistance.

Time Trial A way of training that is solo and the measurement of elapsed time as in time trialing a fixed distance for time.

Training Any sustained cardiovascular exercise at a heart rate or intensity level sufficient to result in metabolic adaptation in the muscles involved. The commonly accepted lower threshold or floor for training is considered to be 50% of maximum heart rate.

Training Effect The response to the level of fitness or functional capacity as a result of a dosage of exercise.

Training Load The total amount of exercise as determined by frequency, intensity, time and mode of the exercise experience.

Training Volume The amount of time and frequency or time and distance of a workout or series of workouts.

Triglycerides The chemical name for the fat stored in the body; most of the fat in foods is also triglyceride.

VO$_2$ Max The maximum volume of oxygen that the body can utilize, regardless of intensity increases; it is synonymous with "maximum oxygen consumption" and "maximum oxygen uptake."

Index